A
SHORT HISTORY OF
FRANCE

A SHORT HISTORY OF
FRANCE
FROM EARLY TIMES TO
1972

BY

HERBERT BUTTERFIELD, D. W. BROGAN
H. C. DARBY, J. HAMPDEN JACKSON

WITH CONTRIBUTIONS BY

SIR ERNEST BARKER, A. EWERT
I. L. FOSTER

EDITED BY

J. HAMPDEN JACKSON

SECOND EDITION

WITH NEW MATERIAL BY N. J. M. RICHARDSON

CAMBRIDGE UNIVERSITY PRESS

0635147   115543

Published by the Syndics of the Cambridge University Press
Bentley House, 200 Euston Road, London NW1 2DB
American Branch: 32 East 57th Street, New York, N.Y.10022

Chapters 1 to 6. Crown copyright

Chapter 7. © Cambridge University Press

Library of Congress Catalogue Card Number 74–76584

ISBNs:
0 521 20485 2 hard covers
0 521 09864 5 paperback

First published 1959
Second edition 1974

Photoset and printed in Malta by
St Paul's Press Ltd

CONTENTS

063514   115543

CONTENTS

POSTSCRIPT

LIST OF MAPS AND DIAGRAMS

PUBLISHER'S NOTE

Most of the material and all the maps in this book were originally published by the Naval Intelligence Division of the Admiralty as part of a Handbook on France, in four volumes, for service use. By arrangement with the Controller of Her Majesty's Stationery Office, the original owner of the copyright, the historical sections are now reissued in this shorter form. The publishers are grateful to the principal original contributors for permission to reproduce their work; they were Professor D. W. Brogan, Professor Herbert Butterfield, Professor H. C. Darby, Sir Ernest Barker, Professor A. Ewert and Professor I. L. Foster. Mr J. Hampden Jackson has unified the material and added a chapter bringing the book up to date.

A companion volume, *A Short History of Germany, 1815–1945* by E. J. Passant, with contributions by C. J. Child, W. O. Henderson and Donald Watt, was published in 1959.

NOTE ON THE SECOND EDITION

For this edition Nicholas Richardson has written a chapter on Gaullist France and a postscript to cover events up to the elections of 1973.

CHAPTER I

FRANCE IN EARLY TIMES

1. THE EARLY PEOPLES AND THE ROMANS

THE EARLY PEOPLES

FRANCE, situated on the margin of Europe, has been a meeting-place of cultures and peoples moving towards the west. From the Mediterranean lands came peoples and civilizations associated with the spread of cultivation during the third millenium B.C. These peoples found easy access into the interior from the Mediterranean seaboard up the valley of the Rhône; some even spread through the Straits of Gibraltar to reach the western coasts, especially Brittany. The second main line of movement lay along the Alpine zone. The civilization which spread along this zone was a peasant culture in which the agricultural community was the unit of social life. It affected particularly the French Alps and the Central Massif. In the third place, the lowland of central Europe formed another route along which came repeated invasions. These northern lands were agriculturally poor, so that in earlier times stock raising was an important feature of their economy, and society was consequently more mobile and martial than among the cultivating peasantries of the more southerly regions.

In general terms, the modern population of France is composed of the descendants of peoples who moved into the country along these three routes in prehistoric and early historic times. The people who spread along the Alpine zone possessed a group of physical characteristics which are common among the bulk of the populations of the mountainous backbone of Europe, and which are usually referred to as the Alpine type. The movements from Mediterranean lands brought peoples with a different combination of physical characteristics—the Mediterranean type. Along the northern lowlands came people who differed markedly from the two southern types in that their colouring was fair—the Nordic type. These terms Alpine, Mediterranean and Nordic, however, do not imply strict physical patterns to which all members of a particular type conform. The terms are merely convenient designations which cover a variety of sub-

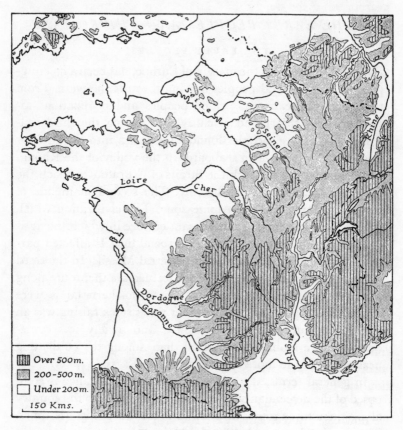

Fig. 1. The relief of France

types and indicate no more than a tendency for particular physical characteristics, such as head form, colouring, stature, to go together in individuals belonging to a particular type.

It was the invasion of France by the Celts, a people of the Nordic type, which gave the country its first approach to a common culture. In the first millenium B.C. the Celts gradually imposed themselves on the earlier inhabitants as a sort of ruling class. Their tribal leaders became the landlords of great estates. They opened communications for trade. Their descendants gave France her first name, Gaul, and the Gauls' dialects became the nearest thing the people had known to a common language. The Gauls fought among themselves, they fought the earlier settlers and they fought other immigrants. Perhaps their greatest enemy was Marseilles, a port founded in about 600 B.C. by traders from the Ionian city of Phocea. Marseilles became a great trading city, connecting France with the civilization of the Hellenic world. The city-states needed protection against the Gallic tribes and called in Roman soldiers for that purpose. Thus began a new chapter in the history of France.

THE ROMANS

The first Roman soldiers came to France in 154 B.C. to defend Antibes and Nice for the Marseillais. A generation later the legions came again, to clear the Rhône valley for trade. This time they settled. When in 58 B.C. Julius Caesar became governor of the Roman province of Gaul, the Gallic tribes were in difficulties with Helvetian invaders. Caesar began his campaign as a liberator, but he soon turned into a conqueror if not an enslaver of Gaul. A number of tribes, led by the young Gaul Vercingetorix, succeeded in combining against him and for a time the legions were hard pressed, but the defeat of Vercingetorix meant the Roman conquest of Gaul. The Roman occupation was to last for nearly five centuries.

The Romans wrought some indelible changes in the country we now call France. They gave her a frontier which after two thousand years of intermittent fighting is still roughly the French frontier. They gave the people a degree of security such as they had never known, security based on a legal system, a standing army and a network of military roads (Fig. 2). They gave her administrative unity centred on Lyons, the Roman capital. They built great cities and set an example of civilized life, and they transformed rural life by imposing the 'villa' structure on the great estates of the Gauls.

And they gave Gaul a common language. After the Roman subjection of the Gauls, the spoken Latin of the soldiers, teachers, colonists and administrators gradually spread among the whole

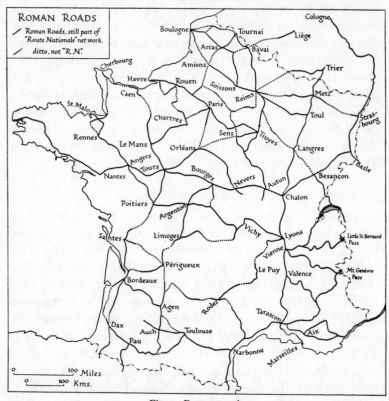

Fig. 2. Roman roads

The Roman roads are still largely represented in the *Routes Nationales* network of today. Where the physical circumstances offer very obvious routes, e.g. in the Alpine valleys, Rhône valley, Loire valley, the modern roads follow the track of the Roman highways over long stretches. Elsewhere the main 'modern', i.e. largely eighteenth century, roads sometimes chose easier if less direct courses, or passed through terrain which two thousand years ago was not in a suitable condition for road building, for example, through poor drainage or forest cover.

population and by the fourth century had virtually replaced the Celtic speech. This spoken (popular) Latin differed from classical Latin in many important features of vocabulary, pronunciation and grammar. While it could not escape the natural

4

changes to which a spoken language is always subject, it nevertheless remained comparatively uniform throughout the Roman Empire until the fifth century, and this later form of Latin is sometimes called Romanic or Romance.

Conversion to Christianity took place in spite rather than because of the Romans. The first missionaries were Greeks and Levantines who made their way along the Mediterranean trade-routes. Their gospel was welcome among the plebians of the towns, especially in Lyons where the first organized Christian community made its appearance. The converts survived persecution, and when the Emperor Constantine proclaimed liberty of conscience in A.D. 313 the new religion spread rapidly among townspeople, although centuries were to pass before the rural population was made Christian.

Meanwhile Gaul was facing new invasions.

2. THE FRANKS

This time the invaders came from the North. When the Roman garrisons were withdrawn from the Rhine early in the fifth century, Gaul was overrun by Tartars and Huns, Goths and Visigoths, Allemans and Burgundians. Still more important were the Salian Franks, who eventually gave their name to France. When they first appeared in history they were occupying the marshy country about the lower Rhine. As the Roman power weakened they moved into north-east Gaul as far as the Somme, making Tournai their capital. Clovis became their king in 481. Five years later he defeated the Gallo-Roman forces at Soissons and extended his powers to the Seine and afterwards to the Loire. The Church then made overtures to the conqueror. Clovis, who could not have held the whole of Gaul without the help of the Christian Gallo-Romans, was converted to Christianity. By his victory at Dijon in 500 he subdued the Burgundians. In 507, by another victory near Poitiers, he freed the country as far as the Pyrenees from the Visigoths. Although the whole of France was now in Frankish hands, the area of Frankish settlement was in the north and east. Here, the Franks blended with the population, while in the south and west the Gallo-Roman element remained predominant. Upon the basis of these conquests in Gaul the Franks succeeded in building up the great Frankish empire, which reached its zenith in the reign of Charlemagne (771–814).

Charlemagne was not a king of France: he was ruler of the Frankish lands whose centre was in Germany and in Gaul, and the city where he most loved to hold his court was not Lyons, Soissons, Laon or Paris, but Aix-la-Chapelle on the German-Gallic frontier. His vision was to hold together and protect all western Christendom now that the successor of the Roman Emperors held court in Byzantium, far away in the east. The bishops were his allies, as they had been of all the Frankish rulers. And indeed he served the Church well. He inflicted a final defeat on the Lombards, capturing their capital, Pavia, and crowning himself with their iron crown. He led expedition after expedition against the Muslim Arabs, establishing in the end a defensive zone on either side of the Pyrenees. (His worst enemy in these campaigns was often not the Muslim Arab but the Christian Basque; the Basques once cut off his rear-guard in the pass of Roncesvalles, and they were never conquered.) He brutally destroyed the heathen Saxons, and he drove the descendants of the Huns as far east as Hungary. He set up military marcher-zones in what later became Brandenburg and Austria, to defend the eastern boundaries of Christendom. It is little wonder that Pope Leo III crowned him Emperor when he was in Rome on Christmas Night in 800.

To hold his empire together Charlemagne had little but his armed forces and the Church. The armed forces depended on knights whose continued service had to be rewarded by grants of land. The Church also demanded privileges in return for its support, for example, immunity from imperial taxation and jurisdiction. Charlemagne might administer justice through professional judges and agents (*missi dominici*) but there was nothing approaching a centralized government. The modern idea of a State was far from the minds of ninth-century Europeans.

6

Charlemagne's reign was a time of increasing prosperity for France. In the north each of a dozen great abbeys was employing thousands of workers on its estates and developing agriculture and industry to an extent never known before. In the Rhône and Saône valleys towns revived as peace brought new trade along the traditional route from the Mediterranean. New routes were opened along the navigable rivers to the west. Charlemagne's Empire, remembered today as an ideal, meant solid material well-being to his contemporaries.

3. THE FRENCH LANGUAGE

Nothing makes for unity so surely as a common language, and this France lacked in Charlemagne's time and was not to achieve until many centuries later. After the fall of the Roman Empire in the fifth century and as a result of the barbarian invasions and the weakening of most of the ties which held that empire together, Latin as spoken in Gaul developed peculiarities which differentiated it more radically both from classical Latin and from the forms of Latin spoken contemporaneously in other parts of the Empire (the Iberian Peninsula, Italy, etc.). But even within the limits of Gaul itself, local variations (the beginnings of later dialects) had begun to develop. In particular, a differentiation between the language of the south and of the north gradually arose during this time, which is called the Gallo-Roman period and which may be said to extend down to about the end of the eighth century. The occupation of northern Gaul by the Salian Franks was partly responsible for this twofold development. Although they subjugated the country and gave it their name, they adapted themselves readily to their surroundings. Their cultural inferiority and their fairly rapid conversion to Christianity were a further inducement to give up their native language. But they introduced a large number of words connected with warfare and husbandry, and their habits of speech had a more profound influence on the pronunciation of the Romance language than did those of the Burgundians in southern Gaul.

The varieties of spoken Romance had thus by the end of the eighth century formed themselves into two main groups, a northern and a southern. Latin had continued to be the written language throughout this period, but had degenerated under the influence of the vernacular Romance speech. The gulf between the spoken and written language was finally made unbridgeable when the Carolingian reform restored written Latin to a purity approximating to that of classical Latin. The way was now open and the need made itself felt for a written vernacular. In the north the dialect of the Ile de France (i.e. of Paris and the surrounding district) gradually established its claim to pre-eminence, and by the twelfth century it had become the standard literary language. It was the language of the capital and of the most influential of the various courts, and it occupied a neutral position between the more extreme and divergent dialects. Its supremacy was never seriously challenged, except for a brief period towards the end of the twelfth century, by the Picard dialect of the prosperous cultural centres of the north-east (Arras, etc.).

In the south a more or less standard literary language developed in a similar way and was the medium for the poetry of the Troubadours. Its reign was virtually brought to a close in the fourteenth century, its fate having been foreshadowed by the ruin and depredations resulting from political misfortunes and particularly from the Albigensian crusade (see p. 26). Various names have been given to this literary language, and to the group of dialects of which it is the written counterpart. 'Langue d'Oc' is a term which is still commonly used, because in these southern dialects the affirmative particle ('yes') is *oc* (< *hoc*). 'Provençal' is perhaps a less appropriate term, because the languages covered by this designation are spoken in the Midi generally and not merely in Provence.

The boundary between French and Provençal is not a sharp line. Linguists have studied the distribution of the main characteristics of Provençal, such as the hard *c* before the Latin *a*, for example, *vaca* (French *vache*), *cantar* (French *chanter*), or the preservation of *s* before certain consonants, for example, *testa*

8

(French *tête*), *escoute* (French *écouter*). When the occurrence of these different linguistic features is plotted on a map, it is found that their northern limits are not the same. The lines approach one another near Bordeaux, but as they run eastward they diverge to form a zone of varying width in which northern and southern features intermingle. This intermediate zone stretches well to the north in the Central Massif, a region of isolation and refuge, but it is pressed southward in the west by influences coming through the gate of Poitou, and in the east by others coming through Burgundy into the Saône valley. It is interesting to compare this linguistic distinction with the legal and administrative differences between north and south that continued down to the Revolution (see Figs. 20, 21).

The dialects north of this line constitute what is called the 'Langue d'Oïl', because in them the affirmative particle is *oïl* (< *hoc illud*) = Mod. Fr. *oui*. This term is also applied to the standard literary language, but the terms 'central French' or 'Francien' are perhaps more appropriate. In any case, the language in question developed into what we now call French. While this literary language of the north achieved complete predominance in the Middle Ages, the dialects continued to be spoken in both the north and the south. Those of the north (that is, the French dialects proper) fell into more clearly defined groups than did the Provençal dialects, and writers from the provinces (Picardy, Normandy, Champagne, etc.) introduced many of their native habits of speech into the literary language. But such dialectal variations gradually became less numerous in the fifteenth and sixteenth centuries, and in the seventeenth century they were no longer tolerated.

The conception of a standard *spoken* language is an ideal which was but dimly envisaged before the sixteenth century and imperfectly conceived by the grammarians of that age. It was in the seventeenth century that, by a unique collaboration of polite society, grammarians and authors, this ideal was realized, and the history of the French language from that time onwards is the story of its gradual extension to all classes of society and to all parts of the country, radiating from the centre at Paris. Whereas in the seventeenth century and the greater part of the eighteenth this standard French was still a foreign idiom in the country districts and throughout the south generally, in the nineteenth century various powerful factors, such as the extremely centralized system of government and administration, compulsory education, conscription, the press, reduced the local types of speech to a subsidiary role. They are now called *patois* and even those who still speak them, whether of the northern or southern type, almost invariably speak standard French also, with a greater or less degree of purity. It is natural that the natives of the various provinces should carry into their pronunciation of French some of their inherited and ingrained habits of speech. Thus there arise regional types of French, that is, French spoken with· an accent (*marseillais, bordelais,* etc.) which are not to be confused with the local dialects and patois, whose roots go deep down into the Gallo-Roman or Romance past. Nineteenth-century regionalism, however, produced little more than a Walloon literature of secondary importance and the Provençal literary renaissance of Mistral and his followers.

As distinct from those inhabitants of France whose mother tongue is French (whether in the form of standard French or of one of the patois), there are computed to be still nearly two million persons of French nationality within the political boundaries as constituted in 1919 whose mother tongue is not French; among them are the Basques, Bretons and Alsatians. But it should be noted that the vast majority of these also speak French as a second language and that many in the course of time have come to regard it as their first.

CHAPTER II

MEDIEVAL FRANCE

1. THE AGE OF FEUDALISM

WITH the death of Charlemagne in 814, the great Frankish empire fell into anarchy and disruption. Its partition by his grandsons in 843 forms a convenient beginning to the historic record of the separate states of France and Germany. Louis the German took most of the imperial territories in which a Teutonic language was spoken; Charles took the lands in which Romance prevailed (Fig. 3). From the realm of Charles grew the modern kingdom of France, but we must divest ourselves of any idea that this development was inevitable. In the first place, the division corresponded to no fundamental facts either of human or of physical geography. The partition proposed by Charlemagne himself, in 806, had not in any way suggested the future French kingdom; 'Francia', the northern lands settled by the Franks themselves, was treated as an unbroken unit stretching across the lower Rhine, while, to the south, the unit of 'Aquitaine' comprised the most romanized part of Gaul. This difference between north and south comes out again and again in the subsequent development of France.

In the second place, the partition of 843 was but one of many. There had already been a division in 817; and now, in 843, the three grandsons of Charlemagne came together only after civil war; the partition was but provisional, liable to change at every death in the family, and each of the brothers considered himself a claimant to the undivided Frankish inheritance. Instead of inaugurating an era of peaceful government, the partition was followed by dispute and war. There was another division in 870; then for a brief span of three years (884–7) almost the whole realm of Charlemagne was reunited under Charles the Fat, but when he was deposed in 887, the western unit again emerged, with limits approximately the same as those of 843 (Fig. 3).

Charlemagne's grandson, Charles the Bald, became the first king of the western unit in 843, but he was far from being in complete control of his territory. The Norse pirates who had troubled Charlemagne were attracted by the river estuaries and

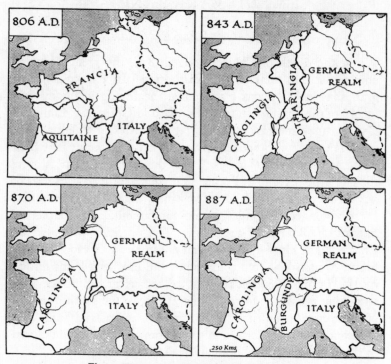

Fig. 3. The partitions of Charlemagne's empire

Based on (1) A. Longnon, *Atlas historique de la France* (Paris, 1885), plates v and vi; (2) *The Cambridge Medieval History* (Cambridge, 1922), vol. iii, map 28.

The map for A.D. 806 is that of a partition proposed by Charlemagne. On all maps, the eastern frontier is only roughly indicated. The facts do not warrant a definite line, and authorities differ in their estimate of where it should run.

by the rich monasteries of western France. In 841 they sacked Rouen, and, until the settlement of Normandy in 912, their attacks never ceased. They came in their ships up the estuaries of the Somme, the Seine, the Loire, and the Garonne. They made four descents upon Paris in forty years, sacking towns, destroying harvests, and slaughtering the peasants or carrying them into slavery. In addition to facing these troubles, Charles spent his life sword in hand against the Bretons and against the people of Aquitaine, both in full revolt. To check the Bretons and Normans, he was obliged to entrust the defence of the north to Robert the Strong, duke of the lands between the Loire and Seine and ancestor of the House of Capet.

Despite all his troubles, Charles spoke authoritatively enough in his edicts. Though incapable of defending western France, his ambition turned obstinately towards the east. He became king of Lorraine on the death of one nephew, and emperor of Germany on the death of another in 875. A year before his own death he took the crown of Italy. But while his titles increased, his authority at home was falling to pieces. Owing to the king's inability to defend the realm, every man made it his business to seek a new protector. The country became covered with strongholds, and the peasant learned to live beneath the shelter of a castle wall. Vassals gave themselves utterly to the lord who guarded them, serving him in battle and labouring for him in peace, for the king was far away and the lord close at hand. Hence the reign of Charles the Bald saw a great increase in the power of the nobles at the expense of royal authority.

After the death of Charles the Bald in 877 the struggle of the Carolingians for power lasted for another century of uncertainty and anarchy. Although the French kingdom in the ninth and tenth centuries formed a single legal conception based upon a definite piece of territory, it was becoming an assemblage of small states, each practically independent and owing little but nominal allegiance to the king. The monarchy was helpless before the local powers that confronted it. The only immediate dominion of the king was the city and district of Laon, lying between Paris and the north-eastern frontier. Laon may perhaps be described as the capital of France during this period.

Just as the royal authority became less effective, so likewise did the power of the great lords for the most part crumble away. A duchy included outlying territories (counties, etc.), in addition to the personal domain of its duke. When by chance he succeeded in acquiring direct control over a number of counties, he was obliged, since he could not be everywhere at once, to provide himself with substitutes in the form of viscounts. Both counts and viscounts endeavoured to enlarge their own authority at the expense of their overlord.

France thus became a loose collection of feudal lordships, each disputing with the others, and it would be vain to attempt a comprehensive view of the State. But some information must be given about each of the main units (Fig. 4).

Aquitaine had never been fully incorporated into the Frankish State. In 781 Charlemagne had found himself obliged to make it into a subordinate but separate kingdom under his own son. It remained separate down to 877, when the Aquitainian king himself became king of France. In the meantime the ducal title had been revived. Long in dispute between the counts of Toulouse, Auvergne and Poitiers, it ended by falling into the hands of the last named in the middle of the tenth century. While everywhere else in France the tendency was towards the minutest subdivision, the dukes of Aquitaine, by a policy almost miraculously skilful, succeeded not only in maintaining effective control over most of their territory but in making good their hold on Gascony. For a time they even succeeded in occupying the county of Toulouse.

Gascony owed its origin to the Vascones, a Spanish tribe who crossed the Pyrenees during the sixth century. In 602 the duchy of Gascony was founded under the vague authority of the Frankish kings. This included 'High Gascony', where Basque was spoken, and 'Low Gascony' from the mountains to the Garonne where Gascon, a dialect of *langue d'oc*, was the native tongue. Under Charlemagne, the duke of the Gascons was allowed to retain his title, and in 864 the area became an hereditary duchy subject, in little but name, to Aquitaine. The line of Gascon dukes ended in 1032 with Sanche VI, but his sister had married the duke of Aquitaine and, eventually, the title of duke of Gascony was finally merged with that of the duke of Aquitaine in 1073.

The Spanish March had been founded by Charlemagne, and extended over the southern slope of the Pyrenees. Subsequently

Fig. 4. France in A.D. 987

Based on *The Cambridge Medieval History* (Cambridge, 1922), vol. III, map 29.
Between Gothia and the Spanish March was Roussillon (R).

it was ruled by French counts, but these soon made themselves independent of France and became connected by marriage with Aragon. The counts of Barcelona, as they were styled, extended their authority even over Roussillon to the north of the Pyrenees.

Toulouse and Gothia lay to the east of Gascony. The territory of Gothia or Septimania, organized by Charlemagne, became a separate duchy in 817, but it gradually lost its individual existence and fell under the control of the counts of Toulouse whom the records of the tenth century style 'Princes of Gothia'—thus preserving the name of the old Visigothic kingdom that once stretched north of the Pyrenees. Less fortunate and less skilful than the dukes of Aquitaine, the rulers of Toulouse nevertheless succeeded during the eleventh century in collecting into their own hands considerable territories. The court of Toulouse was already famous for its art and literature, and the poetry of the troubadours spread its glory. Here lay the rich cities of the most cultured and wealthy portion of the kingdom. But despite this civilization the political unity of the state was weak. The great lords of Toulouse and Carcassonne and a swarm of counts and barons maintained a chronic state of civil war and practically ignored the authority of the distant king of France.

Brittany owed its origin to Celtic immigrants from Britain in the fifth century. They maintained a long struggle against the Frankish kings and were not completely subdued even by Charlemagne. From time to time they continued to send out pillaging expeditions into Frankish territory. In the hope of pacifying the land, one of the successors of Charlemagne nominated a native chief, Nomenoë, as governor or duke in 826. After fifteen years he rebelled, and forced the French king to recognize his independence in 846.

But in spite of its well-marked characteristics, Brittany did not form a very strong political entity. The Gallo-Roman population of the east was in conflict with the Celtic-speaking people of the west, and this antagonism was reflected in rivalry between the counts of Rennes, Nantes and Cornouailles. Complete unity was never achieved. One duke, Conan IV, defeated by the rebellious Breton nobles, appealed to Henry II of England; as a reward for English help, Conan's daughter was forced to marry Henry's son Geoffrey, and so, in the twelfth century, the Plantagenets succeeded in establishing themselves in the peninsula.

Normandy owed its origin to the Norsemen who raided the coasts of France during the ninth century. They first appeared in Normandy in 841 and for the rest of the century they repeatedly attacked and plundered. But these raids gave way to

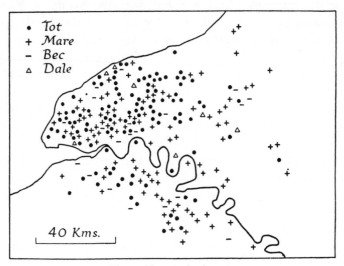

Fig. 5. Norman Settlement

Based on J. Sion, *Les paysans de la Normandie orientale* (Paris, 1909), p. 128.
The map shows the distribution of four Scandinavian suffixes in the place-names of eastern Normandy.

expeditions for settlement (Fig. 5), and, in 911, at St Clair-sur-Epte on the high road between Rouen and Paris, a Norman chief named Rollo was granted the lands along the lower Seine. In return, he consented to receive Christianity and promised homage to the Frankish kings. The Norman territory was extended in 924 and again in 933, when its boundary reached the Breton border. With the establishment of Normandy, Viking activity was practically at an end in the Frankish kingdom; there were still Norsemen on the Loire who raided far inland, while the settlers in Normandy themselves freely raided Brittany, but no fresh settlements were made. Normandy became more unified than any other feudal principality. Its capable dukes were able to keep considerable territories directly under their own control, and to organize the administration of the duchy on a comparatively stable basis.

Flanders was one of the most remarkable units in medieval France. About 863, Charles the Bald had entrusted a group of counties to Count Baldwin to form a northern outpost against the Scandinavian pirates. The successors of Count Baldwin worked unceasingly to extend the limits of their domain. Within a century, the count of Flanders ruled not only all the area between the Scheldt and the Canche but also held the island of Zeeland and some other districts as vassal of the Holy Roman Empire. Situated between two overlords, he enjoyed almost complete independence. 'Kings', says a chronicle of the period, 'feared and respected him; dukes, marquesses and bishops trembled before his power.' By the beginning of the tenth century he was considered to have the largest income in the whole kingdom. He had a regularly organized administration. Important enterprises of clearing and draining were undertaken in the districts bordering on the sea, while, in the interior, the extension of cultivation and of grazing lands went forward. At the same time the cloth industry was so far developed that home-grown wool no longer sufficed the workman. The Flemish fairs were in contact with England, Germany and Scandinavia.

Burgundy is one of the most confusing names in medieval history. At various times there existed a kingdom, a ducal state and a county of Burgundy—all different in extent and all outside the territory of France. But there was a fourth entity of that name in France itself. After the partition of 843, Charles the Bald had found himself compelled to unite under a single ruler some of the Burgundian counties, which had remained French, in order to form a defensive unit along the frontier. But, during the tenth century, the dukes were unable to safeguard the integrity of their dominions, and in the eleventh century they seem to have been insignificant enough, with neither wealth nor policy. Although theoretically they were masters of vast territories, they saw the greater part of their possessions slip from their control to form small semi-independent principalities such as the counties of Chalon-sur-Saône and Mâcon.

Francia had been the largest of all the divisions of early France. Its princes were called 'Duces Francorum', a title in which the word 'Francia' is just beginning to change from its older meaning of 'Frank' to its later meaning of 'French'. In none of the great regional units of France was subdivision greater. The province was cut short by the grant of Normandy in 911, and, during the tenth century, many other portions also became independent. The largest of these independent divisions were the counties of Blois, Troyes and Anjou. There were others as well—all continually changing their frontiers and re-grouping themselves. The duchy of Francia was hardly more than a memory. Outside his immediate domain between the Seine and the Loire, the duke of the Franks preserved nothing save an authority which was being reduced to an empty name. Yet it was from this weak and much-reduced duchy of Francia that the French state was ultimately to emerge. How this transformation was accomplished must now be examined.

2. THE RISE OF PARIS

In the year 987 one of the French vassals, Hugh Capet, duke of Francia, was elected to the kingship. This election may be regarded as a new starting point in French history, for the Capet dynasty continued to rule France for the next 300 years.

There was nothing to mark the greatness of the hour. When the magnates of the realm elected him, they had no vision of a united France. Hugh Capet was simply *primus inter pares*, a fellow-noble. Each of the provincial units which composed France was comparable in strength with that of which Hugh was overlord, and he and his immediate successors understood the limitations of their position. They promised to take no step without consulting the tenants-in-chief of the realm. A powerful duke, Hugh found himself a weak king.

Moreover, the immediate domain of Hugh Capet was far

Fig. 6. The royal domain in France in the eleventh century

Based on (1) R. L. Poole, *Historical Atlas of Modern Europe* (Oxford, 1902), plate 54; (2) W. R. Shepherd, *Historical Atlas* (London, 1930), p. 61.

The duchy of Normandy and the chief counties that surrounded the detached areas of royal domain are named.

from being as extensive as that of his predecessors a century earlier. It extended for about 200 kilometres from north to south, with a general breadth from east to west of hardly 80 kilometres (Fig. 6). It included Paris and Orléans and also the district of Beauce, an area noted for its fertility. Outside this more or less compact block, there were a number of small and scattered territories—Dreux to the west, Attigny to the east on the upper Aisne, and Montreuil at the estuary of the Canche in the north. The capital city, from 987 to the end of the eleventh century, moved with the person of the king. The early Capets resided at Étampes, Poissy, Senlis and, most frequently, at Orléans; they lived but rarely at Paris itself, although there was a royal palace on the island in the Seine where the Palais de Justice now stands.

Outside this restricted domain lay the immediate tenants of the original duchy of Francia but, by now, their allegiance was only nominal. Beyond these were the vassals of the crown, but they, again, were largely independent. The resources of the monarchy were small; the king had to be content with the produce of his farms, and with some tolls, fines and dues, but, as the greater part of the royal domain was granted out in fiefs, these resources did not amount to much. They could fortunately be augmented by illicit gains arising from traffic in ecclesiastical offices.

However wretched may have been his material position, the king had a moral superiority. The tie of vassalage which bound all the great feudal lords of the kingdom to him was not merely a theoretical one; apart from cases of rebellion they did not, nominally, fail to fulfil their duties as vassals when called upon. Contingents of Aquitainians, Burgundians, and so on, were constantly to be found in the royal armies. Moreover, none of the great feudal lords was strong enough to overthrow the Capet dynasty. Their rivalries and their internal difficulties hindered opposition to the crown. With the early Capets there started a process of converting the nominal feudal superiority of the crown into a direct sovereignity over the whole kingdom. Opportunities were constantly found for annexing the lands of a vassal, and, before the end of the eleventh century, the royal domain had already begun to increase through the acquisition of a number of small territories.

During the twelfth century an important stage in the establishment of royal authority was marked by the reign (1108–37) of Louis VI (the Fat). By appearing everywhere as the defender of law and justice, Louis did much to strengthen the institution of monarchy. Vassals, who for long years had been left in peace, were unhesitatingly summoned to appear before his tribunal. Nor, if any of them refused to obey, did he fail to set out upon costly and fatiguing expeditions of reprisal. For thirty-six years he fought against lawlessness in the Paris basin. He freed bishoprics and abbeys, offered the peasants some security, and made the highway between Paris and Orléans safe for travellers.

Beyond the immediate royal domain, Louis VI interfered with success to answer appeals from the more remote Bourbonnais and the Auvergne. But he was not always successful in these more distant enterprises; he failed, for example, to impose his nominee upon the people of Flanders, and his lack of strength showed itself continually in his relations with Normandy.

It is interesting to see how in the reign of his successor, Louis VII (the Young), the arm of the central authority grew longer and longer. The monarchy was recovering from the weakness of the eleventh century, and the king was becoming more and more identified with the whole of what was to become France. Louis VII was as ready as his father to embark upon expeditions to make the royal tribunal respected throughout the country. Thus on two occasions, in 1163 and 1169, the canons of Clermont and Brioude appealed to the king to save them from the violence of the count of Auvergne and his agents. Louis unhesitatingly plunged into the mountains of central France to inflict punishment upon the offenders whom he even imprisoned for a time. To this example of royal interference many others could be added.

As time went on, the royal court of justice became able to take a more commanding attitude, and to insist that the great vassals of the crown should obey its summons. The nobles, too, brought an ever-increasing number of cases to be tried before the king's tribunal. From even the most distant parts of France appeals were addressed to the king. In 1163 the inhabitants of Toulouse, whom he had recently defended against Henry II of England, wrote to express their devotion and to beg for further support: 'Very dear Lord, do not take it amiss that we write to you so often. After God, we appeal to you as to our good master, our protector, our liberator. Upon your power, next to divine power, we fix all our hopes.'

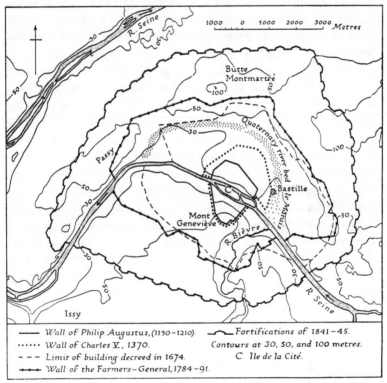

Fig. 7. The site and growth of Paris

Based on G. R. Crone, 'The site and growth of Paris', *Geographical Journal*, vol. xcviii (London, 1941), p. 37.

To sum up: The early Capets had two assets—the possibilities of their kingly office, and a compact though small territory under their own immediate control, as opposed to the rest of France under the control of various feudal lords. The former advantage was reflected in royal interference over France and in the growing importance of the central courts at Paris. The second advantage was increased by successive kings who seized every

115543

opportunity to make additions to the royal domain. Some of these additions were granted out again as appanages, and the extent of the royal domain fluctuated from time to time. But the net result was a steady increase in the direct control of the king over larger and larger stretches of territory. Fig. 8 summarizes, in a general fashion, this control which increased until ultimately the royal domain came to coincide with the whole territory of France.

One indication of the increasing power of the crown was the growth of Paris (Fig. 7). Philip Augustus has been described as the second founder of the city. He seldom left it, save on his military expeditions, and from it he organized a regular system of administration for the kingdom. In 1190 he ordered the burgesses to build walls on the right bank of the Seine, and he himself in 1209 built walls on the left bank; the owners of fields and vineyards within the enclosure were commanded to let their lands for building. For his royal palace, he built the Louvre. Under his patronage, too, the schools of the city were grouped under the title of a university in 1200, and this became the most famous university in medieval Europe. Finally, the cathedral of Notre Dame, founded in 1163, was rapidly approaching completion. Thus Paris was becoming a great city in itself and the centre of an organized realm.

But although the way was thus prepared for the greatness of medieval France, the expansion of the government of Paris over the whole of the kingdom was far from being assured. The territorial problems that this expansion involved fall more or less conveniently into three groups—those of the west, the south and the east. These must be considered separately.

Notes to Fig. 8

Based on (1) W. R. Shepherd, *Historical Atlas*, (London, 1930), pp. 69, 76 and 84; (2) L. Mirot, *Manuel de Géographie historique de la France* (Paris, 1929), Figs. 9, 11, 12, 13, 17, 19 and 20.

The extent of the royal domain fluctuated because portions were frequently granted out as appanages, but the net result was a steady increase—as this sequence of maps shows. By the death of Henry IV in 1610, the areas remaining to be incorporated were the counties of Bourbon (1643) and Turenne (1738)—that is, apart from the fresh acquisition of foreign territory. The enclave around Avignon came under this latter heading (see Fig. 26).

063514

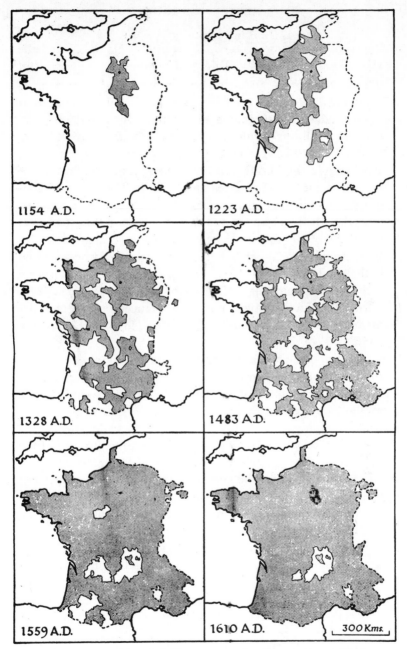

Fig. 8. The royal domain in France, 1154–1610 (for notes see opposite)

25

3. THREE REGIONS OF FRANCE

SOUTHERN FRANCE

The divergence in language between north and south was accompanied by marked differences in ideas and customs; some of these have survived into modern times. Down to the Revolution the north was distinct from the south both legally and commercially. It was, however, the good fortune of the kings at Paris during the Middle Ages that the southern half of France never became as consolidated as the north. The counts of Toulouse, seated in the upper Garonne, by a series of marriages had extended their control to the Mediterranean; their technical vassalage to Paris sat very lightly upon them. It might well have been repudiated altogether had their territories been united with Aquitaine. A southern France opposed to the northern Frankish kingdom might then have come into existence; but, during the thirteenth century, circumstances gave the government of Paris an opportunity of absorbing for ever the separate civilization of the south.

This opportunity was the direct result of religious heresy. In the tenth and eleventh centuries the Balkan Slavonic creed of the Bogomils had already begun to filter, probably by trade routes, into Italy and southern France. In spite of some local persecution it gained ground, chiefly in Languedoc, during the twelfth century, and by 1200 was held by large numbers of the population. The heretics were designated 'Albigenses', but this was hardly exact, for the heretical centre was at Toulouse and neighbouring cities, rather than at Albi itself (Fig. 9). It is exceedingly difficult to form a precise idea of the Albigensian doctrines. What is certain is that the heretics were in opposition to the Church of Rome, and that they raised continual protest against the corruption of the clergy. The Church, on its side, viewed them as wicked rebels, ruining its dominion, and leading souls to perdition. Pope Innocent III launched a campaign of persuasion, but this failed because the count of Toulouse and the other great nobles of the area favoured the heretics. The pope then resolved on force, and in 1209 preached a crusade which assumed the character of a most ferocious war. Fanaticism and greed drew the nobility of the north southward, and for some twenty years horrible scenes of bloodshed were witnessed in the south.

The Albigensian crusade is known chiefly as the most atrocious of religious wars, but it also deserves to be remembered as a great step in the unification of France. The war had become a

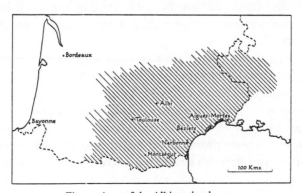

Fig. 9. Area of the Albigensian heresy

Based on R. Muir and G. Philip, *Historical Atlas* (London, 1927), p. 24.

political one—the south against the north. By the Treaty of Meaux in 1229 the king of Paris dispossessed the house of Toulouse of the greater part of its territories, and that of Béziers of the whole of its territories. The heresy itself was not immediately extinguished. There were later outbursts of rebellion, some fomented by the nobles of Languedoc (1240–42), and others emanating from the people of the towns who were embittered by confiscations and by religious persecutions (for example, at Narbonne in 1234, and Toulouse in 1235). The repressive measures were terrible. Thus, in 1245 the royal officers, assisting the Inquisition, seized the heretical city of Montségur and burned 200 people in one day. During the years that followed, the Inquisition continued to terrorize the district, but after about 1330 proceedings against heretics became rare. By fair means or foul, a state of peace and political and religious unity had been achieved. It was not only a strange heresy, but

27

a distinct nationality that had received a death-blow. The domain of the French king now touched the Mediterranean in fact as well as in theory; and Louis IX in 1246 created Aigues-Mortes so as to have a southern port of his own. The name of Toulouse, except as the name of the city itself, passed away, and the new acquisition of France came to be known by the name of the tongue that was common to the whole of southern France. Under the name 'Languedoc' this land of the south became one of the greatest and most valuable provinces of the French kingdom.

The situation in the south had been somewhat complicated by the fact that during the eleventh century Aragon had acquired various rights in French territory; France, likewise, had claimed authority over some Aragonese possessions. Conditions were clarified in 1258 when the French lands were cleared of Aragonese interference; and, in return, the Aragonese counties of Roussillon and Barcelona were relieved of even nominal homage to France.

In spite of these considerable gains, the kingdom of France did not yet extend east of the Rhône—or even reach it in many places. Beyond lay a number of semi-independent units owning allegiance, in name at any rate, to the Holy Roman Empire. By piecemeal annexation the advancing power of France gradually absorbed the whole area right into the heart of the Alps (Fig. 26). In 1305 the bishop of Viviers, after a struggle to maintain his independence, definitely acknowledged the suzerainty of the French king. In 1307 the archbishop of Lyons, temporal lord of the city and county of Lyons, did likewise. Finally, in 1316, the count of Valentinois and Die also paid homage, and the French kingdom now extended eastwards beyond the Rhône. Later in the same century (1349), the Dauphiny of Vienne was acquired by a bargain with its last independent prince. It passed from being an imperial possession into a province of France. But the acquisition of the Dauphiny did not carry with it that of the city of Vienne itself, which escaped for more than a century (1448). Later in the same century came the great annexation of Provence itself (1481). The rule of French princes in that county for two centuries had paved the way for the union. Although practically incorporated with the French kingdom, Provence preserved a separate administrative organization down to the French Revolution, and in laws relating to the county the kings of France still used the title 'count of Provence'.

By these two major annexations of the Dauphiny and Provence, the whole of the land between the Rhône and the Alps had been swallowed up by the French kingdom, with the exception of a group of small states surrounded by French territory. The principality of Orange for a long time was regularly seized by France in the course of every war, and was as regularly restored to independence at every peace, until its final annexation in the eighteenth century (1713). The Comtat Venaissin had become a papal possession in 1274, to which was added the city of Avignon in 1348; and so they remained until their annexation by the National Assembly in 1791.

WESTERN FRANCE

Along the western seaboard of France lay three units each with its own individuality and each presenting a considerable obstacle to assimilation by centralized authority at Paris. Normandy was Viking in origin, and by the conquest of 1066 had become identified with England. Brittany was Celtic, and remote. Aquitaine lay within the region of the *langue d'oc*. For a while, the marriage of Louis VII with Eleanor of Aquitaine united his kingdom and her duchy. A king of Paris for the first time really reigned at the foot of the Pyrenees. But the divorce of Louis and Eleanor, and her immediate marriage in 1152 with the duke of Normandy, who was also count of Anjou, again severed the southern duchy from France. The common lord of Normandy and Aquitaine became the first Angevin king of England, Henry II. Brittany was next added to his domain. Thus, in the course of the twelfth century, the House of Anjou came to control territory in France equal in area to that of the French king and his vassals put together, a dominion which held the mouths of the three great rivers, and which was further strengthened by possession of the English crown (Fig. 10).

It would be easy to exaggerate the cohesion of the Angevin empire. The customs of Brittany were not the same as those of Poitou; and between Normandy and Gascony the difference was very great. The common element in administration was provided only by the English king's wandering court, with its chancery and officials. Accustomed as we are to the associations of the modern map, the Angevin empire might seem most unnatural, but it must be remembered that in the Middle Ages feudal provinces changed hands with their rulers in a manner that today might seem incredible. In many ways, Normandy and south-east England had much more in common than London had with Yorkshire, or Paris with Provence. Communications by road were comparatively difficult; the sea united rather than divided, and so there was nothing anomalous about a state that straddled the English Channel.

But the territories that Henry II had tried to unite with England were, for the most part, lost by Richard I and John. The English cause was ruined by the battle of Bouvines, in Flanders, in 1214. Its results were decisive, and this dramatic triumph created a new sense of unity and power within the kingdom of France. The French king Philip Augustus came back to Paris amid scenes of popular enthusiasm. Beyond Paris, too, French patriotism and national pride were now united in the service of the crown. Brittany still remained subordinate though separate, but Normandy, Maine, Anjou, Touraine and Poitou became part of the French kingdom. By this great acquisition of territory the king at Paris suddenly became incomparably greater than any of his own vassals. The authority of the French crown had never made so great an advance. France was becoming a unified state in which provincial customs and communal privileges were subordinated to a uniform administration. Nor was it by wars alone that Philip Augustus strengthened the throne. He began the development of the machinery of government in France, which subsequently reached an elaboration unknown in Europe since the fall of the Roman Empire.

By the truce after Bouvines, the English were not, however, completely driven from the shores of France (Fig. 10). They

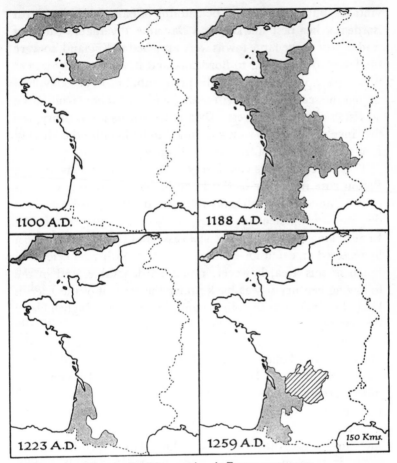

Fig. 10. English possessions in France, 1100–1259

Based on (1) W. R. Shepherd, *Historical Atlas* (London, 1930), pp. 65, 69 and 76;
(2) *The Cambridge Medieval History* (Cambridge, 1929), vol. VI, map 58; and
(3) E. C. Lodge, *Gascony under English Rule* (London, 1926), p. 19.
    The diagonal ruling on the map of 1259 indicates the area nominally transferred
to England by the Treaty of Paris but actually in dispute.

kept the Channel Islands which henceforward remained distinct
estates attached to the English crown. They also retained the
south-western seaboard. This latter may be explained largely
on economic grounds. A market for the wines of the south was
provided, not in France or Spain, where there were rival

vintages, but in England. The triumph of Paris would have cost Bordeaux her best market, and Bayonne a valuable carrying trade. Just as the large towns were attached to England, so were the lesser towns linked to Bordeaux and Bayonne. A system of privileges, approximating to the preferential tariff of today, had united the scattered Angevin realm, and it now bore fruit in the adhesion of the south-west. During the thirteenth century, the province of the south-west continued to be held by the kings of England as vassals of the king of France.

This state of affairs could only lead to dispute; thus in 1242 Poitou rose in favour of the English, but the revolt was suppressed, and the English army retired. An attempt to settle these disputes was made at the Treaty of Paris in 1259. By this, the English king once more became a vassal of France, but in return he received an extension of territory in the south-west (Fig. 10); much of this area, however, remained debatable, and in the following century it was back under the control of the French king (Fig. 11). On the other hand, in 1279, the English claim by marriage to Ponthieu was acknowledged.

Louis IX (1226–70) had taken a great part in the Crusades. His death was lamented throughout Christendom, and he was canonized in 1297. During his reign France had become one of the foremost powers in Europe. The administrative, judicial and financial machinery grew under his successors, especially under Philip IV (1285–1314), and the year 1302 saw the first meeting of the States-General. Assemblies may have been called in 1289, in 1290 and in 1292, but there is no satisfactory evidence to show that the representatives of the towns came together with the nobles and clergy before 1302. In the south-west, Philip occupied much of Gascony in 1294–6, only to restore it in 1303.

In 1328 the House of Capet became extinct, and the crown passed to the related family of Valois. During three and a half centuries the Capets had accomplished great things. The land subject to Hugh Capet in 987 was barely equivalent to two of the ninety modern departments of France. By 1328 the Capets ruled over an area equal to fifty-nine of them. Moreover, the

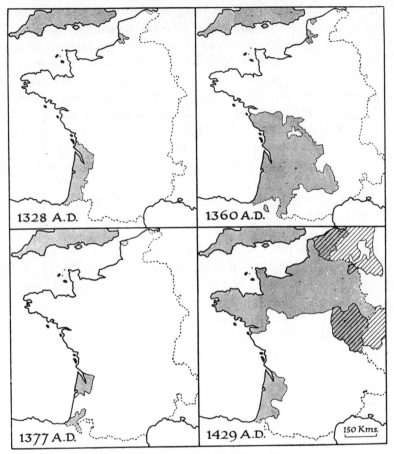

Fig. 11. English possessions in France, 1328–1429

Based on (1) W. R. Shepherd, *Historical Atlas* (London, 1930), pp. 76 and 81;
(2) *The Cambridge Medieval History* (Cambridge, 1932), vol. VII, map 69; and
(3) E. C. Lodge, *Gascony under English Rule* (London, 1926), p. 95.
    The diagonal ruling on the map of 1429 indicates the Burgundian lands.

power of the feudal nobility had been challenged by the beginnings of a centralized machinery of administration. Only four
great semi-independent provinces interfered with the unity of
the kingdom—Flanders, Brittany, Burgundy and Aquitaine.

    But this promising development of French government was
interrupted by the opening of the 'Hundred Years War' with

33

England. The phrase is misleading, for the two countries were by no means at war during the whole of a century; but from 1338 to 1453 their rivalry was always ready to break out into open conflict. One of the main objects of French kings had been to change their feudal superiority over Aquitaine into solid possession, and the Hundred Years War began through the designs of Philip of Valois upon the Aquitainian domain of Edward III. The king of England, in turn, found it convenient to assume the title of king of France. Another important factor in their enmity was a conflict for commercial supremacy in Flanders.

Blow upon blow fell upon the French. They were beaten on sea off Sluys in 1340, and on land at Crécy in 1346, and at Poitiers in 1356. To the perils of foreign invasion were added discontent and the possibility of insurrection at home—in Paris, in the Oise valley, and, indeed, over all northern France. At the Treaty of Brétigny in 1360, Edward III gave up all claim to the crown of France—but only in return for considerable territory (Fig. 12). Aquitaine, including Gascony and Poitou, but not Auvergne, together with the districts of Calais and Ponthieu on the Channel, were made over to England without the reservation of any homage. These lands became politically as foreign to France as the territory of her German and Spanish neighbours. Such a state of affairs could hardly endure for long. Within a few years the treaty was broken on the French side, and when Edward III died in 1377 the territory of the English in France included only some small parts of Aquitaine adjoining the cities of Bordeaux and Bayonne, and the district around Calais (Fig. 11).

But while peace was maintained with the external enemies of France, civil war broke out within the country itself. Charles VI, who came to the throne in 1380, was only twelve years old, and as he grew older he became subject to fits of madness. Two great families were rivals for the prize of power. On the one hand was the duke of Orléans, the king's brother; after the duke's murder in 1407, his place was taken by a relative, the duke of Armagnac, so that the faction is known sometimes as the

Orléanist, and sometimes as the Armagnac party. On the other side were the Burgundians led by the duke of Burgundy. Civil war broke out between these two rivals, and did not end even when danger threatened from England. Indeed, the Burgundians accepted the alliance of the English king, and consented to the dismemberment of their country. The success of the English was rapid and overwhelming. At Agincourt, in 1415, the French were defeated more heavily than at Crécy or Poitiers. The Treaty of Troyes in 1420 formally united the crowns of England and France, and Paris saw the crowning of an English king. Only the central part of France obeyed the legitimate heir of the kingdom, no longer king of Paris, but only of Bourges (Fig. 11).

In 1422 death carried off both the vigorous warrior Henry V of England and the feeble madman Charles VI. Charles VII succeeded to a poor inheritance. There were two French states, each with its king, and the same desolation afflicted the provinces administered from Paris as those administered from Bourges. Both areas were plunged into anarchy. A devastated countryside, terrorized towns and famine—these were the characteristic features of the crisis created by the Hundred Years War. There is, in fact, hardly a more sombre date in the history of France than the year 1422.

Within thirty years, however, France was to make one of the most marvellous recoveries in history, and to emerge bruised and exhausted, but intact in all essentials. For in 1422 the position of the two states was reversed. It was the English king who was now a minor, and England was now torn by the factions that later provoked the Wars of the Roses.

Another decisive factor was the intervention of Joan of Arc. She was a peasant girl from Domrémy, a village on the Meuse near the eastern frontier, and she believed that the 'voices' of saints told her to deliver France and to crown Charles VII at Reims. After much effort she obtained access to the king and persuaded him of the divine character of her visions. At this moment, in 1429, Orléans, the key to central France, was besieged by the English and she was allowed to set out with the relieving force. The siege was raised with success and Charles was persuaded to turn his army towards Reims, where he was crowned like his ancestors. In the following year Joan was captured by the Burgundians and sold to the English, to be brought to trial as a witch and a heretic. She was burnt in 1431,

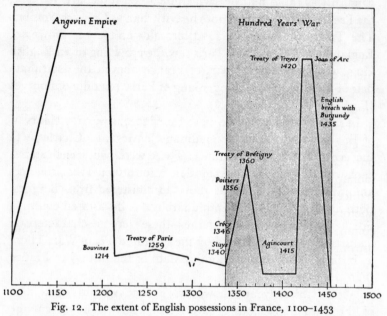

Fig. 12. The extent of English possessions in France, 1100–1453

The graph gives an approximate indication of the extent of territory held by England at different dates. Only Calais remained after 1453—apart from the Channel Islands.

and as the crowd broke up an English soldier muttered 'We are lost. We have burnt a saint.' It was indeed so. The importance of her work lay in much more than local military success. Its effect upon the morale of the French army was immense. Not that all improvement was due to her inspiration, for the clumsy feudal arrays that had met successive defeats were being replaced by professional soldiers properly organized. At her death, the English were still the dominant power in France, but their hold was weakening.

One of the most important facts in the decline of English influence was the loosening of the Anglo-Burgundian alliance. Successive disagreements culminated in 1435 when the duke of Burgundy definitely abandoned the English alliance and made terms with the king of France. From this time onward the victories of the French were uninterrupted, and the French king re-entered Paris in 1436. In 1450 the English fought their last battle in Normandy, and in 1453 the battle of Castillon, in Aquitaine, brought the long contest to an end. The result was the expulsion of the English from all France, except from the single district of Calais. Aquitaine, in English hands since the twelfth century, was now formally incorporated into the French kingdom. Some idea of the way in which the English possessions in France had fluctuated is given by Fig. 12.

The economic result of the war was ruin and depopulation, but the political result was the strengthening of the French monarchy. The defeats at Crécy, Poitiers and Agincourt had reduced both the numbers and the power of the feudal nobility. Victory had come through the agency of hired soldiers, through commanders who were not of the high nobility, and through the use of gunpowder—one of the worst enemies of the feudal noble. A constitutional step taken towards the end of the war strengthened the crown more than men saw at the time. This was the *Ordonnance* of 1439 which gave the king the power to levy a tax (the *taille*) for the support of a permanent army. At first this was restricted to the country of *langue d'oïl*, but it was extended in 1446 to include 'Languedoc'. Further measures promoted the organization of the new standing army, and the main foundations were laid upon which French absolute monarchy rested until its overthrow at the time of the Revolution.

As an epilogue to this story of acquisition in the west came the complete incorporation of the province of Brittany in 1532 as a result of a series of marriages. The liberties of the province were guaranteed, and Brittany retained its own parliament until the Revolution.

EASTERN FRANCE

Throughout the Middle Ages the north-eastern boundary of France had remained comparatively stable. Starting from the North Sea, it roughly followed the course of the Scheldt, but excluded Cambrai; the counties of Flanders and Artois thus lay within France. From the source of the Scheldt, it ran eastwards to the Meuse. Then it turned south, dividing Champagne from Lorraine and the duchy of Burgundy from the county of Burgundy (Franche-Comté), and afterwards approximately following the Saône. Southward, it continued in an irregular line to the west of the Rhône. It is extremely doubtful, however, whether there were many visible signs of these limits on the ground, and only slowly, it would seem, were boundary stones set up along the Meuse. Moreover, there were the inevitable disputed strips of territory, and some lords had territories on both sides of what might be regarded as the frontier. If the inhabitants of a frontier locality were questioned, their replies were not always illuminating. They could only name the jurisdiction to which they were subject, and this was a question of justice and lordship, not of sovereignty; the arguments were feudal, not national. The feudal idea was relatively clear, but the idea of the state or of nationality was obscure. It was quite possible to be a vassal of the king without being his subject. During the thirteenth century, the pope, in a letter to Louis IX, stated that no one in Rome had any exact information about the Franco-German frontier: 'We do not find it determined in any document; although for a long time we have dared to say that, in certain places, it was fixed by rivers, by ecclesiastical provinces, or by dioceses, we cannot clearly demark it; we are in complete ignorance.'

Along this eastern frontier, during the fifteenth century, the holder of one of the great French provinces grew into a considerable European power and became the rival of his French overlord. The dukes of Burgundy rose to the same kind of position that, in the twelfth century, had been held by the dukes of Normandy. In 1361 the territories of the duke of Burgundy had lapsed to the crown, but instead of adding them to the royal domain, the French king had granted them to his fourth son, Philip. In the hands of the successors of Philip, the Burgundian power proved to be an enemy more dangerous than any of the earlier feudal nobles had been. The success of the English in the Hundred Years War (and the Treaty of Troyes in 1420) was largely the result of the Anglo-Burgundian alliance. The reconciliation with France in 1435 left Burgundy no less strong. By an astute and enterprising policy the Burgundian family proceeded to build up a large domain on the eastern frontier of France. Most of the provinces were acquired by the fortunes of marriage or inheritance, some by purchase, some by force of arms. Part of this territory lay within the German allegiance and part within that of the king of France (Fig. 13). Charles the Bold, in the fifteenth century, all but raised his duchy to the position of a middle kingdom between France and Germany, but this ambition was frustrated by his death in 1477. The Burgundian lands fell into three portions—some became independent, some became German, and some became French. In the first place, the ecclesiastical territories of Liége and Utrecht recovered their independence, as also did Gelderland, while Lorraine went back to its duke. In the second place, the greater part of the inheritance passed by marriage to the House of Austria and thereby in the end to Spain. In the third place, France obtained Picardy and the duchy of Burgundy itself. The latter consisted of territory which the kings of France had never before ruled directly, and its incorporation marks an important stage in the advance of French power towards the German lands on its eastern border. The French also claimed Flanders, Charolais, Artois and Franche-Comté, but resigned their rights at the Treaty of Senlis in 1493; and this renunciation was repeated in later treaties—those of Madrid (1526) and Cambrai (1529).[1]

---

[1] The precise status of Flanders, Artois and Picardy in the fifteenth century is difficult to define. At the reconciliation of the duke of Burgundy and the king of France in 1435, the duke, already in possession of Flanders and Artois, received 'the Somme towns' of Picardy together with Boulogne and Ponthieu; he was, moreover, exempted for life from the obligation of homage (Treaty of Arras). The French king, however, reserved the right to redeem 'the Somme towns' for 400,000

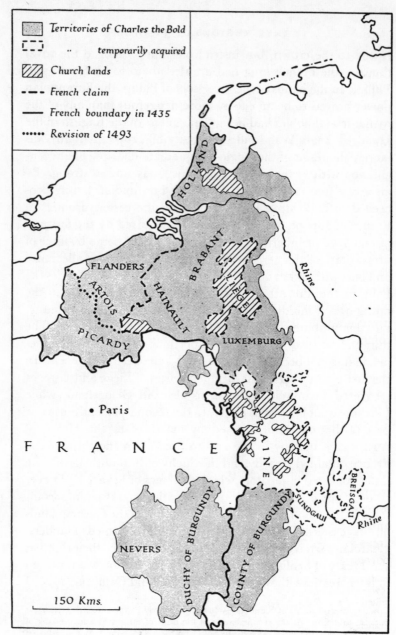

Fig. 13. The Burgundian lands

Based on *The Cambridge Modern History Atlas* (Cambridge, 1924), map 6. For the status of Flanders, Picardy and Artois in the fifteenth century, see the footnote on p. 39.

THREE REGIONS OF FRANCE

It was not until the time of Louis XIV that Artois and Franche-Comté became French territory (see Fig. 18).

Thus by the close of the Middle Ages, the north-eastern frontier of France had retreated and now excluded Flanders and Artois; the eastern frontier still lay along the left bank of the Meuse. But within these limits the kingdom had grown stronger by the inclusion of the duchy of Burgundy which hitherto had possessed something of the character of a separate sovereignty.

4. ECONOMIC AND MARITIME DEVELOPMENT

The break-up of the empire of Charlemagne was followed by a decline in both agricultural and industrial production throughout central and western Europe. Political anarchy on land and piracy on sea were hardly conducive to economic progress, and it was not until the eleventh century that there was a revival of commercial life.

ECONOMIC ADVANCE IN THE TWELFTH AND THIRTEENTH CENTURIES

The great business of colonizing waste land, sketched out in the Carolingian epoch, was taken up again and continued actively for the next century and a half. Both the Capetian kings and the French monastic orders stimulated the work of reclamation. Much forest land was cleared and many marshes drained. Attempts were made to improve the soil by the use of chalk, marl, ashes and calcareous sand. Production developed enormously and land values greatly increased after about 1050. Certain areas in the Paris basin, such as Beauce and Brie, became exporters of grain, while in the south the cultivation of the vine

gold crowns. The towns were actually redeemed in 1463, but lost again in 1465. It was not until after the death of Charles the Bold, in 1477, that Picardy was finally united with the French crown. France also claimed Flanders and Artois (together with Charolais and Franche-Comté), and Louis XI was able to keep Artois and Franche-Comté as a dowry for his future daughter-in-law, Margaret of Austria (Treaty of Arras, 1482). But his son Charles VIII never married Margaret, and by the Treaty of Senlis in 1493 her dowry was restored. By the subsequent treaties of Madrid (1526) and Cambrai (1529), France renounced her claim to Flanders and Artois.

41

was greatly extended, and the vineyards of France acquired a European reputation. This revolution in production in France and elsewhere during the twelfth and thirteenth centuries is one of the capital events of European history.

What was true of agriculture was equally true of industry. Some districts of France were able to turn to industrial specialization and the northern area devoted itself to the manufacture of woollens. The wool came increasingly from England, and the wares of towns like Arras, Douai, Lille, and St Omer were soon appreciated throughout the continent; this northern industrial region of Flanders formed one of the most important manufacturing centres in medieval Europe. Weaving was also carried on in Normandy, especially about Rouen, and in Berry where the country was also suitable for rearing sheep. In the south, too, some manufacture of cloth was carried on near the poor and arid lands of Crau, of Quercy, of Corbières and of the Causses—areas where sheep breeding is still important (Fig. 14).

The result of this industrial development was the rise of a new social group that stood in contrast with the rural agricultural peasantry and the territorial nobles. And it is with the appearance of this intermediate category—wealthy merchants on the one hand, artisans on the other—that the rise of towns was associated. Hitherto, 'towns' were mainly military and administrative centres or the seats of bishoprics, but now a new element was added to the castle or the cathedral. The town, in an economic and social sense, was coming into being, and in a legal sense, too, for it demanded corporate rights and privileges from the feudal lords; from the inhabitants of the French *bourg* has come the term *bourgeoisie*. Despite their many differences, the towns of Italy, Germany, France and England were all manifestations of the same spirit of collective association for the purposes of trade and manufacture.

This economic prosperity, together with the growth of centralized monarchy, was reflected by the astonishing outburst of building during the twelfth and thirteenth centuries, and in particular by the rise of Gothic architecture in the Paris basin, as opposed to the older Romanesque of Normandy and the south.

The Mediterranean Coast

The economic progress of the twelfth and thirteenth centuries only served to emphasize the intermediate location of France in Europe. To the south, the main trade of Europe was carried

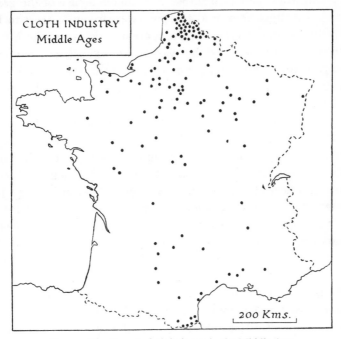

Fig. 14. The French cloth industry in the Middle Ages

Based on the *Atlas de France* (Paris, 1938), plate 43.
    The dots indicate the centres of the industry. For later development, see Fig. 28.

on in Mediterranean waters which gave access to the commodities of the east. This southern commerce was dominated by the Italian trading cities, and there was no question of eclipsing them. Yet, after the French kingdom effectively reached the sea in 1229, the shipowners of the south made progress. To the east, Marseilles remained in the hands of the counts of Provence until the fifteenth century, but Aigues-Mortes, St Gilles, Arles, Narbonne, Montpellier, despite local difficulties of navigation, took an increasingly active part in the trade of the Mediterranean and of the Levant.

Like their English rivals, the French kings of the Middle Ages drew their naval forces from the feudal array, from the national levy and from their own ships. But the obedience of the great vassals was uncertain, and the king was driven to trust to his own ships. These were drawn to a great extent from the Mediterranean seaboard, and he was forced to seek much of his maritime force, by purchase or by hire, from Genoa and, to a less extent, from Aragon. Louis IX created the office of admiral of the fleet, and when he sailed on his first crusade in 1248 he formed a French royal fleet and, with the aid of the Genoese, built a dockyard at Aigues-Mortes. The expeditions of later crusaders, too, stimulated shipping activity. But despite considerable progress, France was unable to support a great Mediterranean fleet of war. When at war with Aragon in 1285, the French had to rely on some hundred galleys collected along the coast from Pisa to Narbonne and, under the control of a Neapolitan admiral, they were defeated.

The Atlantic Coasts

In the north, the maritime activity of the North Sea and the Baltic was complementary to that of the Mediterranean. The great economic centre of Flanders and the activities of the Hanseatic merchants resulted in the development of cities that resembled in some ways the trading republics of Italy. Here, too, the political connexion between France and England increased the commerce of the Atlantic and Channel ports. Bordeaux, with its export of wine, was outstanding. Farther north, Oléron, La Rochelle, St Jean-d'Angély, Niort on the Sèvre, which was then navigable, and Nantes, exported wheat, salt, wool, wines, and did a large amount of business with England and Flanders.

But the attempts of the French kings to fight the English at sea in the thirteenth century brought little success. Philip Augustus collected 1700 vessels and even planned an invasion of England, but in 1213 the ships were surrounded and burnt in the port of Damme near Sluys, and the king could only sadly conclude, 'The French know little of naval methods'. The warfare between the two countries gave ample opportunity for enormous piratical activity centred in part on the Channel Islands. Towards the end of the century another great French armada was assembled against England; almost all Europe was put under contribution in 1294—the Hanseatic towns and the Basques sent ships; Norway promised 300; Provence sent a squadron; the French Mediterranean fleet was marshalled; and from Genoa came shipbuilders to organize an arsenal and dockyard at Rouen. An army was encamped in readiness at Boulogne—but little came of the preparations.

The Champagne Fairs

Standing between the two great commercial centres of northern Italy and Flanders, on the route between Venice and Bruges, was the plain of Champagne, and the Champagne fairs became the markets of Europe in the twelfth and thirteenth centuries, for the fair was the most important mechanism of exchange in the Middle Ages. On these plains of the Upper Seine and the Marne, at the meeting-place of the great routes which united the Mediterranean countries to the lands bordering the Channel and the North Sea, these fairs attracted wholesale merchants and lesser travelling traders from over most of the West—Levantines, Italians, Spaniards, Flemings, Germans, English, Scots, to say nothing of the French themselves. The most important fairs were at Lagny, at Bar-sur-Aube and, above all, at Provins and Troyes.

THE HUNDRED YEARS WAR

The great medieval prosperity of France in agriculture, in industry and in commerce was swept away by the Hundred Years War. The Champagne fairs, no longer the market for English wool and Flemish cloth and eastern luxuries, quickly lost their European importance. At Provins in 1399 there were only thirty looms where formerly some 3200 had been at work. The Venetian and Genoese merchants learned to pass through the Straits of Gibraltar, and sailed direct to Sluys and Bruges in

Flanders and to London, thus leaving France outside the main routes. On the Atlantic and in the English Channel, the consequences were no less grievous. French shipping was almost entirely diverted from its commercial activities to privateering warfare and to preparation for military enterprises against England. The control of maritime trade passed into the hands of neutrals, Spanish or Portuguese. The French kings were obliged even to grant them privileges in French ports, notably at Rouen and Honfleur.

The war opened with disaster at sea. A French fleet of 200 ships and some 25,000 men had been collected in preparation for an invasion of England, when Edward III shattered their force off Sluys, in 1340. Yet, great as the disaster was, it did not mark the end of the French effort in the Channel. Later in the century, some fifty barges and galleys built at Rouen were used to cause repeated diversions (in 1378, 1380 and 1385), which greatly hampered the despatch of reinforcements from England. In 1386 a 'Great Army of the Sea' was assembled at Sluys again, but the stormy season was enough to break it up, and it was never able to threaten England. In the Channel the French no longer had a fleet; the way was open for English transports and ultimately for the transport of the army that brought disaster at Agincourt in 1415. Yet, even during the confusion of these years, French seamen had not altogether lost the initiative. In 1402 Jean de Béthencourt sailed from La Rochelle to conquer the Canary Islands, but, despite his efforts, the reward was reaped by Spain.

In the Mediterranean, the decay of French shipping was accelerated locally by natural causes. The bursting of the dam of the Aude in 1320 and the silting of the estuary ruined the port of Narbonne; the attempt to establish an outport at Leucate could not avert decline. The channel at Aigues-Mortes became so silted up that after 1336 the port was unnavigable. Montpellier was decimated by epidemics, and its population declined to a fraction of its former number. Marseilles, not yet part of France, was involved in the costly wars of the House of Anjou (now rulers of Provence) for the possession of the kingdom of Naples, and was unable to compete with Venice and Genoa for the sea trade of the Atlantic.

This decline on the northern and southern shores, and in the fairs of Champagne, was but an index of the decay within France itself. The anarchy of the Hundred Years War was accentuated by the ravages of the Black Death in 1348–50. In the words of Petrarch (1360) France became 'a heap of ruins'. Thomas Basin, bishop of Lisieux, writing about 1440, described the vast extent of uncultivated land between the Somme and the Loire, all 'overgrown with brambles and bushes'. Some of the accounts may have been exaggerated, but the fact of desolation is borne out by abundant evidence.

FIFTEENTH-CENTURY RECOVERY

Before the long contest with England was brought to an end in 1453, France was already beginning to recover, and the recovery continued with astonishing rapidity. Thus the town of Montpellier, reduced almost to extinction at the beginning of the fifteenth century, was stimulated into new activity by the enterprise of Jacques Cœur about the year 1440. The French competed against the monopoly of the Venetians in the Mediterranean, and re-established contacts with Egypt, Syria and North Africa. The story of Jacques Cœur has become a legend, but his was not a unique case—all the ports of the south shared in the general recovery of the kingdom. Louis XI (1461–83), immediately after the occupation of Roussillon, began work on the harbour of Collioure. Towards the end of his reign, he at last obtained possession of Marseilles (1481) and announced that it was to become the emporium at which merchandise from the east would be unloaded, to be distributed to all the countries of the west. He planned the building of a great Mediterranean fleet, and although he died before his project had been realized, he had at any rate given a great impetus to French trade in the Mediterranean.

Similarly, the seaports on the Atlantic and Channel coasts recovered. Louis XI revived the prosperity of La Rochelle and Bordeaux. But here, foreign co-operation was necessary and favours were granted to Spanish, Portuguese and Hanseatic merchants; Louis introduced commercial clauses into almost every political treaty. He was anxious, too, for a renewal of trade with England—affected adversely by the French recovery of Aquitaine and Normandy—and, in 1470, he even organized an exhibition of French products in England.

This activity on the seaboards of France was symptomatic of the general revival of the kingdom—roads were repaired, navigation by river and canal was resumed, manufactures were restarted. But not all the loss was recovered. The Champagne fairs had lost their European importance for ever, because the great commercial routes of Europe no longer passed through the Troyes country. In the Mediterranean, Turkish victories interrupted commerce at the very moment that French shipping was trying to revive old connexions. On the Atlantic, Spain and Portugal were securing a start that threatened the future of French development. Finally, French industry was being rivalled by the rise of manufacturing in England, Italy and other countries. But despite these adverse factors, the French recovery was remarkable enough. With the passing of the Middle Ages, France was able to take its place with the great commercial nations of Europe.

5. RELIGIOUS AND CULTURAL DEVELOPMENT

What made France outstanding in the Middle Ages was not so much political or even economic development as the contributions made to the religious and cultural life of western Europe. The monastery of Cluny, founded in Burgundy in 910 by a duke of Aquitaine, was to have more influence than any dynasty of kings. Following a new interpretation of the Benedictine rule, Cluny stood for a vision of the monastic life which drew postulants from the length and breadth of Catholic Christendom. Soon there were daughter houses of Cluny not only all over France but as far distant as England and Spain, Italy and Poland.

These houses were held together by a strictly centralized discipline. All took their orders from the Abbot of Cluny, and the congregation they formed became strong enough in the eleventh century to enable the pope to carry through a much-needed reform of the episcopate.

The turn of the eleventh and twelfth centuries saw another extraordinary revival of the monastic ideal. Four great orders were founded in France: the Premonstratensian order of Austin canons; the order of Grammont (*les Bonshommes*); the Carthusians, who combined the hermit's life with the community life of the convent; and the Cistercian order of reformed Benedictines which took its name from the abbey of Cîteaux in the Rhône valley. A monk of Cîteaux, Bernhard of Clairvaux, became one of the most deeply revered of all medieval saints as well as the most influential man in the politics of the twelfth century.

Architecture owed some of its finest medieval development to French genius. The Romanesque style flowered and spread in various forms over all Christendom in the tenth and eleventh centuries, but its main inspiration and drive came from the Cluniac monks. The style known as Gothic might better be called the French style: it first appeared in the Ile de France and its environs. During the reign of Philip Augustus (1180–1223) cathedrals were begun at Paris, Chartres, Bourges, Laon, Soissons, Reims, Meaux, Noyon, Amiens, Rouen, Cambrai, Arras, Tours, Sées, Coutances and Bayeux; nearly all of these were completed before the end of the thirteenth century. In the time of St Louis (Louis IX, 1226–70) French architecture, with its attendant arts of sculpture and stained glass, became famous all over Christendom.

It was in the time of Philip Augustus and St Louis that the University of Paris became the greatest centre of learning that western Europe had ever known. The masters and scholars of Paris had had a great reputation ever since Peter Abelard (1079–1142) first came to teach on the Mont Ste Geneviève and Cardinal Eudes de Châteauroux declared that 'Gaul is the oven where the intellectual bread of all this world is baked'. Now the University of Paris became a self-governing corporation with which neither bishop nor monarch dared interfere. Its foundation was followed by that of the universities of Montpellier, Toulouse and Orléans.

French universities were the chief cradles and repositories of scholarship, and the Romance languages of France were the most widespread forms of literary expression in the Europe of the thirteenth and early fourteenth centuries. The *langue d'oïl* owed its expansion over Europe to the fame of the University of Paris, to the gathering of merchants and other travellers in the fairs of northern France and to the exploits of French arms in the Crusades. It would be a long time before the vernacular of other countries could achieve a written form to equal the prose of Villehardouin and Joinville, the historians of the age of St Louis.

CHAPTER III

CENTRALIZATION AND EXPANSION

1. THE CENTRALIZATION OF THE STATE

An essential feature of French development from the tenth to the eighteenth centuries was the growth of centralized government. By the end of the fifteenth century the monarchy, with the aid of the bourgeois, was beginning to form a professional non-feudal administration. The assertion of Louis XI (1461–83) was more than a mere claim: 'to us alone belongs and is due the general government and administration of the realm.' To keep in constant touch with his officials, and 'to have careful information from every quarter', Louis created the *poste*; on all the main roads in the kingdom relays of four or five good horses, reserved for the king's riders, were arranged under the charge of *maîtres de la poste*.

But centralized government did not necessarily mean a centralized people. While the French monarchy became more and more absolute, France itself remained divided, and during the wars of religion in the sixteenth and seventeenth centuries some of these divisions came dangerously near the surface. The danger was averted and the administrative reforms of Richelieu, in the first half of the seventeenth century, prepared the way for the great measure of centralization under Louis XIV. Not that all differences were obliterated, for, until the Revolution, France retained many evidences of its former disunity.

RELIGIOUS WARS, 1562–1629

It was impossible for France to remain isolated from the general movement of religious reform in Europe during the sixteenth century. The writings of Luther and other reformers found earnest readers, and, in spite of persecution, the reformed doctrines gained increasing support in France. On 29 January 1535 an edict ordered the extermination of the heretics, and with this began that emigration of Protestants which did not cease until the middle of the eighteenth century. The most famous of these exiles was John Calvin, who became pastor of the first French Protestant Church, founded in 1538 at Strasbourg by some 1500 refugees. The first Protestant church in France itself was that of Meaux (1546), organized on the lines of that at Strasbourg. The distribution of the Huguenot centres in France is instructive. Apart from a few outlying centres, of which the most important was Normandy, the bulk of the Protestants lay south of a line from Lyons to La Rochelle; and the last Huguenot resistance, like the Albigensian heresy, lay in the area to the west of the Rhône delta.

Constant warfare with the Hapsburgs prevented any very complete execution of the edicts against heresy, but when peace was made with the Hapsburgs in 1559 a period of religious conflict began at home. Between 1562 and 1570 there was intermittent warfare which ended in the Treaty of St Germain. The Huguenots now obtained, first, liberty of conscience and of worship, and then, as guarantee of the king's word, four fortified places—La Rochelle, a key to the sea; La Charité in the centre; Cognac and Montauban to the south. The religious struggle seemed almost at an end when, in 1572, the unfortunate Charles IX was induced to sanction a general massacre of the Huguenots in Paris on the eve of St Bartholomew (24 August). Other towns followed the example of the capital, and altogether nearly 20,000 victims fell.

The news of the massacre roused the survivors to a desperate resistance. Weakened by the loss of many leaders, they had but little chance of success. The government prepared forces to reduce those towns which refused obedience. La Rochelle held out for six and a half months against the Catholic army which was obliged to abandon the siege after losing more than 20,000 men. A policy of suppression was impossible to carry out, and an edict of July 1573 brought the war to an end by granting a general amnesty and by permitting Huguenot worship in La Rochelle, Nîmes, Montauban and Sancerre. Hostilities, however, soon broke out again, and continued intermittently for the rest of the century.

During these years the issues of the Catholic-Protestant struggle were confused by political considerations. The Huguenot bourgeoisie, mostly drawn from the industrial districts of the south, joined hands with discontented nobles and anticlericals. The defence of a persecuted religion became more and more involved with a struggle for political power. The complications of the time were not diminished by the fact that each side obtained foreign assistance—the Spanish support of the Catholic party was particularly important. 'Men', it was said, 'were combatting not for faith, not for Christ, but for command.'

At this time the heir to the throne was none other than Henry of Navarre who had become leader of the Huguenots, so that in 1589 when the house of Valois became extinct, the legitimate king was a Calvinist. At first it seemed an impossible situation, but the Catholics were so divided among themselves about an alternative that the result was complete confusion. Henry offered a solution—his own accession and religious toleration. In 1593 he decided the fate of France by formally adopting the Catholic faith, and in the following year, supported by the moderate Catholics, he was able to enter Paris in triumph. He at once declared war against Spain, which still supported the extreme French Catholic party. All loyal Frenchmen rallied to his standard. In 1595 he was acknowledged by the Pope, and in 1598 the Treaty of Vervins ended the war with Spain. When peace was in sight, Henry turned to the question of the Huguenots. In 1598 the Edict of Nantes gave them liberty of conscience, full civil rights, and freedom of public worship in those places where it had been celebrated in 1577; it also gave them guarantees in the form of a large number of fortified places to be held for eight years, the cost of garrisoning them to be borne by the crown. Thus, after nearly forty years of dispute, a religious compromise was secured (Fig. 15).

But an end to civil war had not yet been achieved, for the death of Henry IV in 1610 left his great work unfinished. During the minority of his successor, Louis XIII, power fell into the hands of counsellors who were only too ready to favour the Catholic party. The Huguenots once more took up arms in

53

defence of their liberty. Their dissatisfaction was again as much political as religious. Aided by the weakness of the crown, the Huguenot towns had become virtually self-governing communes, independent of the central government. Huguenot organization

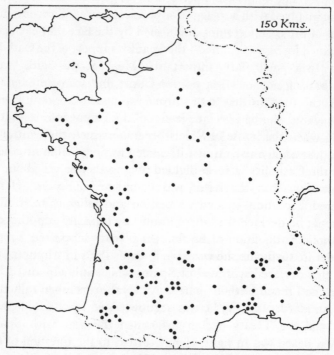

Fig. 15. Huguenot centres in France

Based on *The Cambridge Modern History Atlas* (Cambridge, 1924), map 19. The 'places de sûreté' of the Huguenots are indicated by dots.

had parcelled France out into districts ('circles') under regular officers. In the strong words attributed to Richelieu, the Huguenots shared the government of France with the king.

There were revolts in 1621–2, in 1625–6 and again in 1627–9. The great Huguenot stronghold of La Rochelle was starved out after a gallant defence, and then it was a comparatively easy matter to crush the rebellion in Languedoc and in the district of the Cévennes. By the Treaty of Alais in June 1629, the

Huguenots ceased to retain any political power. Their guaranteed towns were handed over to the government; their fortresses were dismantled; their organization was destroyed, and they ceased to exist as a political party; their liberty of worship alone remained unimpaired. The treaty marked the end of the period of religious wars, and constituted an important step forward in the centralization of the country.

ADMINISTRATIVE REFORM UNDER RICHELIEU, 1624–42

Richelieu had come into power as the chief minister of Louis XIII in 1624, just in time to destroy the political power of the Huguenots. But there was yet much to be done before France was a unified state. As long as the administration of the provinces and the raising and control of the army were in the hands of the territorial nobility, a successful court intrigue was still liable to throw the country back into a state of anarchy. To obviate this danger Richelieu applied himself to the establishment of a bureaucracy—a civil service under the direct control of the crown. The abolition of duelling and the destruction of feudal castles in 1626; the substitution of royal administrative officers for those of the territorial nobles in Brittany and Languedoc after the rebellions of Vendôme (1626) and Montmorency (1632) respectively; the direct administration by crown officials of the Huguenot towns after 1629; the development of a professional army; the more complete establishment of a royal post throughout the kingdom in 1627—all these were steps in undermining the political power of the nobles and in centralizing royal authority more completely at Paris.

An indication of the way in which France was now being governed from the capital is provided by Tavernier's map of post roads in 1632 (Fig. 16). In Roman times, Lyons had been the chief route centre of Gaul; and during subsequent centuries Roman roads still provided the main routes from town to town. But the road network, considered as a system and not as individual stretches, had changed its character; by the seventeenth century the road centre had become Paris. French geographers themselves have emphasized the part that routes play in holding diverse regions together in one political unit. Thus it was that the main roads of France, and the organization of post services along them, were calculated to serve the centralizing policy of its monarchy. The stages in this development are plain to see.

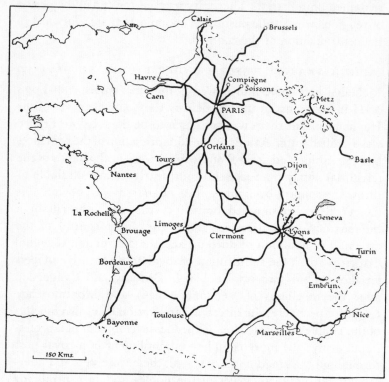

Fig. 16. The post roads of France, 1632

Drawn from the *Carte géographique des Postes* by Michel Tavernier (1632).

Lyons was a focus of routes in the seventeenth century, as in Roman times. The focus at Paris, however, was a new feature not characteristic of the Roman road system.

In 1599 Henry IV's chief minister, Sully, took the new title of 'Chief Road Surveyor of France', and created the nucleus of the administrative machinery of the *Ponts et Chaussées*, the first national highway department of modern times. In 1627 Richelieu improved the post system; in 1672 the transport of letters became a state privilege. Although there was no great technical

improvement in road making until the coming of the eighteenth
century, the implications of Tavernier's map of 1632 are clear
enough. The road system shows a considered combination of ways
and means in accord with the centralizing policy of the state.

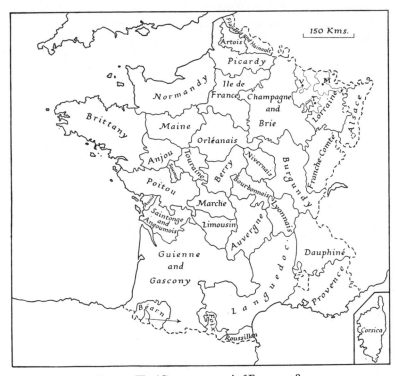

Fig. 17. The 'Gouvernements' of France, 1789

Based on (1) W. R. Shepherd, *Historical Atlas* (Paris, 1930), p. 146; (2) R. L. Poole,
Historical Atlas of Modern Europe (Oxford, 1902), plate 58.
    Under Francis I (1515–47) there were twelve principal *gouvernements*. In 1618
there were twenty-five; and by 1789 there were thirty-eight. The three bishoprics
of Metz (M), Toul (T) and Verdun (V) are marked.

In order to consolidate his political despotism, Richelieu
made use of the system of 'Intendants' established in the latter
part of the sixteenth century. These intendants were commissioners sent out by the king to restore order in the provinces
after the civil wars. Their functions were at first extraordinary
and temporary, but some had been retained as permanent State

officials. In 1637 Richelieu appointed intendants over the whole of France, and placed the complete financial, judicial and police administration in their hands. The centralized monarchy which grew up after the Hundred Years War, under Louis XI and his successors, had divided France into *gouvernements*, each presided over by a governor whose functions were mainly military, but whose chief significance lay in the fact that he represented the crown against the disruptive tendencies of the old feudal nobility (Fig. 17). The new intendants were even more strictly dependent on the crown, and were not drawn, like the governors, from the ranks of the provincial *noblesse*. Their duties became so extended that the power of the governors was reduced to a shadow. Their unit of administration was a new one (the *généralité*), and, in effect, the new system created a permanent civil service that helped to centralize absolute power at the expense of local authority.

THE REIGN OF LOUIS XIV, 1643–1715

Richelieu died in 1642 and his death was followed by that of his royal master, Louis XIII, in the following year. The new king, Louis XIV, was but five years old, and France was once more weakened by a regency and by renewed intrigues on the part of the nobility. Under these circumstances there grew up the movement which is generally known as the 'Fronde'. It was, in effect, the last rally of the discontented elements of French society against the power of the monarchy under the *ancien régime*. It broke out in 1648; but under Richelieu's successor, Cardinal Mazarin, it was brought to an end in 1653. Government by intendants was re-established, and the direct authority of the king was henceforward without rival in France. When Mazarin died in 1661, Louis XIV, now twenty-four years old, declared his intention to rule as well as to reign. For fifty-five years he not only controlled the destinies of France, but was the most prominent figure in Europe.

Many wars were fought during his reign, and the frontiers of France were greatly extended (Fig. 18). But perhaps even more important than his wars and his diplomacy was the type of civilization that now developed in France. He was not a man of

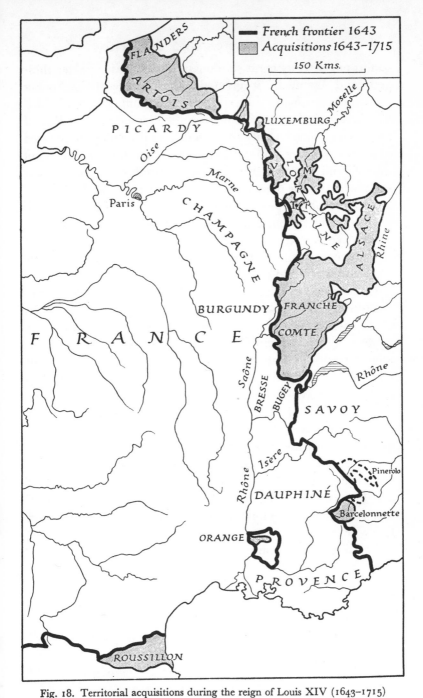

Fig. 18. Territorial acquisitions during the reign of Louis XIV (1643–1715)

Based on (1) *The Cambridge Modern History Atlas* (Cambridge, 1924), map 46; (2) W. R. Shepherd, *Historical Atlas* (London, 1930), p. 126.

At the Peace of Westphalia in 1648, France obtained formal recognition of her sovereignty over the three bishoprics of Metz (M), Toul (T) and Verdun (V) which she had held since 1552. Pinerolo, held since 1631, was lost to Savoy in 1696.

genius nor a really great statesman, but he was capable, energetic and dignified. So great did the prestige of the French monarchy become that its etiquette and manners spread to all other courts in Europe. Moreover, the literary and intellectual movement which had begun in the days of Richelieu culminated in a blaze of glory, and critics in France became the arbiters of taste for all Europe. French drama reached its highest development in the hands of Corneille, Racine, and Molière; among the philosophers of the period were Descartes, Pascal, Bossuet, and Fénelon. The 'Age of Louis XIV' was not only the golden age of French literature but a landmark in the history of European culture; the domination of French thought over the European world of letters was complete.

In the midst of this efflorescence of culture, Louis lived surrounded by servility and adulation, and intoxicated by the idea of his own greatness and invincible power. Everything was made to centre around the king and the court. Any form of opposition was unbearable; neither public nor private criticism was allowed; the police became the chief bulwark of the government. The States-General were never summoned. The centralized system of Richelieu and Mazarin was carried to its logical conclusion. Louis attempted to destroy the provincial differences of France, and to spread a uniform civilization as well as a uniform administration over the country. The destruction of municipal liberties was completed under the pretext of bad financial administration. The intendants were supported and strengthened against all local opposition. 'L'état,' said Louis, 'c'est moi.'

The Huguenots became a particular object of the king's attention. Satisfied with the free exercise of their worship, many Huguenots of the middle class had devoted themselves with great success to industrial employments of various kinds. But now, impelled by his passion for uniformity and by an increasing devotion in the later years of his life, Louis began a repressive policy. In 1682 missions were established throughout France to convert the heretics, and edicts were issued closing Huguenot churches and schools. When numbers of the most industrious of the artisans of France began to leave the country, Louis forbade emigration. In desperation, the mountaineers of the Cévennes rose in tumult in 1683, and were suppressed with inhuman barbarities. Finally, in October 1685, came the Revocation of the Edict of Nantes; the reformed worship was suppressed, and its ministers expelled. Many Huguenots escaped and carried their thrift and skill to the enemies of France—thus Holland dates its industrial revival, and Brandenburg its industrial life, from 1685. It is said that over 400,000 inhabitants were thus lost to France. Those who were too poor or too ignorant to escape continued, in the fastness of the Cévennes, a desultory but fanatical struggle with their oppressor. From 1703 to 1711, under the name of the ' Camisards ', they were able to hold their own, but ultimate triumph was with Louis. Not until 1801 did the Huguenots again attain a legal standing in France.

In Paris itself, Louis had refused to live any longer at the Louvre in the midst of the citizens, and built for himself the enormous palace of Versailles. This became the centre of national life and a model for foreign royalties. While the people groaned under taxes to support this royal magnificence, the nobles of France were content to hold the towel at the king's toilet. Although it had lost its independence under Richelieu, the nobility of France remained a rich body with great social influence. By destroying the political power of the nobles and yet leaving them their privileges, Richelieu and Louis XIV prepared the way for the Revolution.

INCOMPLETE CENTRALIZATION

Despite the centralizing policy of Richelieu, Colbert and Louis XIV, unity was never completely attained in France. Here and there were many anomalies and local independencies—survivals from an earlier age. And, more particularly, France remained divided within itself from the standpoint of administration, of law and of commerce. It was for the Revolution to sweep away these anomalies and to produce a reorganized France more centralized than ever.

Administratively, there was a difference between the *pays*

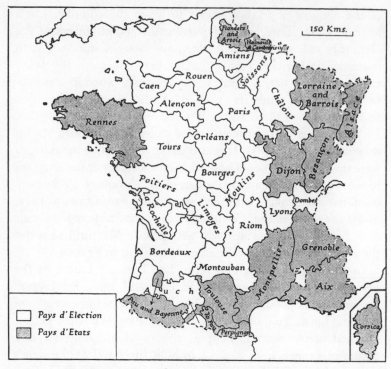

Fig. 19. The 'Pays d'Élection' and the 'Pays d'États', 1789

Based on W. R. Shepherd, *Historical Atlas* (London, 1930), p. 147.

The names of the *généralités* and *intendances* are given. The intendant was in charge of justice, police and finance, and his area of jurisdiction was the *généralité*, a financial division of France, so called because there was in each a chamber of the *trésoriers de France* who were also known as the *généraux des finances*. The name of a *généralité* was usually taken from the seat of its 'chamber'. They were divided into (1) *généralités des pays d'élection* in which the taxes were levied and assessed by royal officials; and (2) *généralités des pays d'états* which had a measure of independence in that they themselves voted and assessed the money asked for by the crown. In addition, there were some districts in which there was no chamber of *trésoriers de France*, but simply an intendant. These were not, properly speaking, *généralités*, but *intendances*. They were Besançon, Flanders and Artois, Hainault and Cambrésis, Lorraine and Barrois, Perpignan, Alsace, Dombes and Corsica (see R. L. Poole, *Historical Atlas of Modern Europe* (Oxford, 1902), plate 58).

d'élection and the *pays d'états* (Fig. 19). The former were those areas in which the royal taxes were assessed and levied by the officials of the crown themselves. Here, the big units of the *généralités* were subdivided into *élections*, each with a royal official

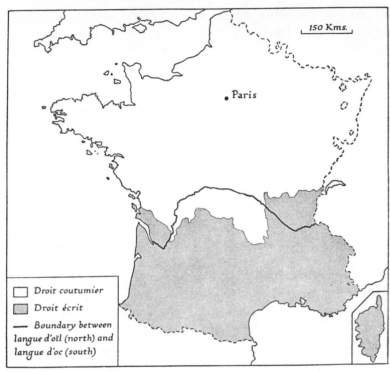

Fig. 20. French law (1789) and language

Based on (1) W. R. Shepherd, *Historical Atlas* (London, 1930), p. 147; and (2) J. Brunhes, *Géographie humaine de la France* (Paris, 1920), vol. 1, pp. 318–19.

(the *élu*). The *pays d'états*, on the other hand, had their own provincial parliaments which voted and assessed the money asked for by the crown. These Estates also controlled local works and industry and they frequently showed evidence of vigorous local feeling. The Bretons, for example, had their own constitution and used to declare that if they were French, it was only by the happy coincidence that the king was also duke of Brittany. The men of Provence and the Dauphiny both felt and said rather similar things. The establishment of intendants did much to diminish the importance of these local bodies, but they still retained their local institutions and an intendant could not afford to disregard their wishes.

63

In law, there was likewise dissimilarity. France was divided into two main legal areas (Fig. 20). The south was the land of 'written' law (*droit écrit*), where Roman law, modified by local usage, was the general rule. The more Frankish centre and north

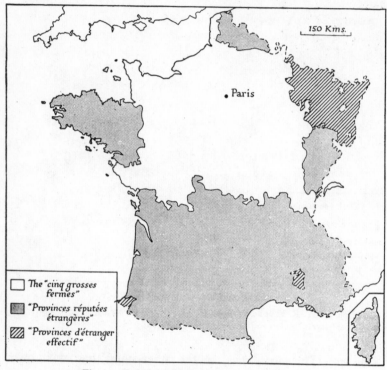

Fig. 21. French internal customs areas, 1664–1789
Based on W. R. Shepherd, *Historical Atlas* (London, 1930), p. 146.

was the land of 'customary' law (*droit coutumier*); here, a large number of different feudal 'customs', such as the *coutume de Paris*, were observed. There was, of course, great variety in both areas but more particularly in the north. It is interesting to note that this division roughly corresponds with that between the *langue d'oc* and the *langue d'oïl*.

Finally, France was not unified even for the purposes of commerce. Sully had failed to abolish the numerous internal dues within the kingdom. To take one example of the diversity: the people of Languedoc exchanged their goods freely with Spain and resisted royal interference with this arrangement. In 1622, accordingly, Louis XIII set up customs houses between this province and the rest of France. Colbert, in 1664, made an attempt to remove all local dues, and to establish a uniform duty along the frontier. But local resistance was so strong that he succeeded only in bringing some uniformity to fourteen northern provinces. These were called the *provinces des cinq grosses fermes*, because he abolished a number of smaller and less profitable duties, reducing the number to five. Besides this, there were two other types of customs area in France (Fig. 21). The southern provinces were 'reputed foreign' (*provinces réputées étrangères*)—they kept their tariffs, and wares passing to and fro from the rest of the kingdom had to pay duty. Then, again, the eastern provinces were 'foreign in fact' (*provinces d'étranger effectif*); these did not form part of France at all, economically speaking, for they were outside the national customs frontier, making their own tariff arrangements with other countries.

2. *THE EVOLUTION OF THE FRENCH FRONTIER*

The sixteenth century opened with a new departure in French development. This was a series of attempts at interference in Italy whose divided condition invited an aggressor. The net result of confused efforts from 1494 onward was the expulsion of the French, from both Milan and Naples, by Spain in 1522.

French interference in Italy became part of a .wider struggle with the House of Hapsburg. By chance, in the late fifteenth and early sixteenth centuries, there had been formed a mighty power which exercised a dominant influence in Europe for more than a century. In 1490 the Austrian Hapsburgs were exclusively a German power, but in 1496 Maximilian of Austria married his son Philip to Joanna of Spain, and their son in 1519 inherited both the Spanish and the Austrian dominions. The Hapsburg empire thus appeared as a vast aggregation of territories surrounding and threatening the French kingdom (Fig. 22), and the Italian

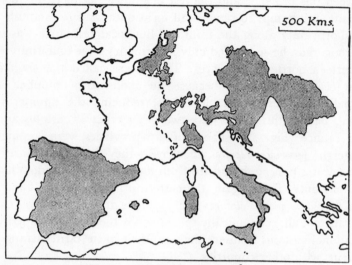

Fig. 22. The Hapsburg dominions, 1556
Based on *The Cambridge Modern History Atlas* (Cambridge, 1924), map 10.

wars developed into a struggle which checked the expansion of France for nearly a century. When in 1529, at the Treaty of Cambrai, the first great settlement between the two combatants was made, France recognized the unquestioned supremacy of Spain in Italy.

The Franco-Hapsburg struggle continued after 1529, but fighting was indecisive and intermittent. In the last of her wars with Charles V, France abandoned all hope of obtaining territory in Italy, and, in 1552, sought expansion along the eastern frontier by occupying three imperial bishoprics in Lorraine—Metz, Toul and Verdun. Seven years later, the Treaty of Cateau-Cambrésis brought a struggle of more than fifty years' duration to a close. Italy was left as she had been left in 1529; Savoy was restored as a buffer state between France and Italy, although France retained Saluzzo which had been occupied in 1548. All these decisions were the termination of long-standing disputes. One other—the retention by France of the three bishoprics acquired in 1552—marked the starting-point of new

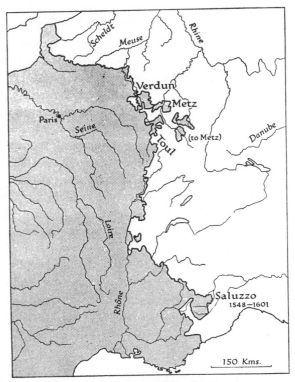

Fig. 23. The eastern frontier of France, 1559

Based on *The Cambridge Modern History Atlas* (Cambridge, 1924), map 11.

debate. These three patches of territory, disconnected from each other and from the main body of the kingdom, could only be a temptation to further advance (Fig. 23).

With the Italian dream over, and with England finally ejected, France now faced the German realm, which was divided within itself by political circumstances and by the Reformation. Henceforward, the continental ambitions of France turned towards the

67

Rhine. But despite the tempting possibilities to the east, no
further advance was made in the sixteenth century,[1] and the
day of French domination in Europe was postponed for roughly
another hundred years.

THE NORTH-EASTERN FRONTIER

One cause of the delay in French expansion was weakness at
home. France, torn by religious dissension, was hardly in a
position to undertake foreign conquest. The Treaty of Vervins
in 1598, which ended another phase of Franco-Spanish rivalry,
only confirmed that of 1559 and left France still hemmed in by
Hapsburg territories. Twenty years later, in 1618, began the
Thirty Years War. It opened in Germany as a contest between
Catholics and Protestants, but foreign powers soon intervened
and the original issues became obscured. In 1638 France,
guided by Richelieu, interfered against the German Catholics,
not indeed with the object of helping the Protestant faith, but
in order to check the Austro-Spanish power and to establish the
French frontier on the Rhine. Richelieu's policy was Catholic
at home and Protestant abroad. To the east and north-east the
French frontier was far from secure. Following roughly the
streams of the Saône, the Meuse and the Somme, it brought
the German realm dangerously near to Paris, especially as the
intervening country was not easily defensible and as the passes
of the Vosges were in German hands.

The war dragged on until, after four years of negotiations, it
was ended by the Peace of Westphalia in 1648. By this great
series of treaties France received formal recognition of her
sovereignty over the three bishoprics of Metz, Toul and Verdun;
she also obtained various rights in Alsace amounting almost to
complete control (e.g. the Sundgau and the ten Imperial cities),
but the wording of the treaty was confused, and provoked
dispute (Fig. 24). The Peace of Westphalia was but a step on the

---

[1] During this period there were side issues, too. In 1550 France recovered
Boulogne, lost to England in 1544; and, in 1588, she recovered Calais, after more
than 200 years of foreign occupation. Calais was again held by the Spaniards from
1595 to 1598, but was restored to France by the Treaty of Vervins.

long road of aggression that France was pursuing under Richelieu and Mazarin. By the war she became the first military power of Europe. By the peace she was planted securely upon

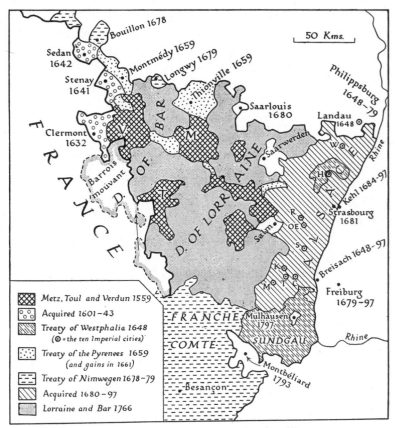

Fig. 24. The extension of the eastern frontier of France

Based on (1) G. Droysen, *Historischer Handatlas* (Leipzig, 1886), p. 41; (2) W. R. Shepherd, *Historical Atlas* (London, 1930), p. 126.

the Rhine and acquired, in the mountains of the Vosges and the strongholds of Breisach and Philippsburg, not merely a strong frontier for defence but also an incentive to future expansion. The French ambition for a frontier on the Rhine, sanctioned in part by the Peace of Westphalia, was to become one of the chief disturbing elements in European politics for nearly two and a half centuries.

The Peace of Westphalia, however, had not secured peace with Spain, and the Spanish war was not ended until the Treaty of the Pyrenees in 1659. By this, the duke of Lorraine received back his territory which the French had overrun; but this loss was balanced by the French acquisition of the province of Artois and of several smaller districts (Fig. 25). These gains still left the northern frontier unmarked by natural features, and left it moreover, discontinuous in character. Isolated points like Philippeville and Marienbourg were held by France within Spanish or imperial territory, and so there grew up a desire for the Scheldt analogous to the desire for the Rhine. As a corollary to this advance, Dunkirk, taken by Cromwell in 1658, was purchased from England in 1662.

The eastern policy, started by Henry II in 1552 and amplified by Richelieu and Mazarin, was developed by Louis XIV to a logical conclusion; and it became the established tradition of the French Foreign Office. In the north-east he suddenly invaded the Spanish Netherlands during the summer of 1667. He soon would have reached Brussels and perhaps even the mouth of the Rhine, had not a combination of the English, the Swedes and the Dutch forced a peace. By the Treaty of Aix-la-Chapelle in 1668 the French abandoned their claim to the Spanish Netherlands, but in return gained some territory along the frontier, together with a number of outlying towns, for example, Courtrai, Oudenarde (Fig. 25). These outlying acquisitions represent the farthest French advance towards the north-east that was recognized by any treaty. To the east, the French had invaded Franche-Comté, and Louis had gone in person to Besançon to receive its submission; now, by the same treaty of 1668, he was forced to give back the province, but with its fortresses dismantled.

The years following the Treaty of Aix-la-Chapelle saw Louis XIV at the height of his glory. Thanks to Colbert's finance, to the army organized by Louvois, and to the diplomatic success of able negotiators, he was in an exceedingly strong position.

His navy, already more powerful than that of Spain, threatened soon to rival those of England and Holland. In 1672 came the great assault. Louis appears to have intended the complete subjugation of the Dutch. Almost without pretence his armies

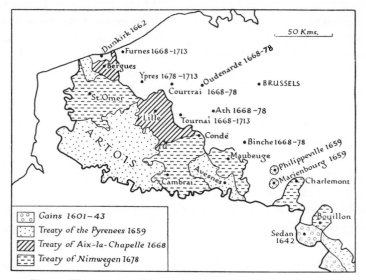

Fig. 25. The extension of the northern frontier of France, 1659–1714

Based on (1) L. van der Essen, *Atlas de Géographie historique de la Belgique* (Brussels and Paris, 1927), map viii/ix; (2) W. R. Shepherd, *Historical Atlas* (London, 1930), p. 126.

It is difficult to plot all the changes at successive treaties because many outlying towns were held for only short periods of years. The map shows, however, the extension of the main frontier, and it also indicates some of the more important, outlying towns that were temporarily occupied by the French. For later changes along the frontier see Fig. 30 (p. 135).

invaded the country, but this act of pure aggression was checked by a European coalition and resulted in the Treaty of Nimwegen in 1678. France restored some towns (for example, Courtrai and Oudenarde), but annexed some nearby areas, including Valenciennes, Cambrai, St Omer and Maubeuge (Fig. 25). The really substantial gain was made to the south, where Franche-Comté was annexed from Spain, thus bringing the French frontier up to the Jura. France even obtained the town of Freiburg-im-Breisgau on the right bank of the Rhine (Fig. 24).

The Treaty of Nimwegen is often looked upon as the summit of the success of Louis XIV. He had obtained much, but not all, that he wanted, and began to cast about for pretexts for obtaining further territory, and, in particular, for consolidating his hold upon Alsace. The ambiguity of the Peace of Westphalia gave great opportunity. In 1679 he appointed tribunals called 'Chambres de Réunion', at Breisach, Metz and Besançon, to adjudge what further territories might be incorporated. The tribunals well understood their duty, and no sooner were their decisions pronounced than French troops occupied the areas. The city of Strasbourg was included in the decision that gave all rights in Alsace to Louis, and at the end of September 1681 all Europe rang with the news that this key to the upper Rhine was in French hands. Moreover, he continued in the occupation of Lorraine because the duke of that country had refused to subscribe to the Treaty of Nimwegen.

The whole of France resounded with preparations for war. It came in 1689 and lasted until 1697, and has been described as 'one of the most exhausting and uninteresting wars of which history makes mention'. France, with four armies in the field, was confronted by a 'Grand Alliance' of the leading states of Europe. At sea Tourville was defeated, and privateering was a poor substitute for the loss of colonies and trade. In 1697 came the Treaty of Ryswick. France surrendered Freiburg, Breisach, Kehl and Philippsburg beyond the Rhine; but, while revoking these and other 'réunions' outside Alsace, the treaty confirmed those within the province in accordance with the construction put upon the Peace of Westphalia by the French diplomatists.[1] Thus the disputes that had been going on since 1648 were ended in favour of France who now obtained practically the whole of Alsace (Fig. 24). Lorraine, on the other

[1] H. Vast, *Les Grands Traités du Règne de Louis XIV* (Paris, 1898), vol. 11, p. 232. 'The most important acquisition was that of Strasbourg, which had been forcibly occupied on 30 September 1681, and subsequently fortified by Vauban. The importance of Strasbourg led to its being expressly ceded to France by Articles XVI and XVII of the treaty, although it was already included under the general article relating to Alsace (Article IV)' (see *Peace Handbooks: Alsace-Lorraine* (H.M.S.O., London, 1920), p. 22).

hand, was returned to its own duke. The frontier in the north-east was left almost the same as in 1678, but, as a precautionary measure, the chief frontier fortresses of the Spanish Netherlands were garrisoned by the Dutch.

The last chapter in the effort of Louis XIV to dominate Europe was the War of the Spanish Succession. When Louis accepted the Spanish crown for his grandson he aroused a second 'Grand Alliance'. This aimed at preserving the balance of power by recovering 'the Provinces of the Spanish Low Countries that they may be a fence and a rampart commonly a Barrier, separating and distancing France from the United Provinces', and, not least, from England. The war lasted from 1701 to 1713 with cruel loss to France. Her finances were exhausted, her government discredited. On the continent, the great campaigns of Marlborough and the battles of Blenheim (1704), Ramillies (1706), Oudenarde (1708) and Malplaquet (1709) marked successive stages in the defeat of France. At sea and in the colonies, Louis likewise failed. The French attempt at negotiations in 1709 produced terms too harsh to be accepted, and it was not until 1713 that the Treaty of Utrecht was concluded. Overseas, England gained considerably. At home, France lost far less than might have been expected. Some outlying towns (for example, Furnes, Ypres, Tournai), gained in 1668 and 1678, went to the Netherlands; the whole Spanish Netherlands were handed over to Austria in order that this critical point in the balance of power might be held safely for the common good of Europe; finally, the Dutch were allowed to continue their garrisons in the barrier fortresses as a surety against further aggression. Two years after the peace Louis died, in 1715, amidst domestic misfortune and public gloom.

The net result of the work of Louis XIV along the eastern frontier of France may be summed up in two statements:

(1) In the north-east, between 1678 and 1713, the balance of forces had attained equilibrium (Fig. 25). A triangle of territory was gained—considerable in extent and offering an adequate defence for the French capital. The arrangements made in 1713 have, with very slight changes, remained permanent, except

for the French annexation of the Netherlands during the revolutionary wars.

(2) To the east, Franche-Comté had been acquired, and, also, the French frontier was firmly planted upon the Rhine (Fig. 24). Lorraine, it is true, remained under its own duke, but in 1738 France obtained a reversionary right to the duchy, which was incorporated in 1766. The outlying lands of Metz, Toul and Verdun ceased to be isolated. The promise held out at Cateau-Cambrésis in 1559 was fulfilled, and the work of Louis XIV completed some fifty years after his death.

THE SOUTH-EASTERN FRONTIER

By the acquisition of the Dauphiny in 1349 and of Provence in 1481, the French crown had extended its control from the Rhône up to the natural barrier of the Alps. Beyond lay the small state of Savoy controlling the Alpine passes and so constituting a critical factor in the strategy of the south-east. In 1536 Savoy paid the price of its position and was occupied by France. The Treaty of Cateau-Cambrésis (1559), however, restored it to independence subject to the French occupation of six fortresses that commanded important routes through the Alps; these included Susa and Pinerolo, and were restored in 1574. Pinerolo was again occupied by France between 1631 and 1696.

In the meantime, a dispute about the territory of Saluzzo had resulted in French annexation (1548), and at the settlement of 1559 Saluzzo remained as a French peninsula thrust into the heart of Savoy (Fig. 23). It was lost in 1588 during the time of confusion in France, and in 1601 Savoy was allowed to keep it in return for Bresse, Bugey, Valromey and Gex. The acquisition of this territory in the angle between the Rhône and the Saône thus brought the French frontier up to a defensible natural boundary (Fig. 26).

Some rectification of the frontier took place at the settlement of 1713 when France received Barcelonnette in exchange for a strip of territory on the Italian side of the Alps (the valleys of Exilles, Fénestrelles and Château-Dauphin). In the same year, the little principality of Orange was annexed to France, leaving

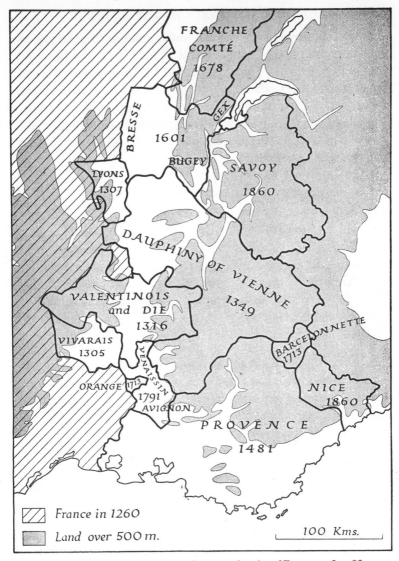

FRANCHE
COMTÉ
1678

GEX

BRESSE

1601

BUGEY

SAVOY
1860

LYONS
1307

DAUPHINY OF VIENNE
1349

VALENTINOIS
and DIE
1316

VIVARAIS
1305

VENAISSIN

BARCELONNETTE
1713

ORANGE 1713
1791
AVIGNON

NICE
1860

PROVENCE
1481

///// France in 1260

▨ Land over 500 m.

100 Kms.

Fig. 26. The extension of the south-eastern frontier of France, 1260–1860

Based on (1) W. R. Shepherd, *Historical Atlas* (London, 1930), p. 126; (2) *The Cambridge Medieval History* (Cambridge, 1932), vol. VII, map 68; and (3) A. Longnon, *Atlas historique de la France* (Paris, 1885), plates xii–xv.

The dates of the acquisitions of successive territories by France are given. The map does not indicate fluctuations of frontier, for example, the gain and loss of Pinerolo (Fig. 18) and of Saluzzo (Fig. 23). For temporary changes in 1814–15, see Fig. 31 (p. 136).

the papal possessions of Avignon and Venaissin surrounded by French territory; these later became French in the course of the Revolution (1791). There the frontier remained until 1859 when the kingdom of Sardinia-Savoy agreed that France should obtain Savoy itself in return for supporting the Italian patriots. But Napoleon III, uneasy at the growth of so formidable a power across the Alps, claimed Nice as well, and in March 1860 the two areas were ceded.

THE SOUTHERN FRONTIER

The Pyrenees, owing to the scarcity and height of their passes, have always been a serious barrier. With their rampart character they form a more definite boundary than even the Alps. But at either end comparatively easy communication is possible, and here grew up two states whose fortunes fluctuated between Spain and France. At the eastern end was Roussillon, and in the west was Navarre.

Roussillon

In the east, Catalonia on the Spanish side of the Pyrenees was occupied by Charlemagne's troops, and was then turned into a Frankish march. Subsequently it was ruled by French counts who soon, however, made themselves independent of the French crown and became connected by marriage with Aragon. Roussillon likewise passed into the Aragonese sphere of influence, and in 1258 both Roussillon and the ancient county of Barcelona were relieved of even nominal homage to France. From that time onward, until the seventeenth century, Roussillon ceased to belong to France except for a period of French occupation between 1462 and 1493.

With the decline of Spain came the opportunity of France, and Roussillon was restored to the French crown by the Treaty of the Pyrenees in 1659; thus the Pyrenees became, by law as well as by nature, the boundary between France and Spain. Catalonia itself was occupied by the French in 1694–7 and again in 1808–13; but neither occupation resulted in the permanent acquisition of further territory.

Navarre

The western end of the Pyrenees was very prominent in the early Middle Ages. Here, in the pass of Roncesvalles, the army of Charlemagne was surprised by mountain tribes in 778, and the event took hold of popular imagination. Early in the following century (835) the discovery of the bones of St James at Compostella in north-west Spain started one of the greatest pilgrim routes in medieval Europe, a route which was as important as that to Rome, and almost as that to Jerusalem itself. The pilgrims followed Charlemagne's route to Pamplona and so through Burgos and Léon to Compostella. Between the eleventh and fourteenth centuries, these pilgrimages grew to enormous proportions.

The pass of Roncesvalles was held by the state of Navarre, which emerged into the clear light of history, about the year 1000, under Sancho the Great. This state straddled the mountains, but its greatness was cut short by the expansion of Castile and Aragon, each of which annexed some of its provinces. From 1234 onwards it was in the hands of various French families, at times connected with the French crown, at other times with that of Aragon, but always maintaining a large measure of independence. In 1516, however, the Spanish side was annexed by Spain. The northern part was called by the Spaniards 'ultra puertos', or the country beyond the passes; and this northern area survived as a small independent kingdom until the accidents of succession brought Henry of Navarre to the throne of France itself in 1589. The nearby semi-independent state of Béarn had fluctuated between French and Spanish allegiance. Now it passed with Navarre to France, although it was not finally incorporated until 1620.

Andorra

Between Roussillon and Navarre, the Pyrenean valleys north of the main crest possessed for long a large measure of independence, although subject to the French crown or its vassals. The only surviving example of this independence is the state of Andorra. Its privileges have remained intact because the suzerainty of the district became equally and indivisibly shared in 1278 between the Spanish bishops of Urgel and the French counts of Foix. The rights of the latter have been inherited by the French State and the two powers, temporal and ecclesiastical, have mutually checked innovations, while the insignificant territory has not been worth a dispute. Thus Andorra is not a republic but is designated in official documents as the *Vallées et Suzerainetés*. It covers some 260 sq. km. (175 sq. miles).

3. THE RISE OF FRENCH SEA-POWER,
1600–89

France in the sixteenth century enjoyed the reputation of being far richer than England. Exceeding the latter in area and population, it had also advantages of soil and climate. Fronting both the Mediterranean and the Atlantic, with easy access to the North Sea and the Baltic, it was in a better position for the European commerce of the period than any other country, while a remarkable system of internal waterways brought the interior of the country into easy communication with the coast.

In the early stages of its development, French oceanic enterprise ran on lines parallel with that of England. First, there was a period of desultory voyages of discovery, inspired by the hope of a short passage to the East, and associated with the fishing off the Newfoundland banks. This period stretched from the discovery of America to the death of Francis I in 1547. In 1534, for example, Jacques Cartier of St Malo sailed to investigate the St Lawrence estuary. Other seamen of northern France followed his example, and at Dieppe there sprang up a school of cartographers who made a notable contribution to the advance of geographical science. Then, in the middle of the sixteenth century, there followed, as in England, a vigorous attempt to open up trade with the regions claimed by Portugal in Guinea and Brazil.

Despite these early beginnings, France was still unprepared to engage extensively in oceanic commerce. The chief part of its trade was with its neighbours; it found the best market for its exports in Spain, and it sought a large part of its imports from Italy. French military expeditions to Italy loomed far larger at the time than the discovery of the New World or of the sea-route to India; the Italians stimulated and gratified new tastes and introduced new methods in business. Moreover, France shared with Venice the profits of trade in the eastern Mediterranean, and had been the first of the European States to secure from the Sultan at Constantinople in 1536 a 'capitulation' in the modern form, defining the conditions upon which foreigners could trade.

This promising development was checked by the religious wars of the later sixteenth century. Anarchy at home had its counterpart in lack of power abroad. Ever since the death of Francis I in 1547, the financial condition of France had gone from bad to worse. By 1600 French merchantmen had almost disappeared from the Atlantic; voyages to foreign lands ceased, and even the coasting trade passed into the hands of the English, the Flemish and the Dutch. Marseilles still maintained relations with the Levant, but the French merchants there were being mercilessly bled by the Turkish government, and were being rapidly driven out of the market by the English and the Dutch. One by-product of the confusion at home alone relieved the gloom; in the later decades of the sixteenth century the religious wars drove many Huguenots to sea and inspired a plundering campaign against the Spanish colonies in the west, which somewhat antedated that of Drake and his followers. Arising out of the same movement were small, ill-supported, under-capitalized efforts to plant Huguenot colonies by Villegagnon (1552) in Brazil, and by Ribault (1562) and Landonnière (1564) in Florida. These, like the undertakings of Gilbert and Raleigh, failed and left no trace. Even details of these enterprises have perished, for France produced no Hakluyt to preserve its record of adventures across the ocean.

HENRY IV AND SULLY

When Henry IV came to the throne in 1594, years of peace and progress were necessary before the kingdom could recover from the civil wars. The task of evolving order from the confusion was entrusted to one of Henry's comrades-in-arms, the duke of Sully. Heedless of the interests of individuals, Sully instituted a series of sweeping reforms. For twelve years, from 1598 to 1610, these two men were continuously and inseparably engaged upon the great work of setting the affairs of France in order.

Sully devoted all his efforts to the development of agriculture. He aimed at turning France into the great producer of food for Europe. By the draining of marshes and the careful management of forest land, large tracts hitherto unproductive were brought under cultivation. Thus all the swampy district of Bas-Médoc was reclaimed, and the work was so successful that it served as an example for other areas. The removal of all export duties on corn enabled France to sell her surplus to less favoured nations at considerable profit without rendering herself dependent upon them for any prime necessity of national existence. National self-sufficiency was the political creed of the day, and Sully was its greatest exponent in Europe. While encouraging agriculture as much as possible, he deliberately deprecated manufactures, imposed duties on manufactured goods, prohibited the export of gold and silver, and showed little favour to the establishment of new industries.

The greater statesmanship of the king corrected the prejudices of the minister. Silk manufacturing, which has become so important an industry in France, was introduced by Henry IV; Lyons and Nîmes flourished with the new industry, and the gardens of the Tuileries were planted with mulberry trees. The glass and pottery works of Paris and Nevers were encouraged. Various metal works received favour and prospered; so did the making of tapestries, carpets and linen (Fig. 27). The construction of roads was promoted, and regular services established along the post routes. The first of the great canals of France, that between the Loire and the Seine, was built; many stretches of river were canalized and made navigable. Marseilles became a great mercantile port, and Toulon a great naval centre. In 1604 commercial treaties were concluded with the Hanseatic League, with Denmark, and with Sweden. Discoverers were

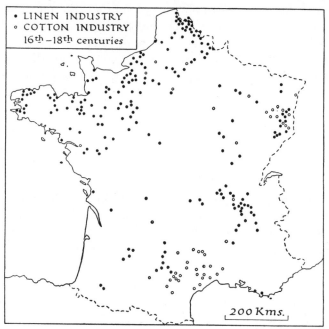

Fig. 27. The French cotton and linen industries, sixteenth to eighteenth centuries
Based on the *Atlas de France* (Paris, 1938), plate 43.
    Under Henry IV, French *linen* manufacturers were enabled to compete with the Dutch in the Spanish market. Towards the end of the seventeenth century, the growth of the industry was checked by competition from the Irish industry, originally founded by a group of French refugees established at Belfast. The manufacture of *cotton* was not important until the latter half of the eighteenth century when cotton goods came to be in great demand.

sent out under royal patronage to establish colonies in America; Port Royal (Nova Scotia) was founded in 1604, and Quebec in 1608. Henry even aimed at the foundation of an Indian company that might rival the enterprise of the English and the Dutch in the East. Both in commerce and in agriculture the reign was a period of reconstruction. But for the government of Henry IV, there could have been no 'Age of Louis XIV'.

RICHELIEU, THE FOUNDER OF THE NAVY

The brilliant and rapid recovery that took place under the government of Henry IV was too soon interrupted by his death. But with the rise of Richelieu to power in 1624, something of the economic work of Henry IV and Sully was continued. The plans formulated in the early years of Richelieu's career for the most part failed, but it must be remembered that during the eighteen years of his administration there were not above three in which the country was at peace both at home and abroad; the intervals of peace were more rare than in the reign of Napoleon. Despite these difficulties he left behind a substantial legacy of maritime achievement.

Richelieu was not slow to realize that France, with her extended seaboard and her great resources, was well equipped for becoming a maritime power. It was he himself who declared: 'France, bounded by two seas, can maintain herself only by sea-power.' He therefore took the colonies and the marine under his special charge, and in 1626 became superintendent of navigation and commerce. He at once applied himself to the construction of a navy that should be worthy of a powerful kingdom. Henry IV had left not one man-of-war to his successor, and when Richelieu assumed office in 1624 France had no navy deserving of the name. French ships, unwilling to salute the English flag but afraid to refuse, sailed under the Dutch flag. This condition of affairs was changed by Richelieu. The English of this period called themselves 'kings of the sea' and dubbed him a 'fresh-water admiral', but during his administration the French navy counted twenty men-of-war, besides eighty smaller ships. Probably it could have met on equal terms the navy of any other European nation.

The encouragement of naval enterprise was but part of a wider policy of economic and maritime development. Despite the complications of the Thirty Years War (1618–48), Richelieu found time to·encourage overseas expansion. His methods were influenced by his passion for bringing every manifestation of French energy within the grip of government control. He therefore chose the chartered company as the ideal method of expansion. The middle of the seventeenth century was in France the great age of chartered companies, far more numerous than in England, and on the whole less successful. Whereas in England the chartered company was a form of private enterprise, Richelieu's companies were managed as departments of state. The number of French commercial companies founded between 1599 and 1642, including reorganizations, amounted to twenty-two, covering Canada, the West Indies, Guiana, the west coast of Africa, Madagascar, the East Indies and the Malay Archipelago.

In 1627 Richelieu chartered the Company of New France to take control of Canada and to claim the whole coastline of North America. However successful it may have proved as a trading venture, it did little for the cause of colonization. By 1663 the French population of Canada numbered only 2500. This question of emigration was the rock upon which the old French empire split. It produced daring soldiers, seamen and explorers in great profusion, but never a sufficiency of sober hard-working cultivators of the New England and Maryland type.

The comparative success of the French West India plantations[1] indicates what might have been done elsewhere, for it took place in spite of, and not as a result of, the efforts of the Company of the Isles of America. But even here Dutch traders reaped the benefit, and the French company fell into a state of bankruptcy.

The French were also active in the East, and French eastern companies were chartered in 1604, 1611 and 1615, but none of them endured for long. Little further was done until 1642, when Richelieu founded the Company of the Indies, which went so far as to plant settlements in Madagascar as bases for the eastern trade. The plan proved unsound owing to the large and hostile native population, and the Madagascan harbours were abandoned after a few years. But despite these failures in east and west, the fact remains that Richelieu took a wider view of

[1] In the West Indies, the French occupied part of St Kitts in 1625, part of St Martin, Martinique, and Guadeloupe in 1636, part of San Domingo in 1664, and they made a settlement in Guiana, of which Cayenne became the capital, in 1624.

colonization than any of his predecessors had done. And, too, he must be regarded as the founder of the French navy.

Richelieu's chosen successor, Mazarin, carried his work to glorious success in the sphere of foreign affairs, but internal discord hindered economic development, for a time, and maritime affairs were neglected. In spite of the efforts of Sully and Richelieu, France seemed to have lost all sense of its destiny as a sea-power. Jean Éon of Nantes, writing in 1646, was 'dumbfounded to see into what a low state it has sunk....I am seized with a feeling of disgrace and of sorrow when I see the greater part of our merchants idle, our sailors without employment, our harbours without vessels, and our ships wrecked and stranded upon the beach.' This is only one of many striking passages in his interesting book, *Le Commerce honorable*, which describes in mournful sentences the state of France of his day. The industries established by Henri IV and fostered by Richelieu, were in a state of decay. The woollen industry had almost ceased to exist in Languedoc which had been its thriving centre. The silk mills of Tours and Lyons were declining. The foundries and the forges had almost been abandoned. Both at home and abroad the condition of French economic life was disappointing.

THE WORK OF COLBERT, 1661–83

At Mazarin's death in 1661, Colbert was made intendant of finance. He rapidly rose in the favour of Louis XIV, and was given charge not only of finance, but of commerce, of colonies and of the navy. He took office with a policy already framed. Some years earlier he had written to Mazarin: 'We must re-establish or create all industries, even those of luxury; establish a protective system in the customs; organize the producers and traders in corporations; ease the fiscal bonds which are harmful to the people; restore to France the marine transport of her productions; develop the colonies and attach them commercially to France; suppress all intermediaries between France and India; develop the navy to protect the mercantile marine.' This was the system that was becoming the doctrine of all the sea-powers, and in France, for some twenty years, it produced most striking results.

In 1664 Colbert initiated an inquiry to find out 'the number and quality of vessels which were in the ports of the realm'. The result showed a total of only 2368 vessels above 10 tons, representing a total of 129,605 tons. There were only 329 vessels of more than 100 tons. Some of these, even, were too old or disabled for service. Indeed, Colbert went as far as to say that France had not 200 vessels in good condition in her ports, and had to confess that, while 'the power of the king by land is superior to that of all others in Europe, by sea it is inferior'. He estimated that out of a total of 20,000 vessels in the merchant marine of Europe, 16,000 belonged to Holland. Dutch ships were upon every sea and in every harbour. The ports of France were no exception to the rule, and even 'in the islands of America occupied by the French, there are 150 Dutch ships annually'. Likewise, the Canadian fur trade went not to Rouen or La Rochelle, but to London and Amsterdam. The only French slave-market, Senegal, was selling no slaves. And in the Mediterranean, France sent only thirty ships a year to Turkish ports, for her coasts were blockaded by the pirate fleets of Algiers, Tunis and Tripoli; every night, from watch-towers built at intervals along the French coast, beacons gave warning of the presence of the corsairs.

The greatest and most lasting of Colbert's achievements was the re-establishment of the French navy. One of the features of the seventeenth century in Europe was the rise of navies. In the preceding century, even the great sea-power of Spain had never possessed a navy in the strict sense of the term—an organized maritime force provided and governed by the State for the purpose of war alone. Neither, at the time of the Armada, had her opponents. The small nuclei of specialized men-of-war which belonged to England and Holland were surrounded by a miscellaneous crowd of pressed and hired merchantmen more or less adapted for the different tasks of warfare. Beyond money and commanders and dockyards, the state directly supplied few of their requisites. The minor operations of destroying commerce were carried out by privateers, subject to a supervision so elementary that they were often indistinguishable from pirates.

The Anglo-Dutch wars now began a new era. They showed that in future the naval battle must be an affair of purely fighting ships; the pressed and hired merchantmen disappeared from the line of battle. Discipline was codified. Tactical principles were emerging. One change, which was also taking place in armies, came to the navies as well—the formation of a regular corps of officers.

These new ideas were exploited to the full by Colbert, and the whole theory of sea-power was put into practice in the systematic, centralizing French way. It has been said that in 1661, when he took office, there were but thirty armed ships in France, of which only three had over sixty guns. When he died, in 1683, there were 107 ships with from twenty-four to 120 guns, besides many smaller vessels. For the maintenance and use of this navy Colbert reconstructed the works and arsenal of Toulon, founded the port and arsenal of Rochefort, and the naval schools of Rochefort, Dieppe and St Malo; and he fortified, with some assistance from Vauban, among other ports, those of Calais, Dunkirk, Brest and Havre.

To supply the navy with recruits Colbert invented his famous *inscription maritime* which is still in use. This divided all seamen into classes, and each seaman, according to the class in which he was placed, gave six month's service every three, four, or five years. For three months after his term of service, a sailor was placed on half-pay; pensions were promised; prizes for naval construction were founded; and, in short, everything was done to make the navy popular.

Nor was the mercantile marine forgotten. Encouragement was given to shipbuilding by allowing a premium on ships built at home, and by imposing a duty on those brought from abroad. Moreover, Colbert did not hesitate to bribe the cleverest shipbuilders of rival maritime nations to enter French service. Just as French workmen were forbidden to emigrate, so French seamen were forbidden to serve foreigners on pain of death.

These naval and shipping developments were the background for wide economic enterprise. Pursuing a policy of complete centralization, Colbert determined to sweep up all external enterprises into two great companies, one for the East Indies and the other for the West. In 1664 he obtained his edicts, which, in effect, divided the world into two parts and gave a half to each company for its exploitation.

The Company of the West was given a forty-year monopoly covering all American, West Indian and African possessions, the latter—the slaving stations—being rightly regarded as part of the western colonial system. The North Atlantic thus appeared as a quadrilateral, with its corners in Europe, Africa, the Caribbean and North America—all forming one economic system. Temperate America provided foodstuffs for the slaves in the West Indian plantation colonies, and took their sugar and tobacco in return; West Africa sent labour to the same plantations; all supplied Europe with raw materials for manufacture and provided, too, an ever-expanding market for manufactured goods. The Company of the West included colonies as well as vast trading interests. But, taught by experience, Colbert laid down stringent conditions to prevent settlement from being sacrificed to trade, and the crown kept the appointment of all the principal officials in its own hands.

The population of Canada trebled between 1664 and 1674, and reached nearly 10,000 by 1679. The figures would have been even higher had not the country been closed to the Huguenots. The centralized bureaucracy of France would not permit dissent even in a colony 2000 miles away. French exploration beyond the agricultural areas was very spectacular. By 1669–73, the Jesuits had completed the exploration of the Great Lakes. They now struck southwards to the headwaters of the Mississippi. In 1682 La Salle journeyed down the great river to its mouth in the Gulf of Mexico. At once arose the project of colonizing the Mississippi delta and ultimately its whole basin. The new region received the name Louisiana, and La Salle lost his life in a vain attempt to open it up in 1687. The first permanent settlement did not take place until the close of the century, and New Orleans, its later capital, dates only from 1717.

In the Caribbean, the Company of the West was doomed to a short life. It was abolished in 1674, when the administration was continued in the king's name. But if the Company languished, French private traders reaped rich profit. In 1662, said Colbert, only three or four straggling French vessels out of a total of 150 had found their way to the French West Indian possessions; the trade of the islands was then in the hands of the Dutch. By 1683 Colbert had driven the Dutch from the field, and more than 200 French vessels traded annually at Martinique, Guadeloupe and San Domingo. At home, he had awakened the western ports of La Rochelle, Bordeaux and Nantes to new life, and the West Indian trade became the main basis of their development in the eighteenth century.

The East India Company was revived in 1664 and enjoyed a longer life than that of the West. A campaign was pursued by Colbert to persuade all throughout the kingdom to subscribe to the funds of the Company; even the king took up shares. National pride was stirred by pointing out the success and superiority of the Dutch in the eastern seas. Everything was done to make the enterprise appear attractive as an investment. It was granted an absolute monopoly of all the coasts of the Indian and Pacific Oceans for fifty years.

The new company attempted at first to resume the project of a colony at Madagascar, but found the opposition of the natives too strong. As an alternative, it occupied the smaller islands now known as Réunion and Mauritius. Here, after many years, it was successful in founding naval bases in the Indian Ocean. In India itself, the first French trading port was founded at Surat in 1668. Another port followed at Masulipatam in 1669. The company, acting with vigour, sought to gain other footholds. Evicted by the Dutch from Trincomalee, the French proceeded to St Thomé, only to be evicted again in 1674. The French commander then led his followers to a third site at Pondicherry. Here he remained working hard to establish his countrymen in the good will of the native powers. At home, in 1666, Lorient and Port Louis were created to serve as the headquarters of the ships of the India Company, and for more than a century they were the chief French *entrepôts* for the produce of eastern Asia.

The other companies founded later by Colbert also had interests in very diverse fields—the North, the Levant, the Pyrenees and Senegal. The Company of the North was organized in 1669 to trade with the ports of northern Europe, especially with those of the Baltic. A forward Baltic policy was essential to any aspiring sea-power because Baltic commodities were vital for naval strength. From 1652 onwards, for over 200 years, the problem of naval timber was acute in Europe. Before the Anglo-Dutch war of 1652 there was no real naval timber problem, because fighting at sea was carried on for the most part by private ships gathered for the occasion. But late in 1652 a severe shortage of wood began. For building and rigging their ships of commerce and war, France, Spain, Holland and England became dependent on timber and naval stores from the north—hemp, sailcloth, tar, pitch, etc. These commodities became matters for diplomats as well as for traders. Colbert offered premiums for the export and import of cargoes to and from the north, and agreed to take masts, lumber, tar, etc., on liberal terms for the navy. Not that home resources were neglected for, thanks to Colbert's efforts, the forests of the Landes began to compete with Norway in providing tar for the French navy. Indeed, Colbert's naval timber policy was far more enlightened than that of the English Admiralty. Predicting that France would perish for want of timber, he evolved an elaborate scheme to postpone that evil day.

It was in the same year of 1669 that Colbert organized a new company to re-establish commerce with the Levant. The Sultan granted to the French the privilege of transit between the Mediterranean and the Red Sea, and enterprising merchants advised Louis XIV to occupy Egypt—and even to reopen direct communication between Asia and Europe by means of a canal.

The Company of the Pyrenees was organized in 1671, in preparation for war with the Dutch, lest trade with the north might be interrupted and in order that the royal fleet might not lack masts and timber.

Finally, in 1673, a company was organized for the exploitation of Senegal. French enterprise, however, did not show itself equal to the task of supplying the West Indies with all the slaves the latter needed, but many new trading ports were founded in West Africa, and the basis was laid for the building up of a prosperous traffic in human lives.

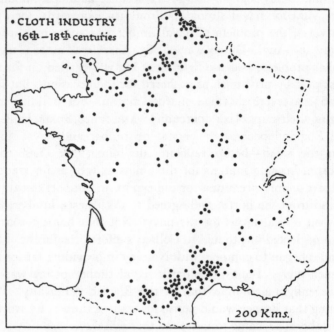

Fig. 28. The French cloth industry, sixteenth to eighteenth centuries

Based on the *Atlas de France* (Paris, 1938), plate 43.

The manufacture of cloth was greatly stimulated by Colbert, who, for example, reorganized the industry in Languedoc so that it was able to compete in the markets of the Levant.

As a background to this overseas activity, a sound economic foundation was being laid at home. Colbert spent much effort reforming the finances of the country. Manufactures were stimulated. It was Colbert, for example, who reorganized the old cloth industry in Languedoc (Fig. 28) so that it was able to compete successfully in the markets of the Levant. French workmen were prohibited from emigrating, and foreign workmen were invited from abroad. Communications were improved. It was Colbert who sponsored the great project of a canal between the Atlantic and the Mediterranean, completed in 1681. This magnificent waterway, nearly 300 km. long, greatly reduced the cost of transport in Languedoc. It was Colbert, again, who tried unsuccessfully to abolish the internal customs on the passage of goods from province to province in France; at any rate, he did something to improve conditions.

But, despite these great achievements, the work of Colbert was not as successful as it might have been. His excessive centralizing policy brought its own penalty. The narrow and rigid government regulations possibly constituted one of the main causes of the ultimate failure of so many of his economic and colonial ventures. There were other causes also. To carry out his programme of economic and naval expansion Colbert needed peace; but the war department was in the hands of his great rival Louvois, whose influence gradually supplanted that of Colbert with the king. France stood at the parting of the ways—advancement by land or by sea; strong as she was, France had not the power to move with equal steps along both paths. Louis XIV did not lack advisers. Thus, the philosopher Leibniz proposed that France should select the latter alternative and base its greatness on the control of the sea and of commerce. He said that France needed peace at home to permit the expansion of its power abroad, and urged the occupation of Egypt to give France control of trade to the Levant and the Far East. But Louis thought the French frontier was too near Paris and saw tempting provinces on the other side of it. He found the arrogance of the Dutch galling to his pride; he wished to place a French prince on the Spanish throne. France therefore was to spend its resources in a series of continental wars continuing nearly fifty years, at the cost of its commerce and its colonies.

4. THE ANGLO-FRENCH STRUGGLE,
1689–1789

When Colbert died in 1683 many of his financial and economic reforms had already been sacrificed to the emergencies of the moment. Henceforward, until the Revolution, the ruling circle at the French court, although patronizing overseas interests in times of peace, sacrificed them to the possibilities of military conquest on the Rhine. As the territory and military power of France increased, the establishments of Colbert languished, and the order he had brought into the finances of France was overthrown. Agriculture, industry, commerce, and the colonies were all smitten. The mercantile marine was stricken and the splendid growth of the royal navy, which excited the jealousy of England, was like a tree without roots. It is true that the fighting ships were kept up for some time and the zeal of Colbert's son continued the work of his father, but naval operations were always made subsidiary to the military ambitions of the French kings.

These military ambitions so completely upset the balance of power in Europe, that for a period of well over a hundred years—from 1689 till 1815—France and England were engaged in one long struggle. France endeavoured to dominate the continent and to defeat the power of England at sea. England supported the continental foes of France and was consciously fighting for maritime supremacy. There were naturally variations and intervals of peace, and the main phases of acute conflict can be summarized as follows:

(1) The war of the League of Augsburg, 1689–97, concluded by the Treaty of Ryswick.

(2) The war of the Spanish Succession, 1702–13, concluded by the Treaty of Utrecht.

(3) The war of the Austrian Succession, 1740–8, concluded by the Treaty of Aix-la-Chapelle. This began in 1739 with the war of Jenkins's Ear between England and Spain. France and England were not at war until 1744.

(4) The Seven Years War, 1756–63, concluded by the Treaty of Paris.

(5) The war of American Independence, 1778–83, concluded by the Treaty of Versailles. This was a purely naval war as far as Europe was concerned, and France was at peace with her continental neighbours.

(6) The Revolutionary and Napoleonic wars, 1793–1815, concluded by the Treaty of Paris and the Congress of Vienna. There was an interval of peace in 1802–3.

THE EARLY CONFLICTS, 1689–1713

The European war against Louis XIV began in 1689, the year after William of Orange came to the throne of England. The continental aspects of this struggle are dealt with on p. 71. Here, maritime and colonial affairs must be considered. The victory of Tourville over the English fleet off Beachy Head in July 1690 made the French masters of the Channel and enabled Louis to pour French troops and stores into Ireland and even to threaten an invasion of England itself. 'Most men were in fear that the French would invade', wrote the English Admiral Torrington. But the threat was dissipated when in 1692 a fleet under Tourville was defeated by Russell off La Hogue, the last general action fought by the navy of Louis XIV.

The French colonies in Canada were left very largely to carry on against the English with their own resources and they did brilliantly. At the outbreak of war in 1688 the Governor of New France, the Comte de Frontenac, kept the frontiers of New England in constant alarm, and later he recaptured Acadia which had been overrun by the New Englanders in 1691. But for the lack of naval support, he would certainly have done more. The favourable colonial terms obtained by France at the Treaty of Ryswick in 1697 were largely due to Frontenac's work. In the renewed war of 1702–13, Canada was less enterprising and the home government even less able to afford assistance. The Treaty of Utrecht in 1713, therefore, gave the fringes of Canada—Newfoundland, Acadia and Hudson's Bay—

to England. This loss was due in part to the neglect of the fine navy which Colbert had built up.

In the East an interesting feature of the wars of 1688–1713 is the little record of hostilities between the English and the French. Neither side was sufficiently established to risk a struggle in the presence of strong native powers, and both accordingly entered into local agreements for neutrality. There were some incidents, however, but as the French Company was far from prosperous it was little able to send help to its servants in India. In 1693, therefore, Pondicherry surrendered to the Dutch, but it was restored by the Treaty of Ryswick in 1697 and it became the seat of French administration in the East. Meanwhile the port at Surat had been abandoned, but in compensation the French obtained a footing at Chandernagore in 1688. At this juncture the history of the French Company resembled that of its English rival half a century before—its servants were making headway in India, but its affairs at home were in the utmost disorder. The disastrous wars and the general ruin of French finances had such an effect that the company was reduced to licensing private merchants to carry on the eastern trade. From 1712 onwards, it despatched no ships of its own for eight years, and Colbert's once promising bid for eastern commerce seemed destined to collapse.

THE YEARS OF PEACE, 1713–40

Louis XIV died in 1715, leaving his kingdom in a condition of bankruptcy and distress that contrasted strongly with the prosperous state of England. In both countries, however, the Treaty of Utrecht was followed by a fever of speculation. The duke of Orléans assumed the government as regent for the young Louis XV and gave his countenance to the proposals of John Law, a Scottish financier who came to France at this time. Law's plan for the re-establishment of prosperity bears some resemblance to the South Sea scheme in England, and the end, too, resembles that of the South Sea Bubble. The crash came in 1720 when a panic succeeded the mania for speculation. Nevertheless, some permanent good remained. The East India Company emerged from the chaos with its trade set in motion once more, and there was a general quickening of commerce. After the fall of Law, the French empire enjoyed over twenty years of peace. During this time, both at home and abroad, there was a general revival of prosperity and rebirth of sea-power.

Canada, although still far behind the English colonies in America, participated in the movement towards prosperity. In 1713 its population was about 20,000; by 1744 it had reached 54,000. Although New England alone possessed five times the population of New France, the French Canadians had by no means admitted as final the territorial losses sustained at Utrecht in 1713. In 1720 they began the construction of the great fortress of Louisbourg on Cape Breton Island. This was intended as a refuge for the French fleet and as a base from which to reconquer Newfoundland and Nova Scotia. The latter province was kept in a constant state of insecurity by boundary disputes and by religious propaganda. In the Mississippi valley too, the French were active, building a series of fortified posts along the course of that river, and never losing sight of the project of linking up Canada and Louisiana in one continuous domain. Off Newfoundland itself, the revival of the French fishery did much to rescue French seamanship from the decline into which Louis XIV had allowed it to fall.

The French West Indies also saw a forward movement from the days of Law. From 1717 onwards the French West Indian trade enjoyed freedom from the excessive restrictions that had been imposed by Colbert, and the French islands shot ahead of the English. By 1738 San Domingo was exporting twice as much sugar as Jamaica, and both Martinique and Guadeloupe were more prosperous than Barbados. The value of the French half of Haiti alone was equal to that of all the English West Indies. French sugar and coffee were driving those of England out of European markets. A like advantage over England in the Mediterranean and Levant trade is asserted by French historians.

The East India Company resumed its independent life in 1723, having already recommenced its trade under Law. Pondicherry became a large and well-governed town, with growing fortifications and with a trade that in 1730 enabled it to send five and a half million francs' worth of goods to France. The company's port of Lorient in Brittany was busy with the despatch of cargoes and the building of large merchantmen. At Mauritius, Bertrand de la Bourdonnais, a seaman of established reputation appointed governor in 1735, created a thriving colony and a dockyard capable of repairing warships and serving as a refuge for the fleet. In India itself, the company acquired the additional trading ports of Mahé on the Malabar coast and Karikal in Tanjore. Chandernagore in Bengal, hitherto a minor station, received as its governor in 1730 Joseph François Dupleix, who in eleven years made it the richest European settlement in the province. According to the orthodox accounts, Dupleix during this period meditated and worked out his daring plan for the expulsion of the English from India. This project he continued after his promotion to the governor-generalship at Pondicherry in 1741, and the outbreak of hostilities soon afterwards gave him a chance of putting it to the test.

This overseas activity, both in the East and West, was reflected in the growth of the French mercantile marine. Great as was the advance of British shipping in the generation of peace after Utrecht, that of the French was more striking. In 1715 the French mercantile marine comprised but 300 vessels; by 1735 it numbered 1800, of which sixty, ranging from 400 to 800 tons each, belonged to the East India Company. If these be added to the vessels of all sizes used in the coasting trade and in fishing, the combined total amounted to more than 5000 ships manned by over forty thousand men. It was progress of this kind that excited the forebodings of William Pitt, the violent opponent of Walpole's peace policy. The Anglo-Spanish War of 1739 and the War of Austrian Succession (1740–8) in which England and France fought as auxiliaries and later as principals, thus afforded an outlet to restless ambition long pent up on either side of the Channel.

This great expansion of France overseas owed much to the removal of commercial restrictions in the years immediately following the death of Louis XIV. It was in spite of, rather than because of, the French government. The French minister Fleury watched this growth with distrust. He had inherited the policy of Louis XIV; his eyes were fixed on the continent. The navy was allowed to decay more and more. The French government abandoned the sea at the very moment that the nation, through the activity of private individuals, was making an effort to regain it. Campbell, the English contemporary naval historian, said that in 1744, after four years of war with Spain alone, the English navy had ninety ships-of-the-line and eighty-four frigates. The French navy at this time, according to Campbell, included forty-five ships-of-the-line and sixty-seven frigates. In 1747, near the end of the first war, he said that the royal navy of Spain was reduced to twenty-two ships-of-the-line, that of France to thirty-one, while the English had risen to 136. The French writers are less precise in their figures, but they agree in representing not only that the navy was reduced to a pitiful number of ships, but that these were in bad condition and that the dockyards were destitute of materials. Thus both the commerce and the colonies of France lay at the mercy of England.

THE WAR OF THE AUSTRIAN SUCCESSION, 1740–8

In 1739 the competition between the colonial empires of France and Britain passed from the commercial to the military stage. The English declaration of that year was indeed launched against Spain, but the war, breaking out over Jenkins's Ear and the right of search, soon merged into a more critical struggle. It was a war not made by statesmen in London, Paris or Madrid. Whenever an Englishman met a Spaniard or a Frenchman on the high seas he spied in him a rival and a foe. Unauthorized quarrels grew into authorized war. It was in vain that Sir Robert Walpole endeavoured to avoid being drawn into hostilities over the Spanish right of search in 1739. Popular clamour forced him into war. It was sufficient that English ships, trading in the Spanish main, should have been roughly searched for contraband and that a wicked Spaniard had lopped off Captain Jenkins's ear. The contest thus started lasted with little intermission—for when formal hostilities ceased, informal fighting continued—until the Treaty of Paris in 1763.

In England there lurked a suspicion that behind Spain stood France. The two Bourbon kings, many believed, were preparing to challenge the world power of Britain. The suspicion was in part justified. Six years previously the two kings had signed the Family Compact, a secret treaty designed, amongst other things, for the recovery of Gibraltar and the curtailment of England's commercial privileges. But in France two parties and two tendencies co-existed. The court and the inner circle of statesmen thought first of European aggression—the conquest of the Netherlands, the advance to the Rhine. Outside this circle were those adventurers and poorer noblesse, weary of the tedious subtleties of higher statesmanship, who turned towards maritime and colonial aggression. It was their ambition which commercial England feared. In India it produced its Bussy and its Dupleix; in America, a series of combative governors, the stronghold of Louisbourg, and the line of forts stretching between New France and the Mississippi. But all the while the inner circle of the government at home was betraying this effort across the seas. The French army grew while the French navy stagnated.

France, then, cumbered herself with two ambitions, mutually destructive because she was unable to support the cost of both a maritime and a continental war. England, also, of necessity and not of choice, was hampered by a European commitment. The king of England was also the elector of Hanover. Honour and policy alike forbade the sacrifice of the electorate in an English quarrel, and the obligation went far to neutralize the preponderance of England upon the sea. The great conflict had therefore its continental as well as its oceanic side. On the continent, the war of the Austrian Succession (1740–8) and the Seven Years War (1756–63) sprang from a common source. In 1740 Frederick II of Prussia seized Silesia from Austria; in 1756 he launched a second war for fear that Silesia might in turn be wrested from him. Meanwhile, a controversy springing from a different root was proceeding between England and her commercial and maritime rivals, France and Spain. Such was the dual character of the gigantic struggle that marked the middle years of the eighteenth century.

There were few errors in French history more calamitous than the decision taken in 1740 to join Frederick of Prussia in his attack on Austria. By that decision France became involved in an exhausting continental war, offering so many temptations, and exposing her to so many risks, that she could take little thought for her scattered settlers overseas. Yet in 1744 she joined Spain against England. Thus were the two international rivalries, continental and oceanic, merged into one struggle.

Early in 1744, the French government planned an invasion of England in the Jacobite interest. Over 10,000 troops were collected at Dunkirk and a large fleet at Brest. There were at that moment not 7000 regular soldiers in England, and the old county militia had been suffered to decay out of existence. The Brest fleet went out into the Channel and the invading army began to embark. A British squadron sighted the fleet off Dungeness, but before the opponents could engage an easterly gale scattered them. The French lost twelve transports with their troops and gave up the project.

The war that followed was not very glorious from the English point of view. Dissension at home, interest in the Netherlands, regard for Hanover—these things combined to prevent a second-rate ministry, divided among itself, from giving proper direction to the naval war. Still, the French navy grew steadily weaker as the result partly of capture by the enemy and partly of financial demands made by the French army. Two naval battles in 1747 completed the ruin. In May, off Cape Finisterre, Anson destroyed a joint squadron, part of which was destined for the recapture of Louisbourg taken by the English in Canada, and part for the support of Dupleix in India. Of nine French ships-of-the-line and eight armed Indiamen, the English captured six and four respectively, and thus hampered any further French offensive in America and India. In October, Hawke destroyed six ships-of-the-line at Belle Ile, when the French fought a hopeless battle in order to save a rich West Indian convoy which they were guarding. On land, however, the French army, to which Louis XV had sacrificed his fleet, carried all before it. By the end of 1747 it had a firm grip on the Austrian Netherlands. But eight years' warfare had exhausted all the combatants and they were ready for peace. All three nations had suffered enormously; and it is said that the combined losses of French and Spanish commerce amounted during the war to 3434 ships, and of English to 3238.

The Treaty of Aix-la-Chapelle, in 1748, was little more than a truce. It left unsettled the main questions in dispute between France and Britain. France evacuated Flanders and Madras in return for Louisbourg. Moreover, Gibraltar, Minorca and Georgia (from Spain) remained in English hands. The Anglo-French frontiers in North America were left to be settled by a commission. In the West Indies, four disputed islands were declared neutral—St Lucia, Dominica, St Vincent and Tobago. Not a word appeared about the right of search that had started the war in 1739. To sum up, France was forced to give up her conquests for want of a navy, and England was saved by her sea-power, though she had failed to use it to the best advantage.

THE SEVEN YEARS WAR, 1756–63

The cessation of hostilities in Europe seemed to give fresh impetus to colonial animosities in North America and India. It was a recognized convention of the time that hostilities confined to the colonies did not necessitate an irrevocable declaration of war in Europe. The Seven Years War, as between France and England, really opened in 1755, although the formal declaration was withheld until the following year. France at first obtained advantages. The conquest of Minorca was followed by the occupation of Corsica, providing a strong French grip on the Mediterranean. In Canada, the operations of 1756 under Montcalm were successful despite the inferiority of the French in numbers. At the same time, an attack by a native prince in India took Calcutta from the English and gave an opportunity to the French. In France itself noisy preparations were made in the dockyard at Brest, and troops assembled on the shores of the Channel. Up and down the country in England, men looked hourly for a landing of the French. The English army was small; the navy indeed had many more ships-of-the-line than France (130 to 63), but no admiral had been found with the luck or skill to lend it success. 'To contend with the power of France seemed to many a hopeless task.'

But instead of concentrating against England, France began another continental war, this time in alliance with Austria whom she had opposed in the previous war. England this time saw clearly where her true interests lay. Making the continental war wholly subsidiary, she turned her effort towards the sea and the colonies. Pitt had no misgivings about the right policy to pursue. The war, he said, was for sea-power and America. The strategy of Britain against France can be summarized under five headings:

(1) Britain tied the French down in Europe by supporting Frederick of Prussia and the Hanoverians. Pitt agreed to the payment of subsidies and the employment of some British troops in Hanover under a Prussian general.

(2) A strong blockade was maintained upon all the Atlantic ports, especially Brest, so as to keep the enemy fleet from getting out without a fight. The effect of this was to keep the French in a state of constant inferiority in the practical handling of the ships. The position of the port of Brest was such that a blockaded fleet could not get out during the heavy westerly gales that endangered the blockaders; the latter, therefore, had the habit of moving back to Torbay or Plymouth, sure, with care, of getting back to their stations with an east wind before a large and ill-handled fleet could get much start of them.

(3) Attacks were made upon the Atlantic and Channel coasts with swift squadrons. On the French coast there was perpetual alarm and waste of French resources. In June 1758, the British landed near St Malo and destroyed twelve armed ships and over seventy merchantmen. In August, the British landed again at Cherbourg, and destroyed twenty ships and a quantity of stores. Landing again near St Malo, however, the British were repulsed with heavy loss at St Cast. Pitt claimed, nevertheless, that these

expeditions had kept employed throughout the summer three times their own number of Frenchmen. Again, on 4 April 1761, some 20,000 men under Admiral Keppel were landed on Belle Ile, and remained in occupation until the conclusion of the war.

(4) A fleet was kept in the Mediterranean and near Gibraltar so as to prevent the French fleet at Toulon from getting round to the Atlantic.

(5) Finally, and perhaps most important, distant expeditions were sent out against the French colonies. In Canada, in 1758, the great fortress of Louisbourg was taken and a French squadron destroyed in its harbour. Quebec fell in the following year. In the West Indies, an English fleet took Guadeloupe, the richest French island after Hispaniola. At the same time an expedition sailed for West Africa and captured Gorée; with this fell the whole of the French slave trade—the vital support of their sugar plantations. In the East Indies a squadron was maintained, thereby supporting the English in the Deccan and cutting off the communications of the French. Clive could base his confidence on superior sea-power.

These, then, were the main lines of the English attack. In the latter part of 1758, France, depressed by a sense of failure upon the continent, harassed by English descents upon her coasts, and seeing that it was not possible to carry on both a continental and a maritime war, determined to strike directly at England. A new and active minister had been called into power by Louis XV. The Duc de Choiseul decided to retrieve all things by a blow at the heart, by an invasion of the British Isles, whilst the British fleets and armies were scattered over the globe. Flat boats to transport troops were built at Havre, Dunkirk, Brest and Rochefort. As the summer of 1759 advanced, the project of invasion was seen to be no idle boast. Fifty thousand men were intended for England, twelve thousand for Scotland, while Ireland was to be raided. Choiseul stimulated and fostered a new enthusiasm for the navy. Popular feeling took up the cry, from one end of France to the other, 'The navy must be restored'. Gifts from cities, corporations, and private individuals raised funds. Two squadrons were fitted out, one at Toulon, the other at Brest. The junction of these two squadrons off Brest was to be the first step in the great enterprise. The fleet from Toulon escaped, passed Gibraltar, but was destroyed by the English in Lagos Bay off the coast of Portugal. At Brest, the English maintained a close blockade all the summer. In November the French admiral Conflans determined to risk all before the year closed. With the English under Hawke in pursuit, Conflans sought refuge in Quiberon Bay, and there on a stormy afternoon Hawke followed him regardless of the reefs and shoals and the gathering darkness. The invasion was finished though scarcely one French soldier had embarked.

Success, however, was not entirely with the English, and paradoxically enough their prosperity was indicated by the magnitude of their losses. Thus, in 1761, the British loss in trading vessels was over eight hundred—three times that of the French. But this contrast was due to the diminution of French commerce, to the immense growth of English shipping, to the inattention of merchant ships in convoy, and to the fact that France ventured all her remaining strength in privateering. During the same year, 1761, the British navy lost only one ship-of-the-line and that was retaken.

The maritime exhaustion of France is abundantly testified to by her naval historians. 'The year 1761', says one, 'saw only a few single ships leave her ports, and all of them were captured.' In 1761, with Canada fallen and the Indian struggle over, Pitt turned to secure victory on the continent by reinforcing the armies of Prussia and by continuing the raids against the coast of France; in this kind of enterprise the greatest success was the capture of the island of Belle Ile near the mouth of the Loire. Choiseul opened peace negotiations, but Pitt's demands were exorbitant. It was evident he aimed at the complete annihilation of French naval power. In the meantime Spain, influenced by family feeling and by resentment against England, undertook to enter the war and formally did so in January 1762. It was an ill-chosen moment. Apart from reserves, England had then one hundred and twenty ships-of-the-line in commission, manned by seventy thousand seamen trained and hardened by five years of constant warfare afloat, and flushed with victory. The navy of France, which numbered seventy-seven ships-of-the-line in 1758, had lost as prizes to the English in 1759 twenty-seven, besides eight destroyed and many frigates lost. The Spanish navy contained about fifty ships with inferior personnel. The English had already taken Dominica from France in 1761; early in 1762 they were taking the coveted and wealthy Martinique as well as St Lucia, Grenada and St Vincent. So far from saving her ally, Spain began to lose her own possessions. On 14 August Havana, the capital of Cuba, surrendered, after a two months' siege, with a fifth of the Spanish navy in its harbour. In October, an English expedition from Madras took Manila, capital of the Philippines. There remained scarcely a ship or an island of the Bourbon powers that was not either taken or immediately threatened.

While the Bourbon colonies fell in rapid succession and while Choiseul was meditating one last desperate plan for the invasion of England, the preliminaries of peace were framed. Great Britain received from France the whole of Canada, Nova Scotia and Cape Breton Island, Minorca, Senegal, Grenada, St Vincent, Dominica and Tobago. She restored to France the fishing rights on the banks of Newfoundland and in the Gulf of the St Lawrence, with the little islands of St Pierre and Miquelon as fishing stations; Belle Ile off the Breton coast; Guadeloupe, Martinique and St Lucia; and Gorée in West Africa. In India, Britain restored to France the skeleton of her former possessions—Chandernagore, Pondicherry and the rest—but unfortified and denuded of their supporting districts. From Spain, Britain received Florida, the logwood concessions in the Honduras, and a resignation of Spanish fishing rights off Newfoundland. Manila was restored, as the news of its capture did not arrive before the signature of the treaty. France completed her withdrawal from America by ceding Louisiana to Spain as compensation for Spanish losses. The Treaty of Paris marks the culminating point of that fierce competition for sea-power and colonial wealth which began with the discoveries of the fifteenth century. Its great significance lies in the decision of the quarrel between England and France for colonial supremacy in the New World and in the East.

THE REVIVAL OF FRENCH SEA-POWER, 1763–89

In England, Pitt was out of office before the end of the Seven Years War. He and many others were bitterly opposed to the terms of the treaty of 1763. Criticizing the peace he summed up his view by saying, 'You leave to France the possibility of reviving her navy'. These words, though illiberal, were strictly justifiable. The restoration to France of her colonies in the West Indies and her stations in India, together with the valuable Newfoundland fishing rights, provided an inducement to restore her commerce and her navy. Even before the peace, Choiseul had started upon the reconstitution of the French navy, and after the peace he never slackened. New ships were built, the artillery improved, the maritime conscription overhauled, and officers, seamen and gunners were trained intensively. By 1770 he had doubled the paper strength and probably trebled the value of the fleet as compared with that of 1763. After the seven years of effort there were no less than sixty-four ships-of-the-line afloat, and the dockyards and arsenals were in a high state of efficiency. Nor did the work stop when, in 1770, Choiseul himself disappeared from public life. By 1778 the number of ships-of-the-line had risen to eighty; there were 67,000 seamen on the books, and 10,000 gunners drilled every week. In the two decades following the Seven Years War, the spirit of Colbert returned to the navy of France. French explorers were active too. Bougainville (1766–7) and La Pérouse (1785–8) carried the French flag across the unknown Pacific.

While promoting the naval power of France, Choiseul had paid special attention to the alliance with Spain. That country had many grudges against England—the successive loss of Jamaica, Gibraltar, Minorca and Florida, and the long infringement of trading rights. With the Spanish connexion, Choiseul hoped for a concentration of naval and mercantile effort in the Mediterranean and Caribbean Seas. By control of the former he hoped to make France more secure against European attack; by control of the latter he hoped to influence events in America and so build up a tropical empire to compensate for the loss of Canada. He showed no desire to retrieve the loss itself. Contemporary French thought was against the acquisition of colonies of settlement, and the recovery of Canada after 1763 never formed part of the national plans. In the Mediterranean, Choiseul carried out the occupation of Corsica (1768–9) yielded by Genoa, and so secured a naval station to neutralize the British possession of Minorca. He also had designs upon Egypt, from which, like Napoleon, he had visions of a new line of advance towards India. In the Caribbean, the French West Indies recovered their prosperity, but an attempt to plant new French colonies in Guinea ended in failure.

The mantle of Choiseul fell upon the Comte de Vergennes, a man not less inspired with the thirst for revenge against the English. The opportunity came in 1775, for in that year broke out the rebellion of the American colonies against England. Vergennes at once granted a loan to the colonists, supplied them with munitions, and hurried on with the French preparations for war. The news of the surrender of a British army at Saratoga was a signal for active interference, and, on 13 March 1778, France formally signed a treaty of alliance with the colonists.

In the following year, on 12 April 1779, Spain concluded a treaty of alliance with France, and formally declared war in June. The two Bourbon powers had between them some 140 ships-of-the-line, those of France being extremely efficient, those of Spain well built but poorly handled. Britain nominally had 150 ships, but many of these were not seaworthy. The two powers had planned an invasion of England. In the spring of 1779 France had already attempted an invasion of the Channel Islands with 5000 men in flat-bottomed boats and had been repelled by the local garrison. But now, with the coming of Spain into the struggle, local sea superiority was assured and everything seemed favourable for a descent on England itself. Fifty thousand troops were assembled at Havre and Cherbourg. Evading the English, the French fleet left Brest to join the Spanish fleet from Cadiz off Finisterre. The combined sixty-four ships-of-the-line, greatly outnumbering the English, entered the Channel and hovered off Plymouth. The English reply to this threat was of a twofold nature. The Channel fleet, while cruising about, did not allow itself to be brought to action under unfavourable conditions, but maintained a constant threat to the enemy; while squadrons of frigates and flotilla craft were formed to watch the invasion ports and to prevent the assembly of transport vessels. In the meantime, the Bourbon allies were divided in their counsels; they were stricken by a terrible epidemic of scurvy, and finally a gale drove their fleet from the English coast and it was too disordered to return.

During the subsequent years of 1781–2, the combined fleets continued to cruise in the Channel, but again the French did not effect a landing on the English coast. The two powers made a great display of force, but produced no result, not least owing to divided counsels. In the Mediterranean the Spaniards took Minorca in 1781, but could only continue in an unsuccessful siege of Gibraltar which had been started in 1779 and which continued until the end of the war.

Outside European waters there was considerable activity. In the East, hostilities had begun with the capture of the French settlements. The entry of Holland into the war in 1780 permitted the English to seize the Dutch stations in India and Ceylon, and the French were without a naval base nearer than Mauritius and the Dutch East Indies. With the arrival of the brilliant French naval commander Suffren, in 1782, the situation changed. Upon the English fell the anxiety of the defensive—with a local inferiority in naval strength, with many assailable points and with uncertainty as to the place where the blow would fall. In 1782–3 Suffren and the English commander, Hughes, fought no less than five desperate actions, in which neither obtained a decisive victory over the other. The net result, however, was that by the arrival of news of peace from England, Suffren's activities had placed him in a position to attempt the reconstruction of French power on the mainland.

It was in the West Indies and off the American coast that decisive action had taken place. At the outbreak of war in 1778, a French fleet from Toulon appeared in the west. By the summer of 1779, Dominica, St Vincent and Grenada had passed into French hands. During the following year, the English managed to keep the balance of power in the islands unchanged, but in 1781 Admiral de Grasse conveyed French forces from the West Indies to co-operate with the colonists on the American coast. At Yorktown, on Chesapeake Bay, the English were hemmed in by the French from the sea and by the colonists on land; their surrender marked the end of the American war. De Grasse then turned to the conquest of the British West Indies which were only saved by Rodney's timely victory in 1782 near the Saints, some small islets between Dominica and Guadeloupe.

The destruction of the commercial and maritime wealth of all the combatants had been enormous. Exhaustion rather than decisive fighting led to the opening of peace negotiations in 1782. By the Treaty of Versailles in the following year the independence of the American States was acknowledged. Between France and Britain there was in the West and East Indies a mutual restoration of conquests except that France retained Tobago and St Lucia. In Newfoundland the French fishing rights were reaffirmed and strengthened. In Africa the French kept Senegal, taken in 1779, and Britain returned Gorée, taken in the same year. Spain retained the reconquered possessions of Minorca and Florida. A separate treaty restored to Holland her lost ports in the Caribbean and in India, except for Negapatam, which was kept by the English East India Company.

The treaty of 1783 was, in a sense, an epilogue to the earlier peace of 1763. But it also registered new movements that were to produce cataclysmic effects in France and in Europe. The American Revolution had meant the triumph of the theories of a great number of idealists among whom Frenchmen had been the most prominent. The framers of the American constitution of 1783 often had the phrases of Montesquieu upon their lips. The example could not be lost upon Frenchmen and the occasion for its emulation followed directly from the war itself. The struggle with England had exhausted the finances of France. Within five years the bankruptcy predicted by Turgot faced the Bourbon government, and the summoning of the States-General could no longer be put off. The opening moves of the French Revolution were to begin.

CHAPTER IV

FROM REVOLUTION TO SECOND EMPIRE

1. THE AGE OF NAPOLEON

THE FRENCH REVOLUTION

In the reign of Louis XVI (1765–93) centuries of disorder in the royal treasury seemed to have come to an inevitable climax. It was clear that the fiscal system needed radical reform and, in particular, that the privileged classes must be made to sacrifice their immunity from taxation. The Assembly of Notables and the 'Parlement of Paris' asserted that so great a breach of custom needed the sanction of the States-General. By this argument they appeared to have checkmated the king, who was not likely to convene parliamentary machinery that had been out of use since 1614. It was, therefore, a great moment in the history of France when the king, in August 1788, decided to summon the States-General to give authority to the required work of reform.

Such a procedure was not likely to eliminate his difficulties; for in the traditional States-General each House or Estate had its veto on legislation, and the privileged body which corresponded to the English House of Lords could still obstruct and defeat any proposals that might be to its detriment. Before the meeting of the States-General, the claims of the Third Estate, the unprivileged class, became the subject of an exhilarating pamphlet literature. The theories of the French 'philosophic' movement of the eighteenth century were now brought into the realm of action, and popular passions were aroused. Louis XVI conceded that the Third Estate should have double the number of representatives of either the nobles or the clergy, but this numerical advantage was of no use to them if nobles and clergy were still to act as separate orders, each with its power of veto. The immediate controversy after the first meeting of the States-General therefore was concerned with the popular demand that

nobles, clergy and Third Estate should meet in one body, legis-
lating in accordance with the wishes of the majority of the
combined assembly.

In former times a French king desiring to tax the privileged
orders would have combined with the Third Estate to crush the
classes that chiefly menaced his power; but Louis XVI and his
queen, living in an artificial world at Versailles, out of touch
with their people, were moved, perhaps, rather by their social
sympathies than by their knowledge of the interests of the
crown. They failed to support the radical demands of the Third
Estate, and the first revolutionary act occurred when the Third
Estate—what we should call in England the House of Commons
—declared themselves the sovereign of France, and invited
members of the nobility and clergy to sit with them (17 June
1789). On 20 June they met in a tennis court and took the
famous oath never to separate until they had established a constitution for France. On 23 June it became obvious that this
Third Estate, calling itself the National Assembly, would not
retreat at the order of the king. The Revolution had begun.

On 14 July the first grand insurrectionary act occurred, when
a Parisian mob stormed the Bastille. It was followed by risings
in the provinces—by the burning of châteaux, the destruction
of title-deeds, and the murder of government officials. This was
the revolution from below, the upsurging of a peasantry to whom
feudal dues and obsolete services had become intolerable. The
leaders of the National Assembly trembled, but knew that if the
king brought troops to Paris to quell the populace, those troops
might be used to disperse the Assembly itself. They made alliance
with the mob, therefore, and used it against the king, glorifying
the men who had stormed the Bastille and keeping the government too weak to restore order. On 4 August they responded to
the provincial risings by decreeing the liquidation of feudalism,
and the abolition of dues, serfdom and tithes. The one thing that
can be secured by insurrectionary action is expropriation; and
the freeing of the peasantry remained the principal permanent achievement of the Revolution. Yet after the exultation
of 4 August it was found that the hopes raised by this decree

could not be completely fulfilled. And no government could satisfy the recalcitrant populace of Paris, who wanted not abstract rights but bread and better economic conditions. The result was that the National Assembly, having allied with the 'insurrection', soon became the prisoner of the mob, which in October 1789 marched to Versailles to bring both the king and Assembly to Paris—more directly under its control. The sessions were opened to the public and, from the galleries, an importunate populace could terrorize the elected representatives of the people. Agitators exploited the growing hysteria and glorified this 'direct action' of the holy people, even when it was directed against the legislature. So the mob, the 'insurrection', gained the lead in the Revolution, driving it ever to the left.

After the disorders of the summer many nobles left France, and at later stages this 'emigration' was joined even by some who had inaugurated the Revolution but had come to appear too moderate. In this way the country was gradually denuded of its conservative elements. Financial dislocation and economic distress gave an impulse to more radical measures, and in the autumn of 1789 the vast endowments of the Church were confiscated. In 1790–1 Mirabeau, one of the ablest men thrown up by the Revolution, saw that the constitution-makers in the National Assembly were running to extremes, and he tried to promote something like the English system of limited monarchy. He advised the king to identify himself with the popular cause, but he died in April 1791. The National Assembly not only made the clergy the paid servants of the government, but redistributed dioceses, abolished monastic orders and reorganized the ecclesiastical system without consulting the Pope, making even the bishops subject to popular election. Many of the lower clergy who had hitherto supported the Revolution now turned against it, and the imposition upon them of an oath of fidelity to this civil constitution of the clergy only provoked a schism. This religious policy of the National Assembly intensified the antagonism of Louis XVI, who on 20 June 1791 escaped with the royal family from the Tuileries, leaving behind him a denunciation of the Revolution. He was captured at Varennes and brought back to Paris. From this moment republicanism gathered force.

The National Assembly completed its work in September 1791—having liquidated feudalism, drawn up the Declaration of the Rights of Man, created a constitution, and divided France into new units, the *départements* (see p. 162). The Legislative Assembly met under this new constitution on 1 October 1791, but France did not return to normality, for the Revolution was by no means finished. The party of the 'Left' in the new Assembly was represented by the Girondins, who achieved a dominating position. They were doctrinaires, disciples of the 'philosophic 'movement, apostles of *laisser-faire*, and enemies of the Church. They represented the bourgeois class which had secured to itself the electoral power under the new constitution. It was they who determined that foreign war would be the salvation of Revolutionary France.

THE REVOLUTIONARY WARS AND THE RISE OF BONAPARTE

The Revolution had already produced repercussions upon the relations of France with other European powers, and these had been particularly important in Germany where the emperor was the brother of the French queen, Marie Antoinette, and where the elector of Trèves, with other rulers on the Rhine, received the *émigrés*, allowing them to arm and conspire against the Revolutionary government. Certain princes in the Rhineland, who had long held seignorial rights in Alsace, claimed that the abolition of these, by the Revolutionary decrees of 4 August, was a breach of the Peace of Westphalia. Finally, in September 1791, after atrocious massacre and civil war, the Comtat Venaissin and Avignon had been incorporated in the French State in conformity with the wishes of a section of the inhabitants, thus infringing the sovereignty which the papacy had enjoyed for hundreds of years in those regions. Opposition to France, however, was hardly practicable until the great states of Europe, particularly the rulers of Austria and Prussia, chose to intervene. The attempted flight of the French royal family in June 1791, together with the dread of republican principles, made the emperor solicitous for the fate of his sister. In August he put an end to his war with Turkey. Diplomatic interest shifted to the west. On 27 August, he and the king of Prussia met at Pillnitz and made a joint declaration to the effect that the situation of the king of France was a matter of concern to other monarchs. He had not yet decided, however, to intervene.

The National Assembly in France had proclaimed, on 22 May 1790, the aversion of the French nation to aggressive wars. The Girondins, however, trusted the revolutionary spirit as a force in warfare and thought that a conflict would either commit Louis XVI to their cause or reveal him as a traitor to the Revolution and to France. The declaration of Pillnitz was regarded as an insult to the French nation, and, though the emperor did not wish to attack, the Girondins were ready to take the initiative out of his hands. They demanded the disbandment of the *émigrés* on their frontier. After months of diplomatic controversy, the Girondins declared war exultantly on 20 April 1792.

Their army was disorganized; many of the old officers had deserted or had been driven away; the fortresses were out of repair. Frenchmen scarcely hated the foreigner so much as they feared treachery within and distrusted one another. The shortage of food had led to risings, and Robespierre had begun to attack the bourgeoisie who had destroyed the nobility only in order to enrich themselves. The troops at their first contact with the enemy fled in disorder, and accused their officers of treason. Everything contributed to alarm and to the intensification of the Revolution. On 20 June, thousands of persons carrying any weapon that lay at hand marched to the Legislative Assembly, and thence to the Tuileries where for hours they intimidated the king, inducing him to put on the revolutionary red cap. Then, when Austrians and Prussians were collecting on the Rhine, the threat to Paris developed. On 26 July the duke of Brunswick, the commander-in-chief of the allied forces, issued a manifesto requiring the French to submit to their king, denouncing all resistance as rebellion, and promising military execution upon the city of Paris in case any harm should befall the royal family. In the capital, fear and hysteria reigned. The mob again stormed the Tuileries on 10 August, and this time they massacred the Swiss guards and sacked the palace. A remnant of the Legislative Assembly, in the presence of great crowds, deposed Louis XVI, and the royal family was committed to prison. A national convention was summoned—based now on universal suffrage—and it was to decide on a future form of government for France. In other words, a fresh Revolution was decreed, and on 2 September—while the allies were marching into France—the 'September massacres' began in Paris. The provinces took their cue from the capital, and in this atmosphere the elections were held. The convention met on 21 September 1792 and immediately decreed a republic.

The immediate foreign danger soon passed. Prussia and Austria put only a small proportion of their armies into the field, and the invading troops, who suffered from weak and divided leadership, discovered to their disappointment that Frenchmen were not ready to welcome the foreign army and rise on behalf of the king. New volunteers gave the French forces a preponderance in numbers and the advantage of a revolutionary *élan*, while the artillery, which had suffered less than other parts of the military organization in the disturbances of the recent years, proved superior to that of the enemy. At the cannonade of Valmy, on 20 September, the French held their own; and the duke of Brunswick's forces, hampered by heavy rains, by difficulties of supply and by the ravages of dysentery, were ordered to withdraw. The French, though they had achieved no great military success, took heart, and now proceeded with a number of military 'diversions'. They occupied and annexed Nice and Savoy. They attacked the ecclesiastical states of the Rhineland and took Mainz and Frankfurt. On 6 November, by their victory at Jemappes, they became masters of Belgium. They entered Brussels on the 14th. On the 16th they contravened international treaties and struck a blow at the Dutch by declaring the Scheldt an open river. On the 19th they promised their assistance to all foreign peoples who might wish to recover their liberty. On 15 December, the French generals were ordered to proclaim, wherever they went, the 'sovereignty of the people', and to suppress existing authorities and overthrow the feudal order. It was these decrees—and the threat to Holland—which drew Great Britain into the war. English indignation had been growing from the time of the September massacres, and the execution of Louis XVI (21 January 1793) intensified English anger. But Pitt broke with France on diplomatic issues, and steadfastly refused in the following years to make the war an ideological one. It was in fact the French who declared war on England and Holland on 1 February 1793. On 7 March they declared also against Spain, and other states were soon involved.

The climax of the Revolution was still to come. At this very time, in March 1793, the tide of war began to turn again. The French armies in the east were driven back to the Rhine. Dumouriez, who should have invaded Holland, was defeated at Neerwinden (18 March), and retreated to the frontier where he negotiated with the Austrians. A few days before this, a dangerous counter-Revolutionary rebellion had broken out among the peasants of La Vendée. The *assignats*, the paper money issued on the security of confiscated lands, had depreciated and France was faced with financial collapse and a shortage of food. On 9 March was formed that Revolutionary Tribunal which proved to be the great instrument of the Terror. On 6 April the famous Committee of Public Safety was established. Early in June, the Jacobins, using the 'insurrection' in Paris again, overthrew the Girondins, who had been too weak to conduct war or quell disorder. Even now Marseilles, Toulon, Lyons, Bordeaux and other regions revolted against the capital, though France was being invaded from both north and south and threatened from the east. Toulon put itself into the hands of the British (August 1793), from whom it was captured (by the agency of Napoleon Bonaparte) in the following December.

It was in this situation that the Jacobin dictatorship, represented by Robespierre, arose—a dictatorship with the populace of Paris behind it. A Revolutionary army was organized on the basis of conscription. Corn, cloth, butter, flour, meat, fodder, cattle, carts, horses, etc., were requisitioned for it. 'Deputies on mission' levied troops in the various departments, made the requisitions, and dismissed administrative officers whose fidelity was questionable. The needs of the army necessitated that economic dictatorship for which the Jacobins and the masses had been clamouring; the maximum price of corn was fixed and this entailed further measures of compulsion in other spheres, entailed, for example, a maximum rate of wages. The Revolution was magnified and now it came to appear as a complete transformation of society and a species of totalitarianism. A new calendar was instituted; a religion of state was set up against Christianity; a new code of laws was projected. Here was a Revolution that demanded all of its citizens. Speculators and capitalists were denounced as traitors to the Revolution. By the Law of Suspects (17 September 1793) the nobles, the relations of *émigrés*, the rich—all who were suspected of ill-will to the Republic—were made liable to summary justice.

The terrorism saved France and created a new kind of army transported with revolutionary *élan*. Before the end of the year the rebellion in La Vendée had suffered successive defeats; in the north, the Austrians had been defeated at Wattignies (16 October); Austro-Prussian forces had been driven out of Alsace. In June 1794 the allies evacuated Belgium, and the French soon proceeded to the conquest of Holland, while Spanish invaders were driven back beyond the Pyrenees. The enemies of France quickly broke up, handicapped by the fact that Austria, Prussia and Russia had jealousies in eastern Europe during the final stages of the partition of Poland. In May 1795 Holland submitted and became a client-republic. In September, the Prussians, jealous chiefly of Austria, made the Treaty of Basle, agreeing to the extension of the French Republic to the Rhine. Other states that had been at war with France—Tuscany, Spain, Switzerland, Denmark and various German principalities—contracted out of the war in the same year.

One further transition was to bring events to their full cycle—and to accomplish the passage to the military dictatorship which some observers had long ago foreseen. There were many reasons why the Revolution which had begun with Liberty, Equality and Fraternity in 1789, and since then had passed through the Terror, should come to this result. If the power of the insurgent masses had made itself felt on successive occasions, the year 1795 and following years were to show that it was helpless before the military arm wielded by a determined government. The Jacobin dictatorship, calling out revolutionary ardour in an emergency, had given a foretaste of the modern high-powered state organized for purposes of war. The Revolution itself had produced the drive for 'natural frontiers' and the policy of guaranteeing these by client-republics on the fringe of France—a system of aggression and conquest. And finally, at home, political regimes succeeded one another, while after 1795 politicians seemed corrupt and self-seeking, and the view began to prevail that soldiers were the selfless ones—the purer type of patriot. Everything was ready therefore for the military dictator who should make himself the real heir of the Revolution.

In July 1794 Robespierre fell, and later went to the guillotine. As Terror could go no further, reaction supervened. In 1795 there was established a new constitution which showed grave faults but which sought to avoid the excesses of the earlier experiments. And when the mob came out into the streets again Bonaparte demonstrated his thesis—that they could not hold out against 'a whiff of grape-shot'. The peace treaties of 1795 were really the fruit of the military achievements of the preceding year; for the armies seemed to suffer from the relaxation in the government, and in 1795 success was again in doubt. It was in these circumstances that first of all the military situation was saved—and real glory achieved for the Revolution—by Napoleon Bonaparte.

In 1796, before he had completed his 28th year, Bonaparte was put in command of the army of Italy. It was intended that the campaign should be subsidiary. The Directory, the new government in France, wanted the left bank of the Rhine, not new commitments in Italy. Using all that had been achieved in the art of war during the last fifty years, and generating again that revolutionary ardour which had transformed the character of the French armies, Bonaparte swept across north Italy, cowed the smaller states to the south, and proceeded north-wards into Austrian territory. His success gave him a dominating position even against the government in Paris, which could not dispense with his military victories and the money that he des-patched. The French army was able to intervene in politics—Bonaparte sent General Augereau to support some of the Directors in a *coup d'état* (4 September 1797). In October the court of Vienna submitted at Campo-Formio and ceded Lom-bardy, which became a republic under French protection; it even promised support for French pretensions to the left bank of the Rhine.

THE NAVAL WAR AND THE EXPEDITION TO EGYPT

Britain stood practically alone, therefore, and the government of the Directory was now faced by a new kind of problem—warfare with an island power. It was an enterprise for which the French Republic was hardly suited. The Revolution which had galvanized its army had brought its fleet almost to ruin. Crews had become insubordinate, declaring that 'to them alone belonged the right to...judge their superiors'. Under the Terror, aristocratic officers had been liable to denunciation as suspects. The government had even introduced an elective element into the appointment of officers—not reflecting (wrote one Admiral) 'that mere patriotism cannot handle a ship'. The material condition of both men and ships had been neglected. There was a shortage of all kinds of stores. Both the Republic and Bonaparte failed to understand the technical requirements of naval power and the obstruction which the sea itself imposes to the neat operation of the ordinary principles of warfare on land. At the opening of the war the French had 76 ships-of-the-line, the English 115. The Dutch joined the French in 1795 with 49 ships-of-the-line that were of little use; and the Spaniards in 1796 added 76 to this combination—a navy, however, badly administered, badly officered and badly manned.

In 1797 Britain—virtually isolated in her struggle with France and overwhelmed by Bonaparte's phenomenal success in Italy—had decided to propose peace. At one moment she contem-

plated terms which George III said would reduce 'the equilibrium of Europe' to a mere name; but in the end the negotiations came to nothing. The Bank of England suspended cash
payments, and consols fell to 51 and then to 48. Ireland was
ripening for rebellion and the Russian ambassador in London
declared that 20,000 Frenchmen would easily conquer it. The
entry of Spain into the war had frightened English ships for the
time being out of the Mediterranean. Corsica, captured in
1794, was abandoned, and the English fleet was withdrawn from
the task it had been performing since the middle of 1795—co-
operation with the Austrian army in Italy and observation of
the conduct of the minor Italian states. This withdrawal had
taken place at the time of the French advance in Italy and
Bonaparte said that it 'had a great effect on the success of our
operations'. At home, Britain began to fear an invasion, and
there were great outcries against the government. A French
expedition had reached the Irish coast in the preceding year,
and though it had failed, the navy could take no credit for its
discomfiture. The British victory of Cape St Vincent, 14 February 1797—which revealed the weakness of the Spanish fleet—
came therefore at a moment when, as Jervis said, England had
essential need of a victory. It was followed in April, however, by
the famous mutinies in the navy, which lasted until summer,
while in the Texel a further expedition was waiting to descend
on Ireland under the escort of the Dutch fleet. Admiral Duncan,
blockading the Texel when all but three of his ships had deserted,
pretended that the Grand Fleet was at hand; and when in
October sixteen Dutch ships evaded his blockade he, having
sixteen himself now, captured nine of them, and so turned the
year 1797 into one of brilliant naval success.

Such was the situation when Bonaparte, after his return from
Italy, came to organize the invasion. Subscriptions were raised
for the scheme in France, and also a loan, to be repaid out of the
contributions and seizures made in England after the conquest.
Towards the close of January 1798, Collingwood was writing:
'The question is not merely who shall be conqueror...but
whether we shall be any longer a people, whether Britain is still

to be enrolled in the list of European nations.' A visit to the coast, however, convinced Bonaparte that 'whatever efforts we make we shall not acquire the control of the sea for many years. To make a descent upon England without being master of the sea is the boldest and most difficult operation ever attempted.' He now (23 February 1798) had two other courses in mind—an attack on British continental trade, through Hanover and Hamburg, and a threat to the British in the East through the Levant. The latter course was congenial to him because during his Italian campaign he had dreamed of oriental conquest, and had acquired the Ionian Islands by the Treaty of Campo-Formio; he thought of making the Mediterranean a French sea, and announced that the Turkish empire was ripe for overthrow. In spite of the difficulty of obtaining naval stores, provisions and money, he set sail with thirteen ships-of-the-line escorting 300 transports and 35,000 troops (19 May 1798). He hoped to take Malta, conquer Egypt, capture the Red Sea, and move against England's eastern empire. Eluding Nelson, capturing Malta on the way, he reached Alexandria at the beginning of July, and Cairo on the 21st. Unfortunately, the French Admiral, Brueys, did not withdraw to safety in Corfu at the first opportunity, as originally planned; and Nelson caught him in Aboukir Bay at the beginning of August and practically destroyed his fleet.

Here, at the first great milestone in the conflict, the importance of sea-power becomes evident. 'The Nile and Trafalgar, each the grave of a great conception', wrote Mahan. The British were now in control of the Mediterranean; they could disperse their forces for divergent objects, and Bonaparte was cut off from France. Turkey declared war and sent an expedition to Egypt by sea. During Bonaparte's expedition against her in Syria, naval power even decisively influenced the military operations. At the crucial moment during the siege of Acre, Sir Sidney Smith destroyed the seven vessels that carried the French siege train, and the check which Bonaparte received here put an end to the Syrian campaign and to the dream of reaching Constantinople. The battle of the Nile and the influence of Nelson induced Naples to resume the European war. A Second Coalition was formed and Russia, Austria and Portugal, even the United States, came into conflict with the Directory. While Bonaparte was in Egypt, the French were driven out of Italy and defeated on the Rhine. Minorca was captured by the British, and the Ionian Islands by a Russo-Turkish fleet. French intrigues with Tippoo Sahib led to his defeat and death, and Nelson's victory discouraged the other Indian states from hostile action. Britain, who must have hesitated before taking Malta from the Knights of St John, blockaded the French there and wrested the island from them in September 1800.

Bonaparte with a small party left Egypt, and, eluding the English again, landed at Fréjus on 9 October 1799. He did not know that the Directory in its distress had summoned him back to France. Within a month he was the master of the government.

THE CONSULATE

Even apart from its failures in war, the government of the Directory was breaking up. It had only maintained itself in existence by a series of what were virtual *coups d'état*. Some of the politicians had decided to use a soldier as cover for their intrigues, and had chosen Joubert, who, in the meantime, however, had been killed in battle. By ante-chamber manœuvres, by conspiracy with ministers and Directors, Bonaparte prepared his *coup*. On the pretext of an alleged revolutionary conspiracy in Paris he was given extraordinary military powers, and he and his friends, after an anxious moment when their plans nearly came to naught, were 'commissioned' to report on measures that were necessary for the public safety. Hailed by Frenchmen as a saviour on his return from Egypt, he had now the prestige to overawe his own associates and became First Consul, with complete authority, for ten years. He strengthened himself by taking a popular vote; it was the inauguration of the modern system of dictatorship based on plebiscite.

Having declared the Revolution at an end, he announced the reconciliation of parties, and before long men who had been royalists were working with ex-Jacobins for a government that claimed to be national. It was his design to reconcile the best of the *ancien régime* with all that was most practicable in the Revolutionary system. He confirmed the peasants in their land and freedom; but at the same time he restored the Catholic Church. He pressed to fulfilment many schemes (such as the legal code) which the revolutionaries had set on foot; he established the authoritarian state, and made representative institutions but a mask for autocracy. Suppressing political doctrinaires, controlling pulpit, press, theatres, education, claiming obedience and self-sacrifice, he gave the police a place they had never before held in a governmental system.

He came to power as the one person who could give France peace, and he knew that peace was expected of him. After a remarkable surprise crossing of the Alps he secured the victory of Marengo (14 June 1800) which confirmed his power at home and shattered Austrian designs in Italy. Defeated again by Moreau at Hohenlinden in December, the Austrians, by the Treaty of Lunéville (February 1801), conceded again all they had granted at Campo-Formio.

One reason for their surrender was the fact that Russia, under the crazy Czar Paul, had not only withdrawn from the coalition but was moving over to the side of France. By clever diplomacy Bonaparte once again secured the isolation of England. He played upon the Czar's susceptibilities, offered him the custody of Malta (which otherwise was about to fall to England), and encouraged him to support the other Baltic states in a return to the principles of the Armed Neutrality of the North (1780). In December 1800, Paul became the moving spirit in a League which included Denmark and Sweden; and Prussia—having it in her power to do great harm to English continental commerce, and hoping from the favour of Napoleon to derive future benefits in Germany—identified herself with this combination. At the end of March 1801 she closed the Elbe, the Weser and the Ems to British commerce, and attacked Hanover, while the Danes occupied Hamburg. It was the scheme Bonaparte had mentioned in 1798 as an alternative to Egyptian conquest

(p. 120)—the closing of England's main channel of continental trade and her exclusion from the Baltic which was so essential as a source for maritime stores (see p. 89). Already on 30–1 March, however, Nelson had achieved his brilliant success at Copenhagen and then moved into the Baltic. News arrived of the murder of the Czar Paul (24 March) and the accession of Alexander I who was disposed to be friendly towards England. In any case, the trading interests of Scandinavia and Prussia—and those of Russia whose products went primarily to England—militated against the policy of the Armed Neutrality, which was gradually abandoned. England survived this further period of isolation. The second Napoleonic scheme of attack had therefore failed.

Britain concluded the Treaty of Amiens with France in March 1802—agreeing to surrender all her recent conquests except Ceylon which had belonged to the Dutch, and Trinidad which had belonged to Spain. Malta was to be restored to the Knights of St John. France undertook to evacuate Naples and Egypt. Bonaparte had already completed the pacification of La Vendée, and made a Concordat with the Pope (1801). He had made treaties with the United States (1800), Naples, Portugal (1801) and Turkey (1802). This was the magnificent Peace of the Consulate. He was now rewarded with the consulship for life.

For a brief period it would appear that 'appeasement' was the current policy, and even England stood aside while the First Consul gave a demonstration of what could be achieved by peaceful aggression. Undoubtedly he desired to avoid the renewal of war; it would take years to build a navy; peace was necessary in any case to keep open the sea which was 'the only drill-ground for fleets'. Furthermore, he became engaged in overseas designs which were bound to collapse the moment England resumed hostilities. In 1797 Talleyrand had recommended colonies and commerce as an outlet for that restlessness of spirit which follows a period of revolutionary excitement. It would seem that Bonaparte himself shared this view, even if he did not make it the basis for an alternative scheme for empire. Immediately after the preliminaries of peace with England had been signed, it became known that Portugal had ceded so much of Brazil as would give French Guiana control of the northern outlet of the Amazon. Before the definitive treaty, Bonaparte was asking England to give him the sovereignty over the best fishing coasts of Newfoundland, a share in the whale fishery, and an extension of territory in India. To crush the insurgent negroes in San Domingo he sent an expedition so large that Britain complained of having to despatch to the West Indies in time of peace a fleet double the size of the one she had kept there during the war. He obtained Louisiana from Spain, sent General Decaen to restore French fortunes in the East Indies, and showed an interest in Australasia. In January 1803 the publication of the report of Sébastiani (whom he had sent to the Near East) revived all the British fears about Egypt.

Meanwhile, since the signing of the preliminaries of peace with England, he had made himself President of the Cisalpine (now significantly renamed the 'Italian') Republic, and had annexed Piedmont to France. He detached the canton of Valais from the Swiss Confederation and made it nominally independent, so that he could control the Simplon route to Italy. Switzerland herself he had reorganized and subdued; and he was declining to withdraw his troops from Holland (the Batavian Republic), as by treaty he had engaged to do. Recent changes in Germany had also operated in his favour. They were the result of the policy of using the ecclesiastical principalities to indemnify German rulers who had lost territory on the left bank of the Rhine. Bonaparte dominated the transaction, used it to advance Prussia at the expense of the Hapsburgs, and aggrandized Bavaria, Würtemberg and Baden. These latter states, by their situation, were fitted to be brought into the French sphere of influence.

British merchants, meanwhile, lost their interest in the conclusion of peace, for they found that French markets were still to be closed to their goods. Antwerp was being made the centre of a grand design; Bonaparte had determined that it should be the biggest naval base in the world—'a spear levelled at the heart of England'. The British would have risked much if they had given him any long opportunity to revive the maritime and colonial power of France. Realizing the situation, they refused to evacuate Malta until they were provided with a better security, especially for the Near East. And, as Bonaparte made Malta a question of prestige for France, war broke out again on 18 May 1803.

The First Consul compelled Holland to join him in the war. He reoccupied certain Neapolitan ports to balance the British possession of Malta and to add to the anxiety of the British Mediterranean fleet. For some weeks he induced Britain to expect another expedition to the Levant. At the same time he occupied Hanover where his control of the Elbe and the Weser enabled him to exclude British goods in accordance with the policy he had enunciated five years before. Britain replied with a blockade of the river mouths, punishing Germany for her acquiescence in this breach of her neutrality. As before, Britain set out to capture the French West Indies. The excessive compliance shown by Spain to the demands of Bonaparte provoked British retaliation which brought her into the war in December 1804.

THE PROJECTED INVASION OF ENGLAND

In the meantime, flat-bottomed boats, constructed for a second invasion in 1801, were being assembled in the Scheldt and at the Channel ports. In harbours, and on the banks of streams far into the interior of France, more of these boats were built, devouring labour and material that might have gone to more imposing naval construction. Bonaparte intended to have over a thousand of them (each bearing 60–100 soldiers and 2–4 heavy guns), and, as they were constructed, they were brought to Boulogne and neighbouring ports—crawling in groups of 30–60 at a time, hugging the coast in order to be covered by the shore batteries. Soldiers were put to the necessary work of excavation in this harbour, for 50,000 troops were there, practising embarkation and disembarkation. Two tides would be needed to make the exit from Boulogne. From various ports, some 130,000 troops were to cross the Channel (with 6000 horses, and harness for many more that would be requisitioned in England) and they were to land somewhere between Dover and Hastings. Eight hours of favourable conditions at night, wrote Bonaparte, would decide the fate of the universe.

Whatever scorn the British navy had for the project, the British government seemed inclined to take no risk—recruiting volunteers, organizing again the Sea Fencibles of 1801 (those whose pursuits were on the rivers and shores) for a possible emergency, building martello towers from Harwich to Pevensey, and installing the new semaphore telegraphs to quicken the communication with the coast. Beacons were to be the signal of an invasion. Once indeed they were lit by mistake. Plans were made for the systematic removal of provisions, cattle, fodder, etc., from the threatened areas. The royal family and the public treasure were to be evacuated to Worcester. The stores of Woolwich Arsenal were to go to the Midlands by canal.

'Cornwallis off Brest, Collingwood off Rochefort, Pellew off Ferrol, were battling with the wild gales of the Bay of Biscay, in that tremendous and sustained vigilance which reached its utmost tension in the years preceding Trafalgar.' Frigates and smaller vessels—100–150 of them—patrolled the Straits and their approaches, attacked the flat-bottomed boats when they were in transit, and kept in touch with the British ships-of-the-line. And nothing in the history of blockades up to this time had 'excelled the close locking of Brest by Admiral Collingwood, both winter and summer, between the outbreak of war and the battle of Trafalgar'. Bonaparte devised one paper scheme after another for his squadrons—schemes that would lure Nelson to Alexandria or send the British fleet scouring the western Atlantic, while his detachments made their carefully timed departures and their junction (preferably in the West Indies), in order to return and gain a predominance in the Channel for a few days. He contrived these schemes as though the weather, the uncertainty of escape from blockaded ports, the defective vessels and defective seamanship—and the judgements or hesitations of his admirals in the face of so many doubtful quantities—did not enter into the case. Finally, in August 1805, his last grandiose combination was being put into execution and he waited at Boulogne expecting to hear that Villeneuve was approaching the Channel. Villeneuve, however, following instructions intended for a case of emergency (and conceiving himself in difficulties) put into Cadiz. Napoleon knew that his scheme had broken down, and switched the Grand Army eastwards to meet the Austrians. The third great design for the defeat of Great Britain, the invasion plan, was now abandoned. It was defeated before Trafalgar had been fought.

Villeneuve, instructed at the next stage to assist French troops in Naples, sought to redeem his reputation, grew over-bold, and came out of Cadiz. The Franco-Spanish fleet of thirty-three ships-of-the-line met Nelson with twenty-seven at Trafalgar (21 October 1805); and the completeness of the destruction of French naval power at this date made the project of invasion impossible after 1805 (though Napoleon turned to the idea again in 1811). It enabled Britain to extend her conquests overseas. And it threw France back on the plan of subduing Britain through her trade.

THE GRAND EMPIRE AND THE CONTINENTAL SYSTEM

By this time the War of the Third Coalition had opened, and Bonaparte had entered upon a struggle which within two years made him master of Europe. In 1804, plots against his life caused apprehension for the stability of the regime in France and were used to create a desire for a regulation of the succession to his government. He was made emperor, and his Italian republic was turned into a kingdom. This, together with his annexation of Genoa (June 1805), induced the Austrians (still the possessors of Venice) to meditate a renewal of the war. They were encouraged by the Czar Alexander who had come forward in a desire to free Europe from the oppressor. Making a rapid march from Boulogne, Napoleon surprised an Austrian army that had come too far forward to Ulm, and, after securing its capitulation (20 October 1805), he proceeded to Vienna. On 2 December he defeated the Austro-Russian forces at Austerlitz, and on the 26th made the Treaty of Pressburg with the Hapsburg emperor. Now Napoleon was master of Italy; he secured Venice, made Illyria a province of France, and sent a force to conquer Naples. Naples became a kingdom for his brother Joseph, who, however, owing to British sea-power, was never able to complete it with the acquisition of Sicily. Austrian power was broken in Germany also. In July 1806 Napoleon formed a Confederation of the Rhine which put Bavaria, Würtemberg and Baden, with several of the minor states, under French 'protection'. The Holy Roman Empire now came to an end.

Prussia had refrained from joining the Third Coalition, but Napoleon compelled her to close her ports to British goods and thereby involved her in a war with England. Nervous lest she should be his next victim, and anxious to make a bid for dominion in northern Germany, Prussia went to war with France in the autumn of 1806, came to an astounding collapse, and suffered a great defeat at Jena on 14 October. French armies quickly overran the whole of the country, and Napoleon announced that he would make no peace treaty but would remain in occupation until Britain was subdued. There followed a severe winter campaign in Poland against the Russians, who were defeated at Friedland in June 1807; after this Napoleon, unwilling to advance into the heart of Russia, had his famous interview with the Czar at Tilsit. Henceforward, with Russian complicity, he was master of the continent.

Russia, embittered against her former ally, who, she said, had shown too selfish an interest in the capture of sugar islands, now joined Napoleon in his war against 'the tyrant of the seas'. Denmark, Portugal, Sweden, Prussia and Austria were to be forced into the system; there was to be no more neutrality in Europe. The whole continent was to be marshalled for the final stages of an epic conflict of land versus sea. From 1806 it was becoming clear that by merely persisting in the struggle, Britain forced Napoleon to continue conquering on the mainland, and forced him to build up an emergency interim empire that he recklessly exploited for the mere purposes of war. In his course of aggrandizement some country might refuse to submit without a struggle (as Spain in 1808); or an Austria, encouraged by British persistence, might (as in 1809) seize an opportune moment and provide Britain with a temporary ally. On the other hand, Britain was liable to be troubled by the fact that the states she wished to free were forced to be the accomplices of their oppressor —though after Tilsit, the British bombardment of Copenhagen prevented the Danish fleet from falling into Napoleon's hands, and friendly pressure induced the regent of Portugal to escape with court, fleet and treasure to Brazil. Britain was assured that the continental peoples were on her side, and though Sweden, for example, was made to declare war, she was pro-British at heart, and the tact of Admiral Saumarez in the Baltic prevented any serious clash.

In this situation the war became essentially a conflict of en-durance between two politico-economic systems. After Jena, Napoleon, by the Berlin Decree (21 November 1806), had shown his realization of the fact and had drawn the essential lines of his final project. Britain was now declared to be in a state of blockade; all commerce with her was forbidden, all her goods and those of her colonies were banned; no ship which had touched a British harbour was to be admitted to the ports of France or of the countries under Napoleon's influence. This decree came into full operation after Tilsit, and the British replied (November 1807) by what was virtually a paper blockade of the whole of Europe. The British intention, however, was not to stop all neutral trade with Napoleonic Europe, but to secure that the cargoes of neutral ships sailing to and from the continent should be compelled to pass through Britain. The cost of the delays and tolls would fall chiefly on the continental consumer; while the licensing of the ships would subject the course of traffic to the constant manipulations of the Board of Trade.

Napoleon's difficulties in the Iberian peninsula from 1808 and his war with Austria in 1809 prevented him from giving his full attention to the rigorous execution of his policy. There was in fact a revival of English trade in 1809, and the Baltic trade, in particular, was greatly increased; this revival was helped by the departure of the Portuguese court to Brazil and the rebellion of Spanish colonies, which opened South American ports to British commerce. Even now the British wares were openly introduced into Holland and, while Napoleon was in Austria, British trade with the North Sea German ports went on almost as in time of peace. In Heligoland (seized in 1807) and in

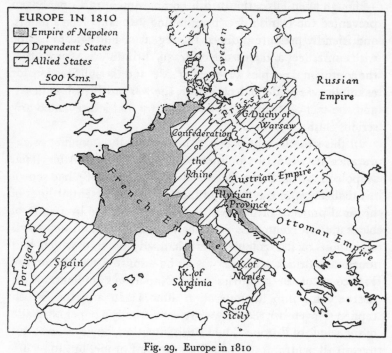

EUROPE IN 1810
Empire of Napoleon
Dependent States
Allied States
500 Kms.

Fig. 29. Europe in 1810

Based on R. Muir and G. Philip, *Historical Atlas* (London, 1927), p. 69.

Malta, Britain established depots from which goods were smuggled to the continent. It was in 1810 that Napoleon set out to tighten his system, and, in order to bring the coasts more directly under French supervision, he drove his brother Louis from the throne of Holland and incorporated the North Sea coast of Germany in the French Empire (Fig. 29). He confiscated even outside the frontiers of France (in Switzerland for example) the colonial goods which had evaded the customs; while in October he publicly burned all the British manufactures he could lay his hands on in Europe, declaring that he would stamp out the smugglers. So the continental system forced him to extend and intensify his conquests, making them more oppressive for the subject populations, and rendering his regime still more burdensome for France.

It was not his intention to starve England—he licensed the passage of corn—but he meant to ruin her commerce, drain away her gold and undermine her credit. The increased severities of 1810 had their effect, and an unusual success was scored when the French seized the greater part of 600 ships convoyed by Britain to the Baltic in that year. Towards the end of 1810, '3% consols sank to 65 and the declared bankruptcies numbered 250 a month'. England, however, had many assets—her manufacturing skill, her supremacy in the tropics, and the possibility of markets outside Europe. The continent lacked tropical goods above all—sugar, coffee, indigo and raw materials; and France had to draw her cotton from the Levant (whence it was carried on horseback from Salonika to Trieste). Napoleon—a great enthusiast for what we should call technology and science—organized research upon substitutes, and after many experiments on various fruits and vegetables, a process was developed for the extraction of sugar out of beet. Like Hitler's Germany (and under similar conditions) he reduced the neighbouring states to a form of economic subjection, repressing any possible competition from Italian industrialists, and forcing the Italians to buy their manufactured goods from France rather than from any other country. Industry gained something from this, but the French ports fell into complete decline, and in 1811 France had to face a commercial crisis.

THE ROMAN CATHOLIC CHURCH

Not the least of Napoleon's achievements was his reconciliation of the secular ideas of the Revolution with the claims of the Church in France. The Roman Catholic Church enjoyed a privileged position in France up to the Revolution, because of its association with the French monarchy—an association which went back traditionally to the baptism of Clovis (496). The deputies of the clergy constituted the first of the three Estates of the realm, and this long-standing prerogative was not abolished until 1789. The Church, moreover, not only possessed great lands and vast wealth, but had a virtual monopoly of education and charitable organization. But the relations of the French State and French clergy with the papacy were not always easy. The all-important position enjoyed by the Church in France led the monarchy (and on occasion the French episcopate) to claim rights of ecclesiastical jurisdiction as against those of the papacy. These tendencies towards independence became known collectively under the name of 'Gallicanism', and, in the modern period, they found powerful expression in the ecclesiastical policy of Louis XIV and in Bossuet's 'Declaration of the Clergy of France' (1682). This declaration was condemned at Rome and later withdrawn, but the Gallican point of view persisted. The attitude of the monarchy towards what came to be described as 'ultramontane' Catholicism was subsequently exemplified by the expulsion of the Jesuits under Louis XV in 1762.

A new phase opened with the Revolution of 1789. The Estate of the clergy disappeared, the religious orders were suppressed, and Church lands were declared national property by the National Assembly in 1789. Pushing Gallican claims to an extreme conclusion, the Assembly made an attempt to set up a national church supported by and owning allegiance to the State. The clergy who refused to take this oath were at first treated with the toleration proclaimed in the Declaration of the Rights of Man, but they soon became identified with the counter-Revolution, and suffered heavily in the violence of the Reign of Terror which followed. In September 1794 it was decreed that the Republic 'no longer pays the expenses or the salaries of any religious cult'; and Church and State were separated under the new constitution of 1795. Napoleon Bonaparte, as First Consul, found it expedient, however, to come to an agreement with Pope Pius VII. A Concordat was signed in July 1801, and became law in April 1802; the Church gave up its claim to the nationalized Church property, and, in turn, the State undertook to support the clergy. The government recognized the 'Catholic, Apostolic and Roman' religion as the 'religion of the great majority of Frenchmen'. The head of the State had the right to nominate bishops, while the Holy See had the right of investiture. Bonaparte hoped by the Concordat to limit ecclesiastical power, but in reality many of the privileges which the Church had lost under the Revolution were restored to it. This Concordat, with a short suspension at the time of Napoleon's excommunication, remained in force until 1905.

THE FALL OF NAPOLEON

Though Napoleon had transferred his brother Joseph to the throne of Spain in 1808, he said somewhat wildly at a later time that anybody might have the crown who would keep the ports closed against the British. The spontaneous rebellion of the Spaniards gave Wellington (with British sea-power behind him) an important foothold on the continent. In 1810 the attempt to tighten the continental system received poor support from the Czar, who, even if he had dared to ruin his subjects by greater severities, had reason to distrust Napoleon's resurrection of a Polish State and to complain of the expulsion of his uncle from the Grand-Duchy of Oldenburg. By an edict of 31 December 1810, the Czar made a more definite break in the continental system just when Napoleon imagined that he was screwing it to its climax. This led to the Russian campaign of 1812 which drew the French Emperor and his Grand Army to Moscow. Great Britain received the co-operation of Russia, therefore, at the very moment when her measures against neutrals had involved her in war with the United States (June 1812). Napoleon's last attempt to deal with England had broken down.

The disasters of the retreat from Moscow, and the ragged remnants of the Grand Army that straggled back to Germany, were the prelude to the landslide that takes place around a conqueror whom fortune for a moment deserts. Prussia, in a period of political regeneration, slipped out of the enforced alliance with France (30 December 1812) and soon attached herself to the Czar (26 February 1813). Then Austria withdrew and adopted a policy of neutrality which proved to be a step towards an actual declaration of war (12 August). The defeat of Napoleon at Leipzig (16–18 October) and the retreat to the Rhine left his protégés, the minor German states, ready to turn against him. From this time onward, Italian troops sent to join him in France melted away, and provinces (for example, Holland), weary of conscriptions and confiscations, took the opportunity to rise up against him. During his brilliant defence of France against the enemy armies that were converging on Paris, his own collaborators turned against him—his brother-in-law, Murat, now king of Naples, negotiated with the enemy; Talleyrand conspired for the restoration of the Bourbons; Marmont (30 March 1814) delivered Paris to the invaders. Finally, the Napoleonic marshals refused to prolong the war. The emperor was forced to abdicate (11 April).

The allies had repeatedly declared that they were fighting not France but Napoleon; and in the Treaty of Paris (30 May) they left France with her old frontiers of 1792, and even gave her certain extensions of territory—a region in the north, around Philippeville and Marienbourg, with a neighbouring area around Gedinne; a small region around Sarrebruck and another that brought Landau within the frontier (Fig. 30); and a more considerable section of Savoy, enclosing both Annecy and Chambéry (Fig. 31), was brought under French sovereignty—as also various enclaves of the pre-Revolutionary period, Avignon, the Venaissin, Montbéliard and certain 'islands' in Alsace (Fig. 24). The Bourbon government ceded to England some of the captured colonies—Tobago, St Lucia, Mauritius and the Seychelles. Finally, at the Congress of Vienna—where Talleyrand, representing the new king of France, Louis XVIII, was able to secure a diplomatic advantage owing to the mutual jealousies of the victorious powers—the British desire for 'security' led to the union of Belgium and Holland as a more imposing barrier, and to the strengthening of Prussia on both sides of the Rhine.

Napoleon, who had been granted the sovereignty of the island of Elba, landed back in the Golfe Juan on 1 March 1815. 'I shall get to Paris without firing a shot', he said, before starting on that remarkable journey which brought him to power again for a

hundred days. He had heard that the allies were on the brink
of war in Vienna, and that dissatisfaction with the Bourbons in
France had begun to issue in conspiracies against the regime.

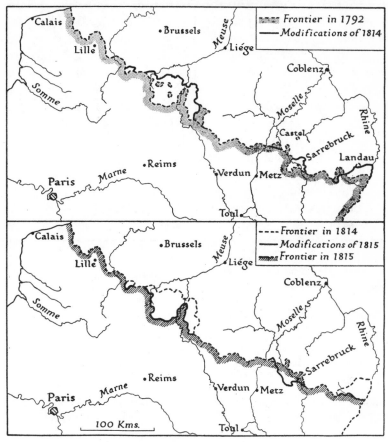

Fig. 30. The north-eastern frontier of France, 1792–1815

Based on E. Hertslet, *The Map of Europe by Treaty* (London, 1875),
vol. 1, pp. 28 and 350.

The allies, however, dismissed their quarrels on the news of his
approach, and defeated him at Waterloo (18 June 1815). In
the second Treaty of Paris (20 November) the French, who had
turned so readily to Napoleon again, were treated somewhat
more severely, though the Prussians failed in their desire to

impose on them the cession of Alsace and Lorraine (Figs. 30, 31). The acquisitions of 1814 were now taken away, bringing the frontier closer to that of the *ancien régime* and even moving

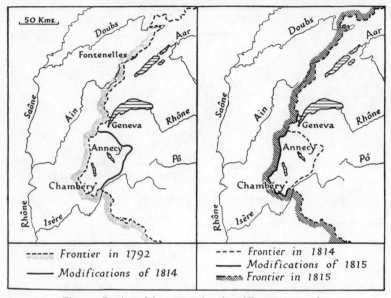

Fig. 31. Portion of the eastern frontier of France, 1792–1815

Based on E. Hertslet, *The Map of Europe by Treaty* (London, 1875), vol. 1, pp. 28 and 50.

The treaty of 1814 gave France the large district of Annecy-Chambéry and the small village of Fontenelles; by that of 1815 France gave up the Annecy-Chambéry area and also lost a small strip of territory so as to give the canton of Geneva direct contact with the rest of Switzerland.

it back a little to join the Rhine at the Lauter River. The 'enclaves' specified above were to remain under French sovereignty. 150,000 allied troops were to occupy French fortresses for not more than five years, and an indemnity of 700 million francs was imposed.

2. THE RESTORATION, 1814–30

The first restoration of the Bourbon dynasty took place in April 1814, the work not of a royalist party in France but of disillusioned Bonapartists, like Talleyrand, who convinced the Czar that only the 'legitimate' ruler could achieve stability. After the allies had entered Paris, the legislative machinery of the Napoleonic empire declared the downfall of the regime, and in the name of the nation called the head of the Bourbon family back to France. Careful not to sacrifice fundamental principles of the monarchy, he took up the government as king, not by election but by hereditary right, counting this the nineteenth year of his reign. His nephew, the Dauphin (the son of Louis XVI), was held to have been king as Louis XVII from 1793 until his death in 1795; the new ruler was, therefore, styled Louis XVIII.

He took care not to be merely the occupant of the throne on conditions—not to accept a diminished crown by virtue of a contract with the representatives of the nation. At the same time he accepted restrictions upon his authority provided the concession should come as a voluntary self-limitation through the promulgation of a charter. By this charter the system of privilege, abolished by the Revolution, was again condemned and the equality of all men before the law was reasserted. The institution of the jury was to be maintained, and the continuance of the honours and pensions of the Napoleonic regime was guaranteed. Those who had purchased from the state the lands which had been confiscated from the nobility and the Church during the Revolution were confirmed in this property, while the new government undertook not to imitate that policy of confiscation. A new House of Peers was created. It contained many royalist aristocrats, but also many functionaries of the recent imperial regime. For the time being, the Lower House was simply Napoleon's *Corps Législatif* prolonged into the new reign. The imperial administrative system was continued, under the direction of its existing officials. And Louis XVIII formed a ministry in which the chief places were occupied by men who had distinguished themselves in the service of Napoleon.

This, then, was nothing like the France of pre-Revolutionary days—the France in which the nobles were immune from taxation, and in which no States-General had met for nearly two hundred years. And perhaps this renewed attempt to fuse the new France with the old—to unite freedom with stability—met with less success than its sponsors deserved. The difficulties facing the restored monarchy are not always realized. For twenty years the name of Bourbon had been in disgrace, and the family with its supporters had been associated with the enemies of France. A succession of revolutionary regimes had produced unsettled minds and faction politics which only the despotism of Napoleon had been able to repress. Coming from exile, the new king had his following of 'royalists', men who had made sacrifices for the monarchy and were superstitiously devoted to the *ancien régime*. Their fanaticism was known to be a danger to the Restoration, yet even a Louis XVIII could not stifle his sympathies so far as to treat them with entire ingratitude. At the opposite extreme there were men of the 'Left' who, forgetting how Parliament and press had been muzzled in the Napoleonic era, thought that the Bourbons were to blame if liberty was not now fully achieved. Comparing the present not with 1812 but with 1791, they judged everything by the freedom they had once known—that excess of freedom which had ruined the Revolutionary governments themselves. The Bourbons inherited problems arising out of twenty-five years of war and upheaval, followed by colossal military defeat. When they had to put thousands of Napoleonic officers on half-pay they were bound to provoke a mutinous spirit in an important section of the people. When they favoured their friends and promoted royalists who had shared exile with them, they were bound to be charged with the crime of rewarding men who had only distinguished themselves by fighting for the enemies of France. It was easy to forget the blessings of the new regime; for example, the fact that so many conscripts could return at last to the tasks of peace.

All these difficulties were multiplied after the Hundred Days. Now, more plainly than before, Louis XVIII was restored to the throne by the enemies of France, and even they for a time had hesitated before committing themselves to a renewal of the experiment. The allies this time showed their hostility not only to the Napoleonic system but to France herself—the France which had acclaimed Napoleon again and precipitated another European war even before the Congress of Vienna had liquidated the old one. They also drew together in a further alliance for the future, one primarily directed against France and against the possibility of renewed revolutionary disturbances. Finally, they instituted a weekly conference of their ambassadors in Paris to supervise the internal government of France.

In general, therefore, the Hundred Days postponed the healing of the country and widened the gulf between the monarchical and the more liberal parties. The second Restoration was accompanied by serious disorders, the murder of Bonapartists—what has been called the 'White Terror'—especially in the south. The government, more distrustful now, and less able to resist the pressure of its royalist friends or of the vindictive foreign powers, took severe action against some who had betrayed it during the Hundred Days. Its position was made more difficult by the election of a lower chamber—the famous 'Chambre introuvable'—much too extreme in its royalism for either the king or the ministers; and this had the paradoxical effect of making the ultra-royalists defy the king and claim the subordination of the government to the wishes of a parliamentary majority. The debts of the Napoleonic empire, which Louis XVIII had agreed to take over, were now increased by the war indemnity and by the costs of the allied army of occupation. In the second Treaty of Paris, also, France had engaged to disburse sums owed to foreign countries by virtue of contracts made in the past with private individuals. On the strength of this engagement private claims dating back to the Seven Years War (even arrears of pay going back to Henry IV, it is said) were brought forward by the countries concerned; the Austrian claims alone amounted to 170 million francs. The Czar Alexander, however, intervened to save French credit, and it was agreed that obligations under this heading should be reduced to a stipulated sum.

Here then was the great problem of the Restoration government. The achievements of that government were first its financial success and the disposal of the foreign debt; secondly, the maintenance of peace by a cautious foreign policy, and the re-establishment of the position of France in Europe; and thirdly, after the dissolution of the 'Chambre introuvable' in 1816, the establishment of a moderate royalist government which in 1819 gave a great measure of freedom to the press and showed sufficient signs of liberalism to provoke protests from the Russian government. During this period, parliamentary life developed in an impressive way, and journalism became a power in politics; but still the enemies of the Bourbons increased their numbers in the Chamber of Deputies every year. In 1819 a famous revolutionary, the Abbé Grégoire, was elected. In February 1820, the Duc de Berry, the nephew of the king, was assassinated. Moreover, revolutionary outbreaks on the continent increased the apprehensions of European governments. These liberal movements were of doubtful character, working by conspiracy and insurrection, particularly by military revolts. At the same time they were based on programmes which in those days, and indeed perhaps at any date, could only lead to anarchy. The French government itself, therefore, moved to the right. Repression on the one side provoked excess on the other; the liberals in France resorted to military plots and to the organization of futile but disturbing secret societies. In 1823 the pressure of the royalists induced the government (with some misgiving) to intervene in Spain to rescue Ferdinand VII from revolution.

The accession of Charles X in 1824 accentuated the conflict between the partisans of the old France and the apostles of the new. He was the brother of Louis XVIII, and up to this date he had been the centre of the extremist royalist faction. In 1825 a project was put forward of a kind which had repeatedly been considered in the previous reign, and of which Louis XVIII would have approved. It was a design to compensate all men, émigrés, nobles or Girondins, whose property had been confiscated during the Revolution; and it could claim to be directed to 'the healing of the last wounds left by the Revolution'. The 'Left', however, denied that compensation was due to émigrés who had fought with foreign powers against their own country. The extreme 'Right', on the other hand, took the opportunity to cry out against the robberies that had been committed in the days of the Revolution; some even claimed that the confiscated lands should be returned to their possessors—it was for the new proprietors to receive compensation (if compensation were necessary). In vain Alexis de Noailles begged the deputies to vote in silence rather than turn a law, which was meant to reconcile men, into an excuse for recrimination. The project was carried, but in fact it had helped to reopen the very wounds that it purported to heal.

The age that restored legitimism in politics saw the re-awakening of medieval ideals in religion, saw the Gothic revival in architecture, and the Romantic reaction in the literary world. From the accession of Charles X it became clear that the throne was about to enter into a closer alliance with the Church. Charles determined to be crowned at Reims with traditional solemnity, though it was agreed that the vow to extirpate heresy should be replaced by an undertaking to obey the Charter, and four Napoleonic marshals performed the functions that had belonged to the great vassals in former times. In 1825 a law decreed the death penalty for sacrilege; 'each year had its memorable anachronism'. The extremists demanded the abolition of civil registration and cried out for a reform of the marriage laws. They desired that the salaries of the clergy, which were voted annually, should be placed upon a permanent footing. Their attempt to recover their ancient control over education produced one of the crucial conflicts of the period. The opposition asserted the traditional independence of the Gallican Church against the Pope, and the traditional independence of the French king against ecclesiastical authority in general. In the face of these attacks the Catholic zealots hardened into the 'ultramontane party', which became so important in nineteenth-century France.

Defeated in the elections of 1827, Charles X, seeing no other course possible perhaps, behaved as a constitutional monarch. He appointed the more liberal Martignac ministry, which reflected the changed temper of the Lower House; but he had no faith in it and seemed to be waiting till the storm blew over.

The influence of the clergy in education and of the government in elections was reduced. The Jesuits were forbidden to teach and the Pope was persuaded to ask the bishops to accept the decision quietly. The press censorship was abolished. Finally, it was proposed to extend the elective principle to local bodies that had hitherto been nominated by the government. The conduct and speeches of Martignac revealed a sincere desire to bring about a reconciliation between the monarchy and the people. The 'Left', however, were dissatisfied; they demanded change more radical and at a quicker pace; and they helped to defeat Martignac's local government project. Charles X, overjoyed, said to Martignac, 'I always told you that there was no way of bringing these people round'.

He decided to defy the parliamentary majority and appointed an extremist royalist ministry under Polignac. The Chamber was dissolved, but in the subsequent elections an exasperated opposition was returned with double the voting strength of the government. It was now that Charles decided on extraordinary measures, saying that Louis XVI had lost his head through unwise concessions. Basing his conduct on Clause 14 of the Charter which allowed the king to 'make regulations and ordinances for the execution of the laws and the safety of the state', he dissolved the new Chamber before it had met, fixed the date for yet another election, altered the electoral qualifications in favour of the richer classes, but to the detriment of the commercial class, and put the periodical press under government control. On 27 July 1830, the day after these ordinances were issued, an insurrectionary movement was set on foot. An inflammatory declaration had been published, signed by over forty journalists. Workers, students, old soldiers of the empire, were gathered together and there was talk of re-establishing the Republic of 1793. The narrow tortuous streets, the fact that the government had not expected trouble, and the unwillingness of soldiers to fire on the people, assisted the insurrection. On 3 August Charles X was in flight. The Bourbon dynasty had had its second chance and had failed.

3. THE BOURGEOIS MONARCHY, 1830–48

The revolution of 1830 was taken out of the hands of the insur-rectionaries, and those who had borne the brunt of the battle did not enjoy the fruits of the victory. Those deputies of the Chamber who had led the parliamentary opposition to Charles X were now alarmed by the sinister forces they had helped to liberate. They found that the overturn had exceeded their expectations, and they set out to curb the movement that was gathering such power in the Parisian streets. They were aware that the new revolution, like the old, driven ever to the left by a popular uprising, might overwhelm France in a flood of uncontrollable change. They knew that the foundation of a republic was likely to provoke the intervention of the European powers. Determined to seize the results of the insurrection for themselves, they—the representatives of the bourgeoisie—stepped in to secure a swift return to the orderly methods of an established government. So the revolution of 1830 stopped, so to speak, half-way, and was tamed into respectability.

France, like England, had had her restoration under a king, not entirely unlike Charles II, followed by a devout Catholic and believer in 'divine right' who recalled the fanaticism of James II. Already men had been saying that France, too, might well have a quiet revolution like that of 1688. It was desirable that 'divine hereditary right' should be destroyed, but that monarchy should continue, peaceably transferred, however, to some obvious relative of the legitimate ruling house, so that the king should be not quite elective but yet not truly hereditary. Fortunately, France possessed the obvious equivalent to Britain's William of Orange. There was the duke of Orléans who had fought at Jemappes for the Revolution and who was already associated in the popular mind with the revolutionary flag, the tricolour. His father had even voted for the execution of Louis XVI, and he himself since 1815, when he was considered as a possible candidate for the throne, had been feared and suspected by the reigning Bourbons. The able bourgeois politicians now succeeded in imposing Orléans on the men who had just driven Charles X from the throne. He disarmed opposition, for example, when he greeted Lafayette, the republican leader, with 'a republican kiss' on a balcony. The Charter of 1814 was modified in a liberal direction, and he ascended the throne on the condition of submitting to its terms; as in England in 1688 there was now a contract between king and people. And to prevent the addition of another name to the long series of 'Louis' who were so reminiscent of the *ancien régime*, he took the title 'Louis Philippe'.

Adopting the demeanour of a mayor rather than that of a monarch, he seems to have proved himself a not unsuitable figurehead for an essentially bourgeois age. Power now passed indeed to the wealthier bourgeoisie (for even now the number of parliamentary electors was only 200,000), and these flourished while France (distinctly later than England) developed towards what by 1850 we can begin to call the 'industrial revolution'. The insurrectionary republicans, however, soon saw that they had been cheated, and the early years of Louis Philippe were disturbed by strikes and risings, and by the agitation of various secret societies. Lyons on two famous occasions was given over to riot, and during one rising in Paris it seemed that the bourgeois king would have to go the way of Charles X. Through the suppression of these disorders Louis Philippe came to be regarded as an agent of reaction, a tyrant not unlike his predecessors; while the bourgeoisie, their object now achieved, came to assume a conservative position. So new revolutionary ideas developed. The workers did not quite follow the middle classes as in former days; they were less confident, now, that their cause was the same. In the reign of Louis Philippe the class conflict began to emerge into popular consciousness.

The revolutionary parties in France had an ambitious foreign policy—it was their aim to wipe out what were considered to be the humiliations of 1815. It became a reproach against all the successors of Napoleon that they had conducted a cautious peaceful policy. While Louis Philippe anxiously set out to persuade foreign powers that his accession was a guarantee that no disorders should proceed from this new French revolution, those who were more radical recovered the missionary fervour of 1792 and demanded that the new government should help the cause of freedom in foreign lands.

Bonapartism had been kept alive in France by discontented officers reduced to half-pay, by the songs which peasant women sang at their looms and the cottage walls hung with cheap lithographs of the triumphs of the Napoleonic wars'. In literature, song and drama, the glories of Imperial France were celebrated. Only the progressive elements of Napoleon's system were kept in mind, and these were expounded in some of the histories that were written in this period. Some of his achievements (the administrative system, the legal codes, the Concordat with the Pope) had remained the heritage of nineteenth-century France. While European liberalism had been repressed by the reactionary governments after 1815, Napoleon in St Helena had industriously set himself to manufacture a legend. He posed as a liberal, who, if only England could have been defeated, would have established a 'new order'—a Confederation of European states, including a united Italy, a united Germany, and an Ireland that would have been emancipated from the tyranny of the English. He claimed that the continued war that had been forced upon him to preserve the benefits of the Revolution had prevented this ultimate liberalism from manifesting itself. As proof of his intentions he drew up in 1820, for example, a liberal constitution for his successor. In 1836 Louis Napoleon, the nephew and now the heir of the emperor, attempted to organize a military rising at Strasbourg, but on its failure was sent into exile. In 1839 he published his *Napoleonic Ideas*, which stressed the Emperor's services to the lower classes, and praised the attempt to combine the liberties of the French Revolution with the necessary principle of authority in society. 'All that I did for the internal prosperity of France', Napoleon is supposed to have said, 'had to be accomplished in the intervals between battles.' In August 1840, a further attempt to provoke a military rising at Boulogne resulted in a period of imprisonment for Louis Napoleon. In the following December, the removal of the remains of the first Napoleon to Paris brought the days of the empire once more into the public mind.

During this period the iron and coal industries were developing, the cotton industry was revolutionized in Alsace, spinning factories, power looms and mechanized paper mills grew rapidly in number. In 1842 a national railway programme was sketched out. Lille developed as an industrial city, while in Lyons the silk industry was highly capitalized. The progress towards the 'industrial revolution', however, was always slow in France, and in 1849 the workshop and the small establishment still remained the rule; the revolutionary Parisian workmen were not factory hands in the English sense. But the evils of the transitional period were apparent—the condition of the silk workers in Lyons, for example, led to serious disorders.

It is not surprising, therefore, that amongst the movements in the reign of Louis Philippe there should be the significant antecedents of modern socialism. The Revolution of 1789 had confirmed the institution of private property and, in its zeal for individualism, had forbidden anything like trade unionism among the workers. The Jacobins had adopted some of the social demands of the working classes. Before 1825 Saint-Simon had heralded the coming of a new industrial age, and declared that the real revolution was the railway. He had deplored the liberal tendency to concentrate on meaningless formulae such as 'sovereignty of the people', and had urged men to turn from mere constitution-making and organize themselves for the exploitation of the resources of nature. He had condemned the exploitation of man by man but seemed to demand a dictatorship, welcoming the industrialists as the leaders, and the scientists as the high priests, of a new order of society. His followers, who became prominent for a time after 1830, attacked the inheritance of property and became the initiators of collectivist ideals. Fourier, though some of his writings were earlier, attracted attention after 1830 by his co-operative schemes. In 1840 Proudhon asked, 'What is property?' and described it as theft; while Louis Blanc proposed the establishment of the social workshop—a system of co-operative producers' societies, each composed of members of the same trade. Apart from these and many other theorists and experimenters, there existed amongst the workmen and the press a general agitation against the tyranny of the rich. From 1840 the *Atelier* appeared, a paper written and edited by working men. The red flag now emerged to signify the new revolution. But though socialism came as the extension of the principle of equality that had been put forward in 1789, it remained somewhat Utopian in France at this time, for it could only come closer to earth as the industrial age became a reality. Because France was slow in her industrial revolution, Karl Marx, who in this period evolved the doctrines of the 'Communist Manifesto', took his materials rather from England. France, predominantly agrarian, and the paradise of the smallholder, was a significant precursor, but (after this period at least) was never the leader of the 'New Revolution'.

The foreign policy of this period is significant because the problem of North Africa came to the fore, the question of Mediterranean predominance became a live issue, and France had her second birth as a colonizing power. Between England and France there arose that tension over Egypt, Algeria and even Morocco which brought the two countries almost to the brink of war by the end of the century. In 1830 Charles X, perhaps hoping to divert attention from the political crisis at home, defied British protests and sent a punitive expedition to Algiers. Most of the reign of Louis Philippe had passed before the whole country was subdued, for French opinion was often indifferent or hostile to the enterprise. The government gave it only a fitful support, while the troops—initially ignorant of the country and inexperienced in the type of warfare required—suffered many disasters, chiefly from the enterprises of the brilliant leader Abd-el-Kader, who had raised a 'holy war' against the invading infidel. The conquest of Algeria was of some importance in the history of the army. In 1830 the *Zouaves* were first organized; and, in 1831, the liberals who had found exile in Paris after the recent revolutionary outbreaks in Europe were organized into a foreign legion that was sent to Algeria. Soon also we hear of *Spahis* under French officers. Before the conquest was completed the episode had brought to the front a type of North African soldier and colonial leader which has been impressive on occasions since that date. The new colony necessitated the extension of French influence over Tunis and Morocco, and before Abd-el-Kader was disposed of, the French had to make a punitive expedition against Morocco, which had provided him with a base of operations.

The famous Mehemet Ali had made himself ruler of Egypt after the departure of Napoleon. He had introduced something of the externals of western civilization, had employed French officers, and regarded himself as the protégé of France. The Turks (at whose expense he had not only created a dominion in Egypt but also conquered Syria) declared war against him in 1839, and the French assembled in the Levant the most imposing naval force that they had collected since Napoleonic times. 'For us this spectacle represented the naval renaissance of France', wrote the Prince de Joinville who was with the squadron, and he stresses the fact that the nucleus of this Mediterranean squadron was given a continuous existence in succeeding years, so that it was trained to act as a unity and France had not to trust to a hastily improvised co-operation between vessels in future. The Turkish fleet on this occasion deserted to the side of Mehemet Ali and the Turks suffered catastrophes that put the rest of Europe in a state of alarm. England, Russia, Prussia and Austria combined to save the Ottoman empire (1840) and the result was a great humiliation—the diplomatic isolation of France. The French were bellicose. 'If we submit to treaties written with the blood of Waterloo', they said, 'we are still in the eyes of the world only the vanquished power of Waterloo.' Most remarkable was the Franco-German hatred that was generated at this moment. 'They shall not have it, our German Rhine', sang the Germans, while the French—remembering only 1815—made preparations for war on a scale that had not occurred since the downfall of Napoleon. The navy longed to renew the conflict with the British fleet. Louis Philippe, however, was determined not to have war and changed his ministers. From that moment his government was discredited.

From 1840 to 1848, Guizot was in power, ruling with a conservative bias, and controlling an oligarchic parliamentary system by the methods which in eighteenth-century England, were technically called 'corruption'. He rejected the demands of the lower bourgeoisie for electoral reform. In February 1848 the assembly of a mob, after the prohibition of a political banquet, resulted in the outbreak of another revolution and the establishment of a provisional government. All the forces that had been gathering power beneath the surface of the 'Bourgeois Monarchy' were now released.

4. THE SECOND REPUBLIC AND SECOND EMPIRE, 1848–70

To placate the socialists in Paris, the republicans gave Louis Blanc a place in the revolutionary government, guaranteed to all men 'the right to work' and founded 'national workshops' for the unemployed. A further split existed between Paris and the provinces; for the latter were more conservative than the capital, and were becoming less inclined to accept the dictatorship that Paris had enjoyed in earlier revolutions. They were not really republicans and were more friendly to Catholicism, so that a National Assembly elected by universal suffrage could hardly fail to come into conflict with the city. The economic crisis of 1847 had intensified the social unrest in the capital. The unemployed from the provinces flocked there to take advantage of the 'national workshops' and strengthen the spirit of discontent. The 'workshops' themselves proved only to be a form of unemployment relief, for men were made to remove earth on the Champ de Mars for two francs (later one franc) a day, and by May there were 100,000 unemployed clamouring for assistance; the whole scheme began to appear a disaster. On 21 June 1848, those between 17 and 25 were told to join the army or go to the provinces. This provoked the extremists, and from the 23rd to the 25th terrible civil war raged in Paris, and cost thousands of lives. The socialists were defeated by the republican Cavaignac; but the lovers of order turned to a new leader, the representative of the tradition that claimed to reconcile the victories of the Revolution with the principle of authority Catholicism with liberalism, external glory with a policy of social amelioration. On 10 December Cavaignac himself was completely outpaced by Louis Napoleon Bonaparte, whom the votes of the nation raised to the Presidency of the Republic.

Louis Napoleon, nephew of the great emperor, on hearing of the February Revolution, had hastened over from England 'to place himself at the service of the Republic'. He was, however, asked to depart, but left friends in Paris to support the Bonapartist cause. In September five departments elected him as their representative in the Constituent Assembly, where he was allowed to take his seat. In December he defeated both the republican and socialist candidates in the election for the Presidency of the Republic.

The makers of the constitution had decided that this officer, like the President of the United States, should possess real executive power, and should not be the nominee and the creature of the legislature. Elected by the whole people for a period of four years, he was to enjoy authority on an independent footing, and, as first president, Louis Napoleon made full use of these powers. His first Legislative Assembly, predominantly royalist in composition, restored the influence of the Church in education, disfranchised a third (and that the most dangerous section) of the existing voters, and put some restrictions on the press. He himself had his own newspapers and toured the provinces, carefully nursing his 'constituency', while a quarrel between President and Assembly almost lay in the nature of the situation. When he desired a revision of the constitution which forbade the renewal of his tenure of office at the end of the four-year period, the Assembly refused its assent, though he urged that a new president, coming simultaneously with a new legislature at a time of political unsettlement, would be a menace to the country. After arresting many of the party chiefs during the night of 1–2 December 1851, he dissolved the Assembly, promised a new constitution, and declared himself in favour of universal suffrage. The republicans and socialists in Paris resisted the *coup d'état*; 26,000 of them were arrested and 10,000 were sent to Algeria. Louis Napoleon represented to a certain degree the victory of the provinces over the capital. He modelled his new system on that of 1800. In December 1852 the President of the Republic became the Emperor Napoleon III.

In much less time than in the case of the first Revolution, this second French Republic had completed the transition to an avowed personal dictatorship. The excesses of the revolutionary parties, the political weariness of many, and the fears of those who were anxious for the maintenance of public order, had brought victory for the thesis 'that it is in the nature of democracy to find its personification in a Man'. The new regime was bound to imply a forward foreign policy. The name of Napoleon meant a revision of the treaties of 1815 if it had any meaning at all.

In 1848 the new President of the Republic had sent an expedition to Rome to destroy the revolutionary government that had succeeded in establishing itself there. He had known that if France did not restore the exiled Pope the Austrians would, and France was always the enemy of Austrian influence in Italy. His Catholic policy therefore was not entirely illiberal, especially as he hoped that Pius IX would take advice from a benefactor and establish more progressive principles of government on his return. In 1850 Napoleon III again showed his solicitude for Roman Catholicism. On the strength of the Capitulations of 1740, which made him the patron of Roman Catholics in the Ottoman empire, he secured concessions in connexion with the custody of the Holy Places. In 1853 he joined England in a war against Russia on behalf of Turkey, and by a maritime feat— by the transference of an army to the Crimea—he avenged the tragedy of Moscow in 1812. The kingdom of Piedmont-Sardinia had been one of the allies against Russia and had secured representation in the Peace Conference of Paris, 1856. Here it was that Napoleon III, who in old days had fought beside Italian rebels, declared that something must be done on behalf of Italy.

Nothing could be more in the tradition of the first Napoleon than the 'freeing' of Italy, and the expulsion of the Austrians from Lombardy and Venice. Austria was the ancient enemy of France and had made herself the principal guardian of the treaties of 1815. By becoming the patron of the Italian movement of liberation, Napoleon could hope to keep it under some degree of control, and to prevent the solution of the problem in a manner detrimental to France—that is to say, the complete unification of the peninsula and the erection of another formidable Mediterranean state.

France and Piedmont therefore went to war in 1859 in order to drive the Austrians beyond the Alps. Even now the 'liberal' policy was streaked with a dash of Catholicism; for the Italian states, freed from Austrian hegemony, were to become a federation under the Pope. Unfortunately, the French emperor carried out only half of the bargain; he put an end to the war when the Austrians had relinquished only their hold on Lombardy; and since the Italians were resentful for what they deemed they had lost rather than grateful for the province they had gained, the emperor immediately found himself estranged from his allies. Tuscany, with other regions, including part of the papal states, instead of entering into Napoleon's plan and joining a confederation, rebelled against their legitimate rulers and, under clever management by friends of Cavour, voted for a union with the kingdom of Piedmont. This state, already enlarged by the acquisition of Lombardy, had therefore now changed the bearings of the whole Italian problem. Napoleon had entered the war with the idea of producing a federation in Italy under the Pope, but Piedmont had emerged as a promising nucleus for a properly united kingdom of Italy. Napoleon now, however, confirmed what was a *fait accompli*, but demanded and secured the cession of Nice and Savoy, to the great indignation of the Italian patriots. In the following year, by a further use of the insurrectionary method (carefully controlled), Piedmont secured the annexation of Sicily, Naples and most of the papal states. Henceforward Rome was the great object of the Italian patriots; Rome was to be the crown of the whole endeavour—but she

was still under the dominion of the papacy. Out of considera-
tion for Catholic opinion, Napoleon III made himself the chief
obstacle to the achievement of the goal. Almost consistently
down to the end of the Empire it was French troops who stood
between the Italians and their capital.

The grand attempt to overthrow the treaties of 1815, therefore, though it may have brought prestige for a moment, resulted
in much embarrassment for Napoleon III, who found himself
unable to stop the ball that he had set rolling. The attempt to
please both Catholics and liberals at once (and to bridge the
tragic gulf the revolution had caused in French opinion and
tradition) failed even in the easiest case; for in 1863 Napoleon
was unable to do anything for the Poles (a Catholic people and
traditional protégés of France), who were then in rebellion
against the rule of Orthodox Russia. Some in France who
watched the results of the principle of nationality as it was
operating in Italy warned Napoleon of the consequences of the
extension of the principle to the parallel case of Germany. The
emperor, however, appeared not unwilling to see Prussia go to
war with Austria for the leadership of Germany and played
with the idea of snatching some territorial advantage out of the
conflict. Since the second Treaty of Paris (1815) the French
had complained of the loss of Saarbrücken, Saarlouis and Landau, and had demanded the more favourable frontiers of 1814.
They had resented the position that the Prussians had gained
in the Rhineland. In 1829 the Restoration government had
thought of a diplomatic combination which would result in the
acquisition of Belgium and the establishment of buffer states
on the Rhine. In the crisis of 1840, the demand was raised that
France should carry her frontier forward to that river. Such
ideas in the mind of Napoleon III in 1866 were gravely imperilled by the thoroughness of the Prussian victory over Austria
at Sadowa. The expectation of a long war between evenly
matched enemies (a war in which France could hold the key
position as a third party) was destroyed, especially when Bismarck hastened the conclusion of a peace treaty with the court
of Vienna. The northern states of Germany now formed a

confederation under the Prussian king whose own territories were greatly increased. Without giving Napoleon III an opportunity to interfere, Bismarck was proceeding to turn the German complex of states into a national unity.

From this moment the diplomacy of the French government became frightened, unreasonable and chaotic. As compensation for the aggrandizement of the Prussian State, the French asked first, in July, for the frontiers of 1814 and the Grand Duchy of Luxemburg, then, early in August, for the left bank of the Rhine as far as Mainz. Bismarck communicated the French demands to the south German states which were outside the new confederation. These states, which might have been expected to lean upon French protection against the Prussian menace, now saw Prussia as the guardian of the integrity of German soil, and accepted treaties of military alliance with her. After proposing the establishment of a buffer state on the left bank of the Rhine, the French suggested that they should be allowed to acquire Luxemburg and to annex Belgium, whose separate nationality Napoleon refused to recognize. In 1867 an outburst of indignation in Germany thwarted a French attempt to acquire Luxemburg by private treaty with its Grand Duke, the king of Holland.

In the meantime, French overseas enterprise had been driven to excess and had come to a great disaster. In the reign of Louis Philippe, apart from the undertaking in Algeria, colonial policy had been marked by extraordinary cautiousness. If the Ministry of Marine projected overseas conquests, the Ministry of Foreign Affairs repressed them, and the efforts were confined on the whole to the establishment of stations for the fleet in the Indian and Pacific Oceans. Tahiti was acquired, not without friction with Great Britain. A French expedition to New Zealand arrived only to find that the British government—after long hesitation—had declared its sovereignty over that region. In the reign of Napoleon III overseas activity was more imposing. Through the distinguished work of Faidherbe, the few dismal trading stations possessed by France in Senegal were transformed (1858–65) into an extensive colony that gave further promise of expansion into the future region of French West Africa. From 1858 a punitive expedition that was not originally intended to lead to colonization gradually achieved the annexation of Cochin-China. During 1857–60 the French and British were at war with China, securing guarantees for merchants and missionaries and receiving reparations for offences committed in the past. In 1860–1 a French expedition to Syria put a stop to the massacre of Christians by the Druses. Finally, from 1861 the attempt to collect money due from Mexico, where civil war was raging, was magnified by Napoleon III into a grandiose project of a Latin and Catholic empire ruled over by Napoleon's protégé, the Hapsburg Maximilian. This was the undertaking that ended in failure and discredit, and in 1866–7 (the very period of the Sadowa disappointment) France came to see the magnitude of the catastrophe. The United States, having brought their own civil war to an end, were not prepared to tolerate Napoleon's breach of the Monroe Doctrine. Napoleon, on the other hand, in view of his relations with Germany at this time, could not afford to dispatch any more troops across the Atlantic to redeem the Mexican fiasco.

Between 1866 and 1870, Napoleon suffered one humiliation after another at the hands of Bismarck. French opinion drove him to repeated diplomatic blunders for, after Poland (1863), Sadowa and Mexico, the very existence of his regime depended on a recovery of prestige. Since 1860 the authoritarian regime in France had been modified somewhat; but now further concessions had to be made to liberal demands, and a relaxation of the press law, and of the control of public meetings, only loosened the tongues of Napoleon's enemies. In 1869 he had to establish 'the Liberal Empire', giving the *Corps Législatif* the full prerogatives of a parliamentary assembly though retaining his control over the ministers.

This was the situation when, in July 1870, the news leaked out that Bismarck had agreed to the imminent nomination of a member of the Hohenzollern family to the Spanish throne that was now being restored after civil war. French nervousness increased the force and fury of justifiable French indignation, but, partly through the good offices of other powers, the Prussian king gave way, and after a short delay the candidature was withdrawn. The frantic state of public opinion may be responsible for the fact that this was not the end of the matter; but Napoleon III refused to be satisfied with the diplomatic victory and now demanded an undertaking that the candidature should never be renewed. The Prussian king impatiently brushed aside this further demand and Bismarck published a somewhat distorted version of what had happened (the Ems telegram), with the result that popular feeling in both France and Germany was embittered and war became inevitable. For Bismarck it was a war that would unify Germany. For Napoleon III it was the war that would rescue or ruin his regime.

At the opening of the war the French were unreasonably confident, and elsewhere in Europe there was a prevailing impression that they would be victorious. Napoleon III at first hoped that south Germany would be neutral and that Austria, if not Italy, would quickly enter the struggle against the victors of 1866. It was known that the Prussian forces had superiority in numbers, but the French could mobilize more quickly and Napoleon III hoped to attack Germany from the Upper Rhine before the enemy could be completely assembled. In recent years, however, the French had been disinclined for war, and unwilling to undertake the burden of army reforms; detailed preparations had not been worked out even for the mobilization, which began on 15 July. In the first few days anarchy prevailed—'the sidings at Metz were congested with trucks of which no one on the spot knew the contents'—and, though the advance might still have been started before the Germans were ready, the uncertainty of the leaders robbed the French of any initial advantage they might have had. Deficient in numbers, in preparation and in organization, greatly inferior in artillery, and cursed by weak and divided leadership, the French, haunted by a sick emperor whose depression was contagious, suffered some severe checks in the early days of August, losing the fight on more than one occasion even where they had a local superiority in strength. Alsace had to be abandoned. The hope of an Austrian alliance had to be given up. By 19 August one army under Bazaine was besieged in Metz, while another army under MacMahon was first ordered to fall back on the capital, then ordered to go to the help of Bazaine. Suffering greatly from the uncertainty of its leaders, it allowed itself to be hemmed in at Sedan, where, along with the emperor, it capitulated on 2 September.

The news of Sedan was taken in Paris to mean the downfall of the dynasty, and while the *Corps Législatif* was deliberating and delaying, the impatient mob burst in, crying, 'Down with the Empire! Long live the Republic!' The Republic was proclaimed at the Hôtel de Ville and, to curb the dangerous revolutionary movement, the deputies formed a provisional government, consisting of certain members of the 'Left', who had been elected for Paris. The war had to continue because Bismarck was demanding the cession of Alsace-Lorraine, while the new government in Paris said, 'We refuse to surrender one inch of our territory or a single stone of our fortresses'. On 19 September the capital was therefore invested by the Prussians, and the government—so closely identified with that city—chose to stand the siege, sending out a few elderly delegates to conduct provincial affairs at Tours. On 9 October, however, Gambetta escaped from Paris by balloon, and by his energy and enthusiasm quickened the creation of a new army—the army of the Loire. This national resistance, combined with the fortitude of Paris under siege, disconcerted the Prussians, who were now faced with problems for which they were unprepared and who had considered the struggle to be virtually at an end. It was hoped that, as the Prussian troops investing Paris were thinly drawn out, a sortie by the besieged forces could be effectively combined with an attack from the army of the Loire; but on 27 October the capitulation of Bazaine at Metz released a considerable Prussian army that had been investing that city, and on 29 November an attempted sortie from Paris completely failed. On 4 December the Germans finally captured Orléans, and the seat of government was moved to Bordeaux; the army of the Loire had been cut in two. Paris still continued its desperate resistance, but an armistice was concluded on 28 January. France had to pay an indemnity of five milliard francs, to submit to German occupation, and to surrender Alsace-Lorraine.

The position of Alsace-Lorraine in relation to the Great Powers of Europe has been the subject of two main theories—the French theory of the seventeenth century and the German of the nineteenth. The French theory naturally followed the teaching of the Renaissance and the study of Roman history; from which it appeared that France was Gaul, and the Rhine its natural boundary. This was the ideal of Richelieu, who wrote in his *Testament politique*: 'J'ai voulu...identifier la Gaule avec la France.' The aim was in part realized by Louis XIV, and completed in the eighteenth century (see p. 73).

Since then, however, the Gothic revival and the study of medieval history had created a new idea which regarded the Holy Roman Empire as the parent of German nationality and of the modern German empire. According to this theory Alsace-Lorraine was a western borderland of Germany; its Gaulish population had been replaced by Germans. Both banks of the Rhine, up to the Vosges and the Moselle, had been part of the Holy Roman Empire and were needed in order to make the new German empire its successor. This theory, more or less recognized, underlay the sentiment of German poets and popular writers in the early part of the nineteenth century; it was adopted by Mommsen and other German historians, and carried into effect by William I and Bismarck. It afforded the justification of the war of 1870, in which the victory was used to capture the ironfields of Lorraine and the industries of Alsace for German commerce.

CHAPTER V

THE THIRD REPUBLIC

1. DOMESTIC AFFAIRS

THE NEW CONSTITUTION, 1870–84

ONE of the first consequences of the defeat of the French armies in the field had been the overthrow of the Second Empire. Royalists, republicans, catholics, anti-clericals—all had combined against the existing regime, but the republican 'Government of National Defence' that was improvised on 4 September 1870 had no deep roots in the country. Its most prominent member, Gambetta, during his six months' dictatorship, committed the republican party to war to the end, but, by January, France was exhausted. Bismarck, however, insisted on negotiating with a representative body, and the elections to the National Assembly were, above all, a plebiscite on peace and war. The peasants, a few months before, had overwhelmingly supported the Empire. Now they voted against the republicans and in favour of peace—although this involved supporting candidates whom, in normal times, they would have rejected. The peace party, although conservative, royalist and catholic, won an overwhelming victory.

The new National Assembly met in February at Bordeaux. Out of six hundred and fifty deputies, four hundred were prepared to vote for the king. They might there and then have restored the monarchy had not the royalist majority been so divided amongst itself. Some supported the grandson of Charles X; some, the grandson of Louis Philippe; others were Bonapartists. As a result of this division the Republic was allowed to continue its work of reorganization, and Thiers was elected 'chief of the executive power'. This tacit agreement to leave the question of the regime open was known as the 'Pact of Bordeaux', and from this provisional transaction, accepted by a monarchical Assembly, sprang the Third Republic—the most permanent regime established in France since the ancient monarchy disappeared in 1792.

The first duty of the Assembly was to make peace and to ratify the preliminary terms agreed on at Versailles. Distrusting the royalist flavour of the Assembly, disagreeing with its pacific intentions, and exasperated by the spectacle of German troops marching down the Champs-Élysées, the workers of Paris rose in revolt. Paris was a second time besieged—this time by the forces of the Republic. It was an humiliating spectacle of Frenchmen fighting against Frenchmen under the eyes of the victorious Germans encamped outside the city. The siege lasted six weeks, and it came to an end, in the last week of May, only after bloody fighting and after Paris had suffered far more damage from French hands than had been inflicted by the Germans.

The by-elections of July showed that the political tide had begun to run against the royalists. The hour of an easy restoration was over, and in August a provisional constitution was voted with Thiers as 'President of the French Republic'—a title reluctantly admitted. As long as the German army of occupation stayed on, as long as the payment of the indemnity was incomplete, the Assembly could hardly afford to do without Thiers. By 1873, however, the main work of reconstruction had been completed, and the Assembly replaced him by the distinguished, but politically naïve, Marshal MacMahon—an honest soldier of royalist sympathies. A last attempt to restore the monarchy failed. From 1873 to 1875, the royalist majority hesitated and finally decided to give France institutions as like a constitutional monarchy as was possible.

A tacit coalition between disillusioned royalists and practically minded republicans made the constitution of 1875. It provided for a president to be elected for seven years by both Houses of Parliament sitting together to form a National Assembly. The Senate was to consist of seventy-five life-senators elected by the Assembly (to be replaced as vacancies occurred by nominees of the President), and of two hundred and twenty-five senators elected for nine years by panels of local government bodies in a fashion that made it certain that the villages and small towns would easily outvote the cities. Only the Chamber of Deputies was to be chosen by universal suffrage, for a term of four years, and it was hoped that this would be shackled by the President and Senate. If it got out of hand, it could be dissolved by the President with the consent of the Senate. It was a makeshift constitution in which no one very much believed.

When Parliament met, in 1876, after the first elections under the new system of government, there was a large republican majority in the Lower House, and the conservative majority in the Senate was very narrow. The alarmed President, Mac-Mahon, forced out of office the moderate republican ministry of Jules Simon, although it had a steady majority in the Lower House; and, with the reluctant consent of the Senate, he dissolved the Chamber of Deputies. The ensuing elections were a dramatic repudiation of the policy of the President. After over a year of compromise, he resigned in January 1879.

MacMahon was succeeded by the eminent but colourless republican lawyer, Jules Grévy. The first three years of the new constitution had completely upset the plan of the constitution makers. The right of dissolution was completely discredited. As long as the Third Republic lasted, no Chamber had ever again to fear a dissolution; secure in their four years' tenure of office, the members were free to exercise their full powers. The office of President, too, was greatly diminished in importance; Grévy boasted of his subservience to Parliament. Thus were destroyed the hopes of those royalists who, in 1875, had seen in the Presidency a moderating power.

In 1884 the Assembly took a further step forward when it enacted that the republican form of government could never be the subject of revision, and that all members of families which had reigned in France were ineligible for the Presidency of the Republic; a repetition of the career of Louis Bonaparte was thus made impossible (see p. 150). Further, life senatorships were abolished, and the purely elective character of the sovereign body was increased; the large towns, too, received more weight in the election of senators, thus making the Senate more representative. By this time, the Senate was as republican as the Chamber. This meant that there was a cleavage between the old aristocracy and the new plutocracy—between the upper middle classes on one side, and the political ruling classes on the other.

Fig. 32. The departments of France

Most of the rich, aristocratic, socially and economically prominent elements of the country were condemned to exclusion from political life.

The main lines of French constitutional practice did not change notably from 1884 to 1940. Ministerial instability arose from the absence of fixed party lines in Parliament. The loose agglomeration of left deputies who constituted the republican party broke quickly into two wings, the 'opportunists' and the radicals. But the members of these parties did not think themselves bound to follow their chiefs blindly or in any course that seemed unpopular. Ministries were normally short-lived, although it must be remembered that there was seldom a complete replacement of one ministry by another; some members of the outgoing cabinet usually found places in the new. But the executive authority was normally weak and timid. Only rarely and under exceptional circumstances and exceptional men, under Ferry, Waldeck-Rousseau, Clemenceau and Poincaré, did a cabinet face Parliament in any but a suppliant attitude.

In the decades that followed the revision of the constitution, the party system in France, though assuming many forms, was at bottom compounded of three elements—the continued decline of the royalist cause, the antagonism of Church and State, and the rise of the 'Left'. These must be considered separately.

THE DECLINE OF THE ROYALIST CAUSE

The death of the Prince Imperial, heir of Napoleon III, in 1879, had been of great aid to the Republic; the Bonapartes were the only dynasty with widespread popular support, and the prince had been the only pretender with any personal power of appeal. His cousin and heir, Prince Napoleon, was neither liked nor trusted, and many leading Bonapartists went over to the divided royalists; one claimant to the throne was the elderly Comte de Chambord, grandson of Charles X, who died in 1884; another was the Comte de Paris, grandson of Louis Philippe, who was to become involved in an unsuccessful bid for power by General Boulanger.

In the meantime, a new generation of Frenchmen had grown up; it was bored by the tedious parliamentary game, and it was bitterly resentful of the humiliation of 1870 which the ruling politicians seemed to take calmly enough. A potential leader for this new generation was a self-advertising soldier, General Boulanger. As Minister of War, he had introduced some useful and conspicuous reforms. He was at first used by ambitious radical politicians, but the more astute of them, like Clemenceau, saw the way Boulanger's mind was moving and abandoned such a dangerous acquaintance. Boulanger had no political ideas or principles; he was willing to take support from any side. After the radicals gave him up, he tried the Bonapartists, but only some royalists, supported by the Comte de Paris, had money and faith enough to back him. He ran for Parliament and was almost always successful when he was a candidate himself, although he could not transfer his popularity to others. When he was elected for Paris in January 1889, it was assumed by everybody, friend and foe alike, that he had only to walk into power. But at the crisis his nerve failed. After a few futile manœuvres he went into exile; his followers were arrested and he committed suicide at Brussels. The Republic was saved from the humiliating fate of overthrow at the hands of a flamboyant soldier, less by its own strength than by the incompetence and moral cowardice of the potential dictator.

It was probably only just saved in time. If the Panama scandal had been revealed when the regime was being attacked, things might have gone differently. Now, in 1892, it was discovered that the greatest French enterprise, the Panama Canal Company, and the greatest living Frenchman, Ferdinand de Lesseps, had been ruined by the blackmail practised by some deputies and senators. Millions of pounds had been lost to the small investor, and an unknown number of politicians had benefited by the swindle. Some of the most prominent republican leaders were involved. Rouvier was suspected of personal profit and Clemenceau's paper had been subsidized by one of the most shady Jewish financiers of the day, Cornélius Herz. All forms of political activity seemed discredited—the monarchist parties by the failure of Boulangism, the republican parties by the scandal of Panama. France was angered and disillusioned. Only the extreme 'Left' benefited.

THE ANTAGONISM OF CHURCH AND STATE

A close observer of the Boulangist crisis had been Pope Leo XIII, who concluded that the royalists had shot their bolt and who recommended to them the policy of 'ralliement' (1891), i.e. the acceptance of the Republic as the only possible form of government in France and the alliance of all Frenchmen who were friends of the Church and enemies of radicalism. Most of the Catholic leaders gave lip service to the papal policy, but many of the rank and file remained bitterly hostile to a regime which, they thought, persecuted the Church and endangered the social order. The policy of 'ralliement' had come too late to effect any reconciliation between the rising left-wing forces and the Church.

It would be difficult to over-estimate the significance of the antagonism between Church and State in the history of modern France. In no sphere of national life is this more clearly demonstrated than in that of education. A struggle extending for more than a century has split the nation into two camps. On the one side stand the adherents of the Catholic Church—the clerical party—who have not ceased to demand a controlling voice in the education of the young; on the other is the large body of anti-clericals whose policy has been to combat the influence of the clergy in education.

The origins of the antagonism may be traced to the revolutionary doctrines of the eighteenth century. In pre-revolutionary France all education was the handmaid of the Church, whose monopolistic control was, for the most part, unchallenged. French revolutionary philosophy reacted vehemently against ecclesiastical control. By the constitution of 1791, and in accordance with the principles of the Revolution, its monopoly was broken and freedom of teaching was established. Napoleon made education a national public service in 1808. A highly centralized system of education, copied from that of the Society of Jesus, was established. 'My aim', said Napoleon, 'in establishing an educational corporation is to be able to direct political and moral opinion.' The Imperial University, later known as the 'Université de France', was the embodiment of this idea. It prescribed the course of instruction for secondary and higher education, and laid down qualifications of the teachers and the conditions of their appointment. 'No one', said the Emperor, 'shall open a school, or teach publicly unless he is a member of the Imperial University and a graduate of one of its faculties'; and, in accordance with the Concordat between Bonaparte and the Pope in 1801, the Catholic faith was made the foundation of the new scheme. A politico-ecclesiastical monopoly was established with the State as senior partner.

Centralization and uniformity were not, however, complete even under the most despotic of French rulers. Primary education remained outside the immediate direction of the State, and concessions permitting families and religious congregations to keep school under the sanction and inspection of the university were granted. So popular were these institutions that when the Empire fell in 1815 it was estimated that nearly 40,000 pupils attended schools for secondary instruction, as compared with 28,000 children in the State's *lycées* and *collèges*. The dualism of later years was already discernible.

From 1808 to 1880 the imperial scheme of national education was little affected by the successive changes of government. The State continued the Napoleonic policy of co-operating with the Church and so controlling its activities. But the Church, to whom the imperial system was at best but an unsatisfactory compromise, was not content with its position. Changing its traditional policy, it became the defender of decentralization and freedom of teaching, as against the State's centralization and monopoly. With steady persistence it used all opportunities to strengthen its control. Standing as a bulwark against the tide of liberalism and unrest, it rallied to its side the growing number of Frenchmen who saw in the Church the champion of social order. It won its first important success in 1833 when Guizot, then Minister of Public Instruction, completing the Napoleonic system by the organization of primary schools throughout France, authorized the establishment of private schools and demanded from teachers of public and private schools the State's qualifying certificate—the 'Brevet de Capacité'. The number of pupils in the private primary schools rapidly increased. In 1830 it was estimated that 'les frères des Écoles Chrétiennes' taught 87,000 children; and in 1847 no fewer than 175,000.

More significant was the success of the 'liberal Catholics' under the Second Republic in 1850. By the famous Falloux Law of 1850 the legal freedom, already secured to primary instruction, was extended to secondary education. Those teaching congregations which had hitherto been proscribed by law were permitted to teach, and, as membership of an authorized cult or a nun's letters of obedience were regarded, respectively, as equivalent to the State's certificate of teaching capacity, the university's monopoly of control was lost. Education was henceforth shared by two legally constituted agencies. By 1854, the Catholic Church had opened 1081 voluntary institutions.

The liberation of university teaching from the State's monopoly was won as late as 1875. Freedom to establish Catholic universities was permitted, and the granting of university degrees was placed in the hands of a mixed jury of professors drawn from State and voluntary institutions. Thus, in all three grades of education, State monopoly had been challenged with success and freedom of teaching secured.

When the Third Republic established its authority the struggle between Church and State entered on a new phase. In the early years of the Republic, the conservative party allied itself openly with the clericals and with Catholic interests in opposition to the Republic. The government, in order to combat the influence of the Church, abandoned the policy of co-operation of Church and State, initiated by Napoleon some sixty years before, and adopted in its place a policy of 'secularization' and 'neutrality'. During the period of the 'Secular Laws' from 1880 to 1906 it abolished religious instruction from all grades of State institutions, and, in 1904, it 'laicized' the schools by withdrawing the right to teach from members of religious congregations, not only in State but in private schools. But the spirit of the law was often different from the letter, and members of religious congregations continued to play an important part in the education of boys and girls. In university education, the mixed juries of laymen and clerics established in 1875 were abandoned in 1880, and the title of university was withdrawn from voluntary institutions for higher education.

The dualism of Church and State finds expression today in two systems of education, parallel to and very loosely connected with one another. In 1934 some 80% of pupils receiving primary education received it in the State primary schools, and

58% of pupils receiving secondary education went to the State secondary schools. The legislation (1929–33) making State secondary education gratuitous struck a severe blow at the Catholic schools. Financed in great part by fees, they competed under heavy disabilities with the non-fee-paying public schools.

Most of the French upper classes were, or professed to be, zealous Catholics. But the governing class of the Third Republic was, almost without exception, agnostic, Protestant or Jewish. And the most popular slogan of the republicans was that of Gambetta: 'Clericalism—that is the enemy.' There were, too, elements of religious as well as social resentment in the party divisions. Zealous Catholics were notoriously at a disadvantage in all branches of the public service—legal, educational and administrative. Only in the army and navy could they hope to compete on even terms with free-thinkers, Protestants and Jews; and here, it was asserted, they could compete on more than even terms.

The clerical and anti-clerical quarrel took a new turn when, at the end of 1894, the public learned that a young Jewish officer named Dreyfus had been convicted by court-martial of selling confidential documents to the German military attaché. From being a minor military scandal the case became a great political *cause célèbre*. Half France believed he was guilty: the other half, with equal vigour, asserted he was innocent. The old Boulangist and monarchist parties rallied to the defence of the army against the 'syndicate' of Jews, Freemasons, and friends of Germany and England. The radicals, and many far-from-radical republicans saw, in the claims of the army leaders to immunity from legal control, a menace to the Republic. That Dreyfus was a Jew, and his most noisy enemies zealous Catholics, involved the affair in the anti-clerical quarrel. The 'ralliement' had not been popular with the more zealous Catholics who were glad of the chance to attack the Republic; a furious anti-Semitic campaign took place in the Catholic press. In 1900, after a second trial, Dreyfus was 'pardoned', and the case was declared closed. But the victorious enemies of the army were not so easily contented. Nor, indeed, was the Prime Minister, Waldeck-Rousseau. He struck at the religious orders, many of whom had rashly thrown themselves into the struggle against the Jewish, Protestant and atheist friends of Dreyfus. He introduced a bill to control the religious orders, but before the law was applied he had resigned. The left had won a great triumph at the general election, and the application of the law was in the hands of the fanatical Émile Combes who used it to expel practically all the male orders from France—to the bitter indignation of that large section of French society which regarded the religious orders with respect, and in many cases with love. Nor was this their only grievance. As the higher ranks of the army had seemed to be in reactionary and clerical hands, there was much support for a policy of controlling methods of promotion. The Minister of War, General André, undertook this reform in a fashion that still further embittered feeling. Officers were even encouraged to spy on their colleagues, and to report on those who went to Mass or sent their children to Church schools.

The Dreyfus case had been much more than a quarrel about a man. It was made a pretext by all parties for gratifying their animosities. It was utilized by the right against the Republic, by rival republicans against each other, by the military party against the parliamentarians, by the revolutionary socialists against the army, by the clericals against non-Catholics, and by the anti-clericals against the Church. It was, in fact, a symptom of the complicated political condition of France.

One of the main features of French political life in the early years of the twentieth century was a campaign against the Catholic Church, without parallel since the Revolution. The climax came with the Act of Separation (9 December 1905).

The 'Act of Separation of the Churches and the State' began a new era in the history of Catholicism in France. It guaranteed liberty of conscience and the free exercise of public worship; but henceforth no religion was to be recognized or subsidized by the State. All the property of religious organizations (Catholic, Protestant and Jewish) was ordered to be transferred to associations for public worship (*associations cultuelles*) which were to be self-supporting. The Vatican refused to acknowledge the separation, and in 1906 forbade Catholics to take part in the 'associations', but a law passed in 1907 provided a *modus vivendi*. Failing the formation of 'associations cultuelles', the buildings for public worship together with their furnishings were left at the disposal of the clergy and their congregations. They remained, nevertheless, the property of the State, whereas new churches, like the many which sprang up in the Paris industrial belt, became the property of private companies (*sociétés civiles*) in which the donations of the faithful were vested.

One of the results of the separation was a reduction in standard of living for many of the clergy to the level of those among whom they worked; there was a new contact between the Church—long the apparent ally of the propertied classes—and the workers. The Christian Trade Union movement, and the 'Association Catholique de la Jeunesse Française', grew apace. The mobilization of priests and monks for active service and their gallant conduct during the war of 1914–18 also helped to improve relations. The return to France of Alsace-Lorraine with its large Catholic population, which under the German rule had escaped the anti-clerical policy of the Third Republic, was among the reasons which decided the government to renew diplomatic relations with the Vatican in 1921. A solution acceptable to the Vatican of the vexed question of 'associations cultuelles' was found in 1924 when they were reconstituted as 'associations diocésaines' under the chairmanship of the bishops.

It seemed as if the anti-clerical struggle was over. But a left ministry of 1924 sought to carry out a new anti-clerical programme involving the withdrawal of the embassy from the Vatican, the stricter enforcement of the laws concerning the religious orders, and the introduction of purely secular teaching into Alsace-Lorraine. The embassy was in fact suppressed in January 1925, but unrest in Alsace-Lorraine resulted in special treatment for these provinces; the Council of State declared that they were still under the regime of the Concordat and that they should therefore continue to be represented at the Vatican. A few weeks later, in April 1925, the policy was reversed; the French embassy to the Holy See was restored and has been maintained since that date.

In this atmosphere of diminishing anti-clericalism there was a marked growth of the Catholic 'Left', signalized by the parliamentary activity of the 'Parti Démocrate Populaire', and accompanied by improved relations between the Church and the Republic. A number of Catholic papers were founded as declared opponents of totalitarianism, particularly of the 'Right'. The Archbishop of Paris, Cardinal Verdier, with his hundred new churches in the industrial region of Paris and his team of energetic young priests, did much to re-christianize the so-called 'red belt'. Both he and the 'red cardinal', Liénart of Lille, had a moral authority, outside their own fold, enjoyed by few of their predecessors.

This Catholic revival, which was such a notable feature of French life since the turn of the century, had not only these left-wing manifestations as indicated above, but also a very considerable right-wing. Writers like Bourget, Barrès and Charles Maurras, the editor of the royalist *Action Française*, were among the most noteworthy representatives of this tendency, which took a more constitutionally conservative form in the activities of the 'Fédération Nationale Catholique'.

Throughout this period members of the religious orders gradually returned to France and their activities were tolerated. In 1928 a prominent Jesuit Father could even write that the laws against religious orders were 'universally and flagrantly violated'. When Laval, as Foreign Minister, went to Rome to sign the Franco-Italian agreement of January 1935, he was received in audience by the Pope; such an unprecedented encounter had not taken place for seventy years. Cardinal Verdier was able to state just before the outbreak of war in 1939 that the relations between the Catholic Church and the French State, except for the still unsolved question of education, had 'never been better'. Though there are no statistics available to show that Catholicism was still 'the religion of the great majority of Frenchmen', the rites of the Church (for example, baptism, marriage and burial) still remained important in the lives of the majority of Frenchmen, even of anti-clericals.

Before the armistice of 1940, the Catholic Church in France

comprised seventeen archbishoprics and sixty-eight bishoprics together with the two bishoprics of Metz and Strasbourg. The total number of Catholic clergy was about 51,000.

The separation of Church and State marked the complete triumph of the radicals, and it was fittingly consummated under their veteran leader, Clemenceau, who took office for the first time in 1906 and remained in power for the phenomenal period of almost three years. The 'notables' were now put down from their places in all departments of French official life—in the army, navy and administration, as well as in Parliament; their great ally, the Church, was disestablished and the religious orders were in exile. But this great and bloodless victory, like all victories in civil war, left much bitterness behind; and the defeated party turned in increasing numbers to the violent, anti-parliamentary and authoritarian doctrines of the *Action Française*, a royalist league and newspaper, preaching doctrines that some years later became one of the parents of Italian fascism.

THE RISE OF THE LEFT

The quarrels over the Church and over the regime were not the only political questions agitating the country. The suppression of the Paris insurrection in 1871 had, for a time, put an end to an organized socialist movement in France. But the amnesty that came with the republican triumph of 1877–9 brought back to France many exiled leaders; and some of these had been affected by Marxian doctrines learned abroad. The steady though slow industrialization of France increased the market for such teaching, and the economic depression of the eighties had permanent results in stimulating the growth of economic discontent.

Moreover, in French Lorraine was the second greatest iron-ore field in the world. When the frontier was drawn in 1870, the ore could not be worked because of its high phosphorus content. But the Gilchrist-Thomas process solved the problem, and France became an important steel-making country and a still more important exporter of iron ore. Around Paris, the new automobile industry, in which France was the European pioneer, was only the most striking sign of the change in French economy. This change was reflected in the growth of socialism and syndicalism. Before 1905 socialism had found its chief scope in anti-clericalism. Now, after the separation, economic questions came to the fore. Socialism found a great parliamentary leader in Jean Jaurès, and the number of socialist deputies in the Chamber continually increased.

The syndicalists were determined to break all connexions between the trade-union movement and politics. They wished the workers in their own indigenous organizations to oppose all forms of the bourgeois State, including Parliament; the general strike and sabotage were to be the true weapons, not the vote. The intellectual spokesman of this doctrine was George Sorel, who had some influence on the ideas of the young Italian socialist leader, Benito Mussolini. Over-production of wine produced an agricultural strike in the south, and there were bloody mining strikes in the north, but the most menacing result of syndicalist teaching was the great railway strike of 1910: it collapsed when the strikers were called up as army reservists. The syndicalist weapon was broken, but French unity seemed fatally compromised. Yet in 1914 it was shown how superficial this apparent disunion was. For the overwhelming majority of Frenchmen, the great reality was still France, not any creed or party.

2. COLONIAL AFFAIRS, 1870–1914

In 1870 the French empire consisted of a few relics of the old colonial possessions of the Bourbon kings together with the foundations of a new empire begun under the Restoration and under Louis Philippe. A few islands in the Antilles and in the Gulf of St Lawrence; a few decaying trading posts in India; a few islands in the Indian Ocean; the stagnant swamps of French Guiana—these had survived the wreck of Napoleon's empire. They decayed all through the nineteenth century. Only the posts at the mouth of the Senegal had any future. Charles X had begun the conquest of Algeria which was completed under Louis Philippe. An abortive rebellion early in 1871 was the last flicker of serious native resistance. It was confined to eastern Algeria, and it was easily suppressed, even by a France that had suffered defeat at Sedan. Some Pacific islands, Tahiti, New Caledonia and the Marquesas, had been occupied under Louis Philippe; and Napoleon III had seized the fertile and half-empty delta of the Mekong, the colony of Cochin-China. An advance from the mouth of the Senegal had begun, and scientific and commercial exploration, combined with missionary effort, prepared France to take her share in the scramble for Africa. But in the early days of the Republic, France was too weak and too distracted to profit by the enterprise of her agents. She abandoned the fruits of the daring of François Garnier who had moved north from Cochin-China to attack the empire of Annam. In Egypt, she was a timid and reluctant partner of England. She allowed the Khedive's shares in the Suez Canal to be bought by Disraeli, and when misgovernment and bankruptcy in 1881 led to intervention by Britain, France refused to share the risks—or profits—of the task. It was part of Bismarck's policy to encourage French colonial activities as a diversion from her eastern frontier, and, at the Congress of Berlin (1878), he and the British government conveyed to the French delegates that whenever France wanted to occupy Tunis, her action would meet with the support of Britain and Germany. The time came in 1881, and one result of the establishment of a French protectorate was to drive Italy into the arms of Germany, for Tunis was the only colonial territory that Italy could easily and profitably have exploited. During the same epoch, the advance into Annam was resumed, an advance that ended in an undeclared war with China and in long and expensive guerilla fighting that continued after China had accepted the French occupation of Annam and Tonkin in 1885. The western kingdoms of the Indo-Chinese peninsula, Cambodia and Laos, were also occupied and, by 1890, France was the nominal ruler of the fertile eastern peninsula of Asia. It was some years before General Gallieni made the occupation effective, and it was then his duty to do the same in the great island of Madagascar, where a nominal suzerainty was transformed into annexation in 1896.

In Africa, soldiers and traders, advancing from the Senegal, fought wars with the Arab slave traders, and moved into the Niger valley and down to the ocean on the Ivory coast. Farther south, they disputed with Belgium the opportunity of entering the heart of Africa by the Congo. Cut off from the main basin of the river, they established themselves on the northern bank from Stanley Pool to the sea.

By 1898, France had become the second greatest colonial power in the world. In that year, however, one of her boldest schemes came to naught. An expedition under Captain Marchand, advancing under great difficulties from the Congo, reached the upper waters of the White Nile at Fashoda. There it was to have been met by an expedition starting from the French enclave of Jibuti on the Red Sea and reinforced by Abyssinians, flushed with victory over the Italians. But a few weeks before, Kitchener had destroyed the Dervish power at Omdurman, and now advanced to Fashoda to find the French flag flying and Marchand in occupation. The British government instructed Kitchener to demand the withdrawal of Marchand. Relations between the two countries became at once seriously strained; the fleets were mobilized, and war seemed inevitable to many. But France was torn by the Dreyfus affair and, in any case, was not in a position to fight the first naval power. The French government decided not to maintain the Marchand mission at Fashoda, and he was ordered home.

Germany had continued the policy of encouraging French colonial enterprise as a diversion and as a means of alienating France from Britain and Italy. It was British support that saved Siam from the fate of Cambodia and Annam. It was British activity that kept France from securing all the Niger valley. British missionaries stimulated resistance to French penetration in Madagascar. It was Britain that profited by the feebleness of the French in Egypt. There were also minor grounds of irritation—the condominium in the New Hebrides, and the old quarrel over fishing rights in Newfoundland. To the French colonial party, Britain was almost or quite as bad as Germany. And the French colonial party was often identical with the French navy. Naval officers had conquered Indo-China, and had begun the conquest of Madagascar and the penetration of the Congo. The humiliation of Fashoda was largely a humiliation of the navy, which had to admit that it was not prepared for a war with Britain. There was, therefore, in France an influential party that saw little if anything to choose between Britain and Germany—a party on whose ambitions and resentments German policy could play in its endeavours to prevent a union of the two western powers.

3. FOREIGN POLICY, 1870–1914

The defeat of France in 1870 marked important changes in the balance of power in Europe. The new united Germany, proclaimed at Versailles in 1870, not only acquired two French provinces and a vast indemnity, but also gained immensely in prestige. The efficiency of the Prussian army lent glory to all German institutions, and the intellectual as well as the political and military weight of France was correspondingly diminished. Nor was this all. The combatants of 1870 had met more or less on equal terms. With a better military organization, or with better leadership, France might have won. By 1880, however, it was evident that the relative advantages of Germany were increasing. First of all its population was growing faster than that of France (Fig. 33). Secondly, the new heavy industries that were the basis of economic and military power were far further developed than in France.

It was, therefore, becoming evident to all clear-sighted Frenchmen that, single-handed, their country was no match for Germany. Only by alliances could the wrongs of 1870 be redressed. But the conviction of inferiority that led the preachers of revenge to seek allies for war, led more prudent persons to seek insurance against another German invasion. The policy of finding an ally had thus two different bases—one, adventurous and militarist; the other, cautious and pacific. The idea of an independent French policy disappeared. So did, though less completely, the dream of renewing Napoleonic conquests.

Not the frontiers of the First but those of the Second Empire became the ideal. France was no longer a crusader power spreading ideas of revolution, but a nation in a dangerous situation, needing all her strength for her own safety.

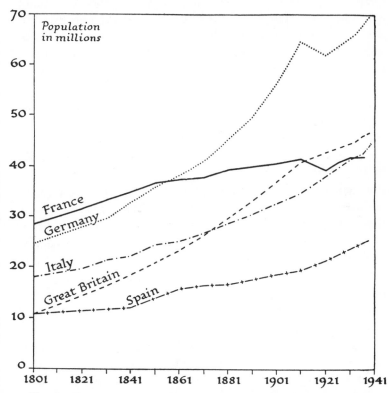

Fig. 33. The growth of population in France and neighbouring countries, 1801–1939. (The growth shown after 1936 is based upon estimates.)

As long as Bismarck could keep on good terms with both Russia and Austria and on not too bad terms with England, France had no chance of escaping from the isolation and impotence to which she had been condemned by her defeat in 1870. But with the fall of Bismarck and the open favouring of Austria rather than Russia by William II, the Czar had to look around for an ally. He needed support and he needed money. He could only get them from France and, swallowing his monarchist and religious principles, he accepted the lay Republic of 1890. A series of agreements bound the two countries together in defence of their common interests, notably their common interest in the prevention of German hegemony. Credulous souls in France dreamed of Russian aid for the recovery of Alsace-Lorraine, but wiser heads were content with the Russian guarantee of French security; it was a relief from the nightmare of a new German invasion, a nightmare that had seemed near reality on more than one occasion.

The Russian alliance helped to reassure French public opinion; a sudden German attack was no longer so much to be feared. But it did nothing to better the general position of France as a great power. Only when Russian interests were involved did St Petersburg take Paris into its confidence. Thus France was dragged into supporting Russia and Germany in depriving Japan of the fruits of her victory over China, but at the time of Fashoda the coldness of Russia was one of the causes that determined the French surrender to Britain. The lesson was not lost on Théophile Delcassé who had to conduct the French diplomatic retreat, and he determined to free his hands by settling all outstanding questions at issue between Britain and France. Britain, too, had her own reasons for settling with France. 'Splendid isolation' no longer seemed so splendid. The new German navy was beginning to be a factor in British policy, and British overtures to Germany had been barren of comforting result. The 'Entente Cordiale' of 1904, accordingly, settled all claims between France and Britain. Some of these claims were old—that of Newfoundland fisheries went back to the Treaty of Utrecht (1713). Others were modern boundary questions. But the fundamental bargain was the surrender of France's special position in Egypt for British recognition of her ambitions in Morocco.

Spain was bought off by a share in Moroccan territory, but Germany was not bought off at all, because there was nothing to buy; Germany had no place in Morocco anyway. But the Germans thought differently. So considerable a change in the African *status quo* as the acceptance of French control in Morocco was not to be permitted—except at a price. The French position was weakened by the folly of her ally. Russia had blundered into war with Japan, a war that diverted her military and naval strength to the Pacific, and showed, too, how overrated that strength had been. Defeat was followed by revolt, and France could not count on her ally. The Germans exploited the situation; the Kaiser went to Tangier to declare his interest in the independence of the Sultan of Morocco. The Germans were anxious to break the 'entente', but Britain stood firm. France, however, was in no position to fight, and the Moroccan question was referred to at an international congress which met at Algeciras (1906).

At Algeciras, France got most of what she wanted, in effect an option on Morocco, and the bonds with Britain were strengthened. An attempt by the Kaiser to separate his weak cousin, the Czar, from France was prevented by the action of the Russian ministers and, in 1907, most of the outstanding questions between Russia and Britain were settled. The 'entente' was now the 'Triple Entente', and was recognized as the counterpoise of the Triple Alliance whose junior member, Italy, was obviously open to the offers from the other camp.

If Algeciras was a German defeat, it was soon followed by a German—or Austrian—victory. The Turkish revolution of 1908–9 reopened the Eastern Question in an acute form. Bulgaria threw off her nominal dependence, and Austria annexed the provinces of Bosnia-Herzegovina which she had occupied since the Treaty of Berlin (1878). This was a blow to the position of Russia as patron of the Balkan Slavs, and especially as patron of the Serbs; but, weak after her defeats in the Far East, she was in no position to resist. The instability of the European situation was more and more obvious. Germany proved unwilling to facilitate the working of French 'influence' in Morocco, and France was obviously preparing to make Morocco another Tunis. In 1911 the feeble authority of the Sultan collapsed, and a French army invaded Morocco. Germany retorted by sending a gunboat to Agadir—an Atlantic port whose possibilities interested the British Admiralty. Britain stood by her partner and a new diplomatic deal was made. France surrendered a considerable part of her Congo colony and made over her reversionary rights in the Belgian Congo to Germany. In return, her protectorate in Morocco was recognized.

By now the international situation was generally disturbed. Italy took her chance to invade the Turkish territory of Tripoli. The Balkan states, encouraged by Russia whose risky policy was kept secret from France till it was too late, attacked European Turkey. The Balkan war surprised the world; the Turks were easily defeated, and the victorious armies had been armed and trained by French firms and French officers, while the Turks had been armed and trained by Germany. The victors fell out among themselves and, in the Second Balkan War, Bulgaria, the protégé of Austria, was defeated by Serbia and Greece, the protégés of Russia. Nor was this result important only from the point of view of prestige. Serbia was now certain to turn her ambitions north, and to strengthen her position among the kindred peoples of Austria-Hungary. Could Austria afford this? The rulers of the Dual Monarchy thought not. It was now or never. As soon as Serbia gave an opening, she must be taught her place as a satellite, not as a rival of Austria.

So the assassination of the Austrian heir, at Sarajevo, on 28 June 1914, was hardly even the lighting of the match; the match was already lit. Austria wished for a local triumph over Serbia, but was willing to risk a European war to bring it about. Russia was resolved to prevent the destruction of Serbian independence, and willing to risk a European war. Germany, after giving Austria a blank cheque, discovered too late that she was involved in a situation from which there could be no escape without a general war—except by a surrender on one side or another. France was dragged along by her obligations to Russia, and Britain by her obligations to France. But although neither of the western powers had much interest in the Balkan policy of Russia, they had been convinced by the tone of German policy, by her military machine, and by her naval power, that retreat meant surrender. So the war came.

4. THE WAR OF 1914–18

The French army entered the war of 1914 suffering under two sets of disadvantages. One unavoidable handicap was inferiority in numbers. In 1870 there had been as many Frenchmen as Germans; an equally rigorous system of conscription would have produced an equally numerous army. By 1914 there were only two Frenchmen for three Germans, and although the French system of conscription was now more rigorous than the German, it did not produce an army equal in numbers. The initial British contribution was quite inadequate to offset this handicap, and it was only the Russian alliance that gave the French any hope of meeting the Germans on equal terms. Some German troops would have to be kept in the east to aid the Austrians. The restoration of three years' service and improvements in the system of mobilization would, it was hoped, enable the French High Command to assemble an army which at the first shock would be superior in numbers to the forces the Germans could use on their western front. This calculation proved false. The Germans not only took the risk of stripping the eastern front, but, by creating divisions composed of reservists, were able to put into the field a western army that greatly outnumbered the French. The French did not know this and, even if they had, they could not have done much about it.

As a result, the French plan of campaign was doomed to failure from the start. The French commander-in-chief, General Joffre, believed that he could invade Alsace, attack the German centre in Lorraine, and guard his own left against a German turning movement through Belgium. He could, in fact, do none of these things. The Germans were strong enough not only to hold French attacks but to extend their right so far through Belgium as to imperil both the French left and the British Expeditionary Force. These dangers were made greater by the tactical inferiority of the French. French tactics were simple: a mass of infantry trained to attack in face of very high losses, supported by a very mobile field artillery, was intended to break through the German front, and this breach was to be exploited by cavalry. French field artillery was the best in the world, but the inferiority of the German '77' to the French '75' was more than outweighed by the superiority of the German heavy field guns over the '75' in range and trajectory. The French had no heavy field artillery at all; the new '105' and '155' existed only as prototypes.

The French attacks were bloody failures, and the Allied armies were forced back from the frontiers; the Germans reached the great woods north of Paris and were also at the gates of Nancy. What saved France was the resilience of the French High Command. Joffre stripped his right of every unit that could be spared and accumulated reserves on his left. These latter were thrown against the Germans, who perceived their danger in time to avoid complete disaster, but not in time to avoid defeat. They retreated in haste; the Battle of the Marne was won and lost, and the fundamental German plan of campaign had gone astray even more completely than the French (Fig. 34).

Attacking on the Aisne, the Allies discovered the power of an entrenched force. Both sides, looking for a flank, moved west till they reached the sea. October and November of 1914 were the months of the second great German offensive in Flanders; and this showed the futility of attack on entrenched troops without an overwhelming superiority in guns and munitions that neither side had as yet.

All through 1915 France tried vain offensives; French equipment got more adequate as new heavy guns were provided and old ones drawn from store, but Germany provided even more guns and munitions for the defensive. German industrial resources were much greater than those of France, and most of French industry was either in German hands or in the battle zone. So France became dependent on Britain and on the United States for the means of waging war. All she had in comparative abundance was trained infantry. They were lavishly expended.

In 1915 Germany not only disposed of Russia for the moment, but conquered Serbia. In 1916 she turned to France, and for nearly six months, in successive battles of Verdun, tried to break

the French army before the new British forces were ready to take
a major part in the war. Germany failed; her last attacks at
Verdun were defeated after the great Somme offensive had
opened. But the defence of Verdun had cost the French at least
as many men as the assault had cost the Germans—and the
French could afford such losses far less.

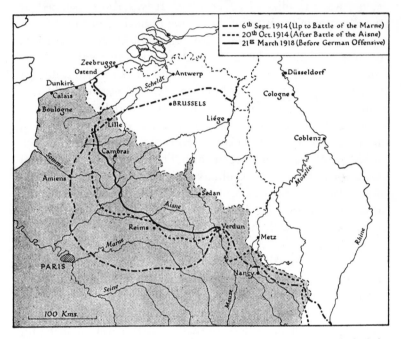

Fig. 34. The Western Front to 21 March 1918. The territory of France is shaded.

The slow, patient and costly tactics of Joffre were increasingly
discredited in a country that was bleeding, if not to death, at any
rate to the edge of a deadly anaemia. A new commander was
tried, Nivelle. He promised not merely victory, but speedy
victory. His April offensive of 1917 showed, however, that there
was no easy recipe for victory. The effect on French morale was
catastrophic; mutinies broke out and were stopped only by the
firmness and tact of the new commander, the hero of Verdun,
General Pétain.

The year 1917 saw the Russian Revolution, and, in France itself there was a great wave of war weariness of which the French mutinies were one symptom. The French socialists and trade-union leaders were increasingly pacifist, and an agitation for a compromise peace found many advocates. Among them was a group of left-wing journalists whose journal, the *Bonnet Rouge*, was subsidized by Germany. It was also subsidized by the Minister of the Interior, the young radical politician, Malvy, and behind Malvy was the more formidable figure of Caillaux, the one-time idol of the radicals. American intervention barely compensated for Russian defection, and there seemed a danger that French resistance would cease. It was 'peace or Clemenceau'. The veteran wrecker of ministries had been a ruthless critic of the various war governments, but his anger had been directed against their slackness. Poincaré, suppressing his own dislike, sent for Clemenceau, and France got the dictatorial government it needed. Caillaux and Malvy were arrested; the *Bonnet Rouge* group was broken up. Its leaders were executed or committed suicide. Politically France was prepared for the storm that burst with the great German offensive of March 1918.

The first result of that offensive was the creation of the unified command of the Allied armies under General Foch, who had been brought back from semi-retirement by Clemenceau. Foch needed all his courage in the next few months. Further great successes were won by the Germans against the British and then against the French. American reinforcements were pouring in, but it was doubtful if they would be in time. In June the first successful counter-attacks were made; in July the last great German offensive was stopped short and turned into a retreat. In August the British army broke the German front, and thenceforward the end of the war was not in doubt. In Macedonia, an Allied army under Franchet d'Ésperey broke the Bulgarian front and marched on the Danube. When the Germans were ready to accept terms that made them incapable of resuming the war, Foch was ready to advise his political chiefs, the heads of the Allied and Associated Governments, that it was time to stop the battle. On 11 November an armistice was made.

On the military side, the chief author of the Allied victory was France. She had borne the greatest burden on land: the Marne was decisive in that it prevented a lightning German victory; Verdun in that it prevented Germany winning a victory on the western front before the new British armies could attack. In the last great crisis, the French army played a role second only to that of the British, and it was a French general who won the great campaign. But few victors have ever been as exhausted as was France in November 1918. The most destructive of campaigns had been fought on her soil; her richest departments were devastated; her most valuable industries were ruined. Worse still, her losses in men—just under 1,400,000, including colonial troops—had been the heaviest of all the major belligerents. France, with her high average age level, had fewer young men per million than any other great nation; with her low reproduction rate she had less chance than any other nation of recovering from her losses. German losses had been very heavy, but they had been bearable compared with the French, and German soil was untouched. British losses had been less, relatively and absolutely, and, except for the merchant marine, British economic equipment had suffered little. The United States had, at most, suffered a slight slowing down of her fantastic growth.

5. BETWEEN TWO WARS

THE LIQUIDATION OF THE WAR OF 1914–18

At Versailles, France seemed in an extraordinary position. She was one of the victorious powers. Her army had been the chief instrument of victory on land; the Allied commander-in-chief was a French Marshal; the French Prime Minister was one of the three organizers of victory in the eyes of the world as well as of France. But the fact of invasion was as much present in French minds as the fact of victory. And to prevent another invasion, Marshal Foch advised the permanent occupation by France of the Rhine bridgeheads. To secure this occupation, the Rhineland would have to be separated from Germany. But although the dream haunted the minds of French soldiers, neither Britain nor the United States would consider such a scheme. As a substitute they offered: (1) an occupation of the Rhineland for fifteen years; (2) an occupation of the Saar, to be followed by a plebiscite (in 1935) to decide whether the territory should go to France or Germany; and (3) the permanent demilitarization of the Rhineland and a region 50 km. wide on the right bank. More important, they offered an Anglo-American guarantee of the new French frontiers. This was the real bait; it was swallowed, and then the French learned to their horror that the United States Senate would not ratify the treaty and that Britain thought her obligations were thus ended.

The failure of the Anglo-American guarantee presented the directors of French foreign policy with a problem that may well have seemed insoluble—and perhaps was. The collapse of Russia, the dissolution of the Austrian empire, the great losses suffered by France, the weakness revealed by Italy—all combined to make the position of Germany *relatively* stronger than it had been in 1914, if Germany were allowed to escape the burdens of the treaty. The fears of a French hegemony, expressed and even felt in some British circles, seemed fantastically ill-conceived to the anxious rulers of France, the wiser of whom, at least, knew that victory does not keep. To restrain Germany and to secure France, a substitute for the Anglo-American guarantee had to be found; all the powers who had acquired an interest in the *status quo* established in 1919 were to be linked together by a series of military alliances. Poland, Czechoslovakia, Rumania, Yugo-Slavia were to organize their armies on French lines, to receive French financial subsidies and to accept French direction. But France was not strong enough to impose her will on such competing allies as Poland and Czechoslovakia, or strong enough to provide some substitute for the economic unity provided by the dead Hapsburg-monarchy. In the west, Belgium was still too sore to take a kindly view of Germany, and accordingly entered into the closest military and political alliance with France. But none of these alliances was a compensation for the estrangement from Britain.

That estrangement had many causes. Britain was anxious to return as quickly as possible to the economic equilibrium of 1914, and soon perceived that the political arrangements of 1919 were incompatible with such a return to 'normality'. There was, consequently, a readiness to blame the 'balkanization' of Europe for ills that had deeper roots, and to impute to selfish French policy what was in truth the result of generations of nationalist pressure in the area between the Danube and the Vistula. Moreover, France had received Syria as her share of the spoil of the Ottoman empire, under mandate from the League of Nations. Not only was this mandate unwelcome to most Syrians, but it interfered with the British idea of a great Arab state. It was soon believed that French officials in Syria and British officials in Palestine regarded with philosophical calm the difficulties of their opposite numbers, and Damascus was the centre of anti-Zionist activities while Jerusalem gave shelter to enemies of the French mandate.

A more important cause of conflict was economic. The reparations clauses of the peace treaties had imposed great commitments on Germany and her allies. It was soon seen that not much could be got from the minor allies, but hopes of making Germany pay for the war were longer lived. They died first in Britain, where the desirability of getting Germany on her feet economically was accompanied by optimism about the permanent destruction of Prussian militarism—an optimism easier to share on the northern than on the southern shore of the Channel. From 1920 to the end of 1922 a series of conferences defined and scaled down German payments; the British proposals always went too far for the French, and not far enough for the Germans. In January 1923, therefore, France and Belgium occupied the Ruhr; Germany would have to redeem her most valuable province or, alternatively, France and Belgium would collect what was due on the spot. The Ruhr occupation was a failure; it was a failure for France who was now faced with the problems of economic transfer; it was a failure for Germany who completed the destruction of her currency in a vain endeavour to subsidize passive resistance; and it was a failure for Britain who remained an impotent spectator, disregarded by both sides.

By the end of 1923 these lessons were being learned. With unofficial American backing, the Dawes Plan was accepted by all parties. France was to evacuate the Ruhr; American and British banking was to provide the means of giving Germany a new currency; and Germany itself was to make a more serious attempt to pay. Europe seemed to be entering a new and hopeful epoch. But estrangement between Britain and France was not over. At Washington, in 1921, America and Britain had combined to impose on France a naval inferiority that was as rigorous as the military inferiority imposed on Germany at Versailles. Of course, France had neither the means nor the will to enter into naval competition with the 'Anglo-Saxon' powers or with Japan, but the pertinacity with which these powers safeguarded their own primacy on the seas was not very palatable to the French navy.

An attempt to give armed backing to the League of Nations, in 1924, was rejected by the British government that came into power at the end of that year. Military security would have to be organized *outside* the League and without British help. The Locarno Treaty of 1925 was at the time more of a boon to Germany than to France, since it bound Britain and Italy to come to the aid of France *or* Germany, should either be attacked—and Germany was in no position to attack anybody in 1925. Nevertheless, it had, from the French standpoint, this good side—it committed Britain to a military guarantee not only of the French frontier, but of that demilitarization of the Rhineland and of the zone on the right bank which had been the chief French gain in 1919. As long as that stood, a war between France and Germany would be fought *in* Germany; and as long as the Germans knew that, there would be no war—or so the French thought.

In 1926 came what seemed the final liquidation of the war. French finance ministers had ignored the fact that Germany was not going to pay for the war. The left ministries that came into power in 1924 were no more clear-headed than the right ministries that had preceded them. By the summer of 1925 the franc was going downhill rapidly; by the summer of 1926 it seemed to be on the road taken by the mark. A government of national union was formed under Poincaré which, by rigorous taxation and by the good fortune that all the world (except possibly Britain) was benefiting from a boom, balanced the budget and stabilized the franc at 125 to the £. The new rate meant that four-fifths of the savings of the holders of the national debt were wiped out. The French middle classes were very badly hit, but they had saved something. Moreover, the reconstruction of the devastated areas was complete—the greatest effort of reconstruction Europe had seen. It had been paid for by France, not by Germany, but it was done.

THE FRENCH COLONIAL EMPIRE

The French colonial empire was not greatly affected by the peace settlement. The most important acquisition was the greater part of the Cameroons (including the territory ceded to Germany after the Moroccan crisis of 1911). This area was valuable both intrinsically and as rounding off French West African possessions. Held under mandate, it was ruled with great vigour, and public works and public health were fostered.

The other chief addition to the empire was Syria. This, too, was a mandate from the League of Nations, but the situation was far less simple than in the Cameroons. The Syrians were a conglomeration of races and religions, and Syria was remote from any important French interests, not an enclave in the great mass of the French empire. The connexion with France was not contemporary but traditional, and the tradition was weakening. Even among the Syrian Christians, traditional protégés of France, the American Protestant influence was rivalling the old Jesuit influence. Nor did Syria promise such economic returns as did the development of French Africa. France, preoccupied with her own reconstruction, had only a limited amount of capital to export, and preferred to export it to her old empire, rather than to a territory whose future status was in doubt. Experience did not alter this view. Arab nationalism was hostile to the mere presence of the French in Syria, and successive French High Commissioners tried various systems of government in vain. In 1925 the great Druse rebellion began, and continued for nearly two years. All attempts to obtain free collaboration from the Syrians seemed destined to failure, but by 1930 both sides were weary, and in 1933 a treaty was signed promising Syria the status of Iraq. The agreement was bitterly resented by the Christians of the Lebanon and the Turks of Alexandretta.[1] The French were discovering that there was no such thing as a united 'Syria', and that the old historical position of France in the Levant had been largely destroyed, by neglect on one side, and by the rise of Arab nationalism on the other. It is true that useful public works were constructed, and some economic progress was made, but Syria was not comparable with the great successes of French colonial policy.

Two of the great French successes, Morocco and Indo-China, seemed for a moment to be in danger of going the way of Syria. In Morocco, the Resident, Marshal Lyautey, who had held the Protectorate all through the war of 1914–18, with very meagre forces, pushed forward a policy of economic development that rather neglected the military realities of the situation. So when Abd-el-Krim, the victorious leader of the Riff rebellion in Spanish Morocco, advanced into French Morocco, the whole area was imperilled. A joint French-Spanish campaign under Marshal Pétain, however, destroyed the power of the Riff chieftains and Morocco was restored to peace.

In Indo-China, the influence of Chinese nationalism and of communism produced a series of conflicts, culminating in a military mutiny at Yen Bay. This was vigorously suppressed, and Indo-China settled down. Its economic development was extremely rapid, and the favourable contrast between its condition and that of southern China was not lost upon its inhabitants.

All over the empire, as France was able to turn from her own reconstruction to overseas development, great public works, especially in the field of transport, were put into execution. Africa benefited most; only the West Indies and the Pacific Islands

---

[1] Alexandretta was ceded to Turkey on the eve of the war of 1939.

were neglected. As economic nationalism grew all over the world, the traditional French view of imperial policy—the enforcement of a unified tariff policy on the whole empire—was given a new lease of life. By 1939 the French empire had been forcibly made much more of an economic unit and much more important to French economic life than it had been in 1914. And with that change had come a growth in imperial feeling. 'France, a nation of a hundred millions', was the slogan that concealed, or made more palatable, the fact that metropolitan France was only half as populous as Germany.

THE SHADOW OF ANOTHER WAR

The great economic depression that began with the American collapse in the autumn of 1929 seemed, at first, to leave France unscathed. She was less involved in international trade than were the other great powers; she was more self-sufficient, and less committed to an optimistic view of the economic future of Germany and America than Britain was. By 1931 she alone seemed to be immune. The economic crises in Britain, Germany and the United States were all in contrast with the calm and the prosperity of France. To Paris came appeals from London, Berlin and Washington, and, for the first time since 1914, the French public had the delighted experience of being courted for economic favours. France was solvent—with an immense gold reserve, and with client states. When Britain and the United States went off the gold standard in 1931, France alone of the great powers had what was, by orthodox standards, a sound currency.

But France was not immune. The last great effort of French economic policy, the Tardieu plan for the economic unification of the Danube basin, came to nothing, and when it became evident that Germany was never going to resume reparation payments, it was impossible in face of French public opinion to think of continuing war debt payments to America. Increasing economic distress accounted in part for the sweeping left victory at the general elections of 1932. Moreover, condemned by the gold standard to high costs of production, France was passing into depression. At the end of 1933 the Stavisky scandal became public. Serge Stavisky had indulged in large-scale fraud that involved several prominent deputies, including one minister. It seemed to many that the whole republican administration was corrupt. Public opinion was roused to feverish pitch. Irritated by the unsatisfactory handling of the case and inflamed by a violent press agitation on the extreme right and extreme left, the citizens of Paris broke into rioting. The Chamber was attacked and was only saved by repeated police charges; the government had just received a vote of confidence in the Chamber, but it fell before the mob, and resigned. A national government provided a brief respite, but the bloodshed of 6 February was followed by further bloodshed on 12 February, when communists and socialists demonstrated against the 'fascists'; there was continued unease, internally and externally. The Stavisky case remained with a fair share of mystery attached to it. But politically there was no doubt about its lesson. Only an executive far stronger than that provided by the French parliamentary system could protect the authority of the State and the integrity of the administration of justice against a recurrence of similar scandal. The diffusion of authority in the French Chambers was a great weakness.

The dominating fact in French democracy, especially when we compare it with British, is the strength of Parliament as compared with the cabinet. The fundamental cause of the difference is the different systems of parties in the two countries. Great Britain has a system of nationally organized parties, active in each constituency, under which the party possessing a majority in the country at large supports a governing cabinet composed of its party leaders. In France the position is entirely different. There are indeed a number of national parties, but apart from some of the parties of the 'Left' (the communist, the socialist and the radical-socialist) they are floating bodies of opinion rather than established and active associations. Party organizations in the constituencies, depending as they do on local circumstances, and often on personal factors, have generally little relation to any national party. Above all (and this is the main distinction between the French party system and the British) there is in France no necessary—and often no actual—correspondence between (1) the parliamentary groups, established and acting within the walls of Parliament, and either (2) the national parties spread over the country at large, or (3) the local party organizations in each constituency. In Great Britain the same body plays simultaneously three roles: it is at once a national party, a local party organization in each and every constituency, and a parliamentary group. In France, apart from the exceptions already noted, the three different roles may be played by three different and unconnected bodies. Particularly important is the want of connexion between the national party and the parliamentary group. Parliamentary groups are formed *after* general elections; they are formed within the two Chambers, for the purposes of the members of the Chambers (including advancement to cabinet office and representation on parliamentary committees) and for the duration of the Chambers; while, to add to the confusion, the groups in the Chamber of Deputies are different from those in the Senate.

In France, therefore, the party system has adversely affected cabinets, and French cabinets have generally been weak: in the first place, because, unable to appeal to nationally organized parties entrenched in each local constituency, they have been forced to depend on party groups formed and acting inside Parliament; secondly, because those groups number a dozen or more; thirdly, because each cabinet, in consequence, has been compelled to become a combination of leaders or representatives of different groups none of them possessing a majority by itself; and finally, because such combination cabinets readily disintegrate under the corrosive criticism of other parties and owing to the influence of mutual jealousy in their own ranks. The result of this weakness in French cabinets has been to strengthen Parliament.

Too much weight, however, must not be attached to the short tenures of French cabinets. It is true that the Third Republic, in a period of seventy years, had over ninety cabinets, while Great Britain had less than twenty. But while there are many

French ministries, they are composed, as a rule, of much the same ministers. Ministries may have had an average tenure of less than a year, but some of the ministers, especially at the Foreign Office, have held office continuously for as long as seven years; and it must always be remembered that a change of ministry does not involve a change in the country at large. It is simply a change within the walls of Parliament, and this for the simple reason that the parties which make the change exist only within those walls; it is a change within the scope, and subject to the terms, of the general mandate given by the electorate at the last election.

After 1934, the economic situation was becoming increasingly difficult—quite beyond the power of a series of weak governments that tried to grapple with it. Pressure on the franc was increasing, and there was a growing 'realist' party, led by M. Paul Reynaud, who believed that France could not defend the gold standard in a world in which all other great powers had either devalued their currencies (as in Britain and the United States) or had instituted exchange control (as in Germany and Italy). In June 1935 the new Laval Government was given plenary powers and a mandate 'to save the franc'—an abdication of authority that was characteristic of the French parliamentary system. Laval announced a drastic deflationist programme, and by the end of October, when its plenary power expired, the ministry had issued some five hundred emergency decrees. These restored confidence for a time but, in the long run, neither balanced the budget nor saved the franc. The economic depression continued, and paved the way for the more radical remedies of the 'Front Populaire'.

Externally, the situation was equally depressing. The German revolution was in full swing, and the danger to French security was increasing daily—yet no French government seemed prepared to take action. Poland had seen that France was not disposed to react against Nazi Germany's open breaches of the peace treaties, and had made its own terms with Hitler. Britain had made a naval treaty with Germany, in which French interests and French sentiments were subordinated. Italy, which in 1934 had reacted so vigorously against the German threat to Austria, was now asking her price in the form of acquiescence in the seizure of Abyssinia. At this, British public opinion violently reacted. The British government took the lead in opposing Italian designs, and France was reluctantly dragged along. But, since neither Britain nor France was ready to go to war with Italy, their bluff was called, and both the great western powers were humiliated by the success of Mussolini who was moving ostentatiously into the German camp. In May 1936 Hitler occupied the Rhineland and the demilitarized zone on the right bank. The excuse was the military alliance between France and Russia which showed the common fears aroused in Moscow and Paris by German rearmament. But the excuse did not matter. The world noted that France allowed the one remaining guarantee of something like military equality between France and Germany to be lost with only verbal protests.

At this moment France was convulsed by the approaching general election of May 1936; the bitterness caused by the riots of 1934 was hardly abated, while the economic depression and the failure of the League of Nations added to the sense of frustration. The left parties, alarmed by the success of the fascist parties in 1934, had joined in a united front, the 'Front Populaire', and it was obvious that this alliance would win the elections. The new government, formed after the sweeping left victories, had to face a kind of peaceful revolution. In all the great factories of the Paris region, the workers staged 'sit-down' strikes. They occupied the factories and refused to leave until the government forced the employers to submit. These terms included wage increases, union recognition, and the general imposition of the forty-hour week. The last was demanded not only as a gain in amenities, but as a cure for unemployment. At the same time the new government felt bound to announce that it would defend the gold standard, so France was committed to the contradictory economic policy of a currency whose defence demanded deflation and a social policy that demanded inflation or, at any rate, a lavish use of credit.

The new government, led by M. Léon Blum, set out upon a programme of reforms of a drastic character for France. They were designed to bring about great improvements in the standard of living of many sections of the wage-earning and small-salaried classes, and at the same time to give industry a larger home market. By increasing wages and shortening hours the policy set out to expand purchasing power, assuming that the large increase in consumption would permit a large increase in output and thus allow increased wage costs to be offset by mass-production methods. In addition, an easy money programme was followed, a public works programme set up, and the currency devalued to help exports. From the resulting increase in the national income the government hoped to draw a substantially increased revenue and thus eventually to effect a balanced budget.

The principal items of reform comprised widespread wage increases, up to 20%, the establishment of a forty-hour week, and a compulsory annual holiday of fifteen days, for twelve days of which full wages were to be paid, together with improvements in the status of labour. The establishment of a national unemployment insurance scheme was planned, but not put into effect. Many of the reforms were long overdue, and have come to stay, if in a modified form, while the theory by which the national economic structure was to bear the cost of the scheme was not unreasonable. A variety of factors, however, combined to render the success of the legislation impossible, and to discredit the plan more, perhaps, than it deserved. In the first place, the international situation in 1936–7 was hardly favourable for far-reaching experiments affecting French productive capacity. In the second place, the reforms were introduced much too rapidly, imposing a sudden strain. There is little doubt that French industry was ill able to bear the simultaneous wage increases, shortening of hours, and imposition of paid holidays. Many industries had to increase their staff: for example, the railway systems by 80,000 and the public services by 50,000. The coal and iron mines increased their labour force by 12–15% without approaching the previous figure of output, and were therefore unable to secure the old level of receipts save by raising their prices by about 40%; in the first quarter of 1937 imports were 7.6 million tons, 45% greater than in the corresponding quarter of 1936. The carrying capacity of the inland waterways was reduced, for barges took longer to cover journeys.

The economic situation of the country was unable to adapt itself to the new conditions or react in the way which was necessary for the success of the experiment. The wage increases were overtaken by a rise in prices. The wage-earning classes did not spend as much on consumption goods as they were expected to (perhaps not as much as the wage earners of other countries would have spent). The increase of purchasing power went mainly to the organized workers, and thus the total purchasing power, in a largely agricultural country, was not greatly extended. A number of factories had to close owing to increases in the cost of coal and labour, so that unemployment was not appreciably reduced, in spite of the large numbers of men serving in the army and the departure of 400,000 foreign workers. Any increase in production was far below the volume required to achieve the object of the framers of the plan, and was accounted for mainly by the rearmament programme, the Exhibition of 1937, and other programmes of a public works character, which were sources of expenditure rather than of revenue to the government. The industrial activity of the country therefore was unable to impart any buoyancy to the national finances. Anxiety continued over the budget, for the government, like its predecessors, was living at the rate of about twice its taxation revenue, and was obliged to resort to further expedients to keep its treasury afloat. The slowing up of production, anxiety over the budget, and fear in the minds of many over the events in the world of labour, gave fresh acceleration to the spending of capital, to its hoarding or to its export, at a time when France itself needed fresh capital funds.

M. Léon Blum's Government was bedevilled from the beginning by foreign affairs. It had barely liquidated the great strikes, when it was faced with the burning question of the Spanish Civil War. When it became evident that the military revolt was not going to be immediately successful or immediately crushed, the British Government sponsored a scheme for non-intervention. All the great powers undertook to refuse to sell arms or give aid, either to the Spanish Government or to the military party which called itself the Nationalists. In France the decision inflamed already bitter feeling. To the supporters of the 'Popular Front' Government, it was outrageous that the legal government of the 'Frente Popular' in Spain should be denied the normal legal prerogatives of a recognized govern-ment. It also became evident that neither Germany nor Italy was observing the non-intervention pact, and that Soviet Russia was retaliating by supporting the Spanish Government. Non-intervention became a farce. The French Government could neither wash its hands of the Spanish question nor take a firm line of its own. Normally, it followed the lead from London; firm when London was firm, weak when London was weak. France was tied to London by more than mere political ties, for the Blum Government had given up the hopeless defence of the gold standard and had devalued the franc in agreement with Britain and America. But the French economic position did not notably improve, and the international position of France was getting worse as German rearmament grew apace. Her eastern allies were weakening. The pact with Russia was never implemented by staff talks. Belgium, after French ac-ceptance of the occupation of the Rhineland, had renounced her obligations under the Locarno pact. Only Czechoslovakia stood firm.

The first Blum Government fell, and France again passed into a period of weak governments. In the first three months of 1938 three successive cabinet changes occurred, and in April the Daladier Government was established. It attempted to restore confidence and to amend the effects of the recent legislation. From April to September a number of steps were taken—the progressive increase in the length of the working week and in the number of longer weeks worked in factories, some redressing of the budget, and a lowering of interest rates. In May the franc was devalued (making the third devaluation of the franc), and pegged at 179 to the pound sterling. While hardly drastic reforms, these steps encouraged a revival of confidence and hence capital flowed back to France, and the government was able to secure subscriptions to a thirty-year 5% loan of 5,000,000,000 francs. Following the Munich crisis the nation showed a tendency to unite behind the government. In November 1938, M. Reynaud joined Daladier and became Finance Minister. The new government pledged itself to 'return France to work', stabilize the franc and institute economy in government expenditure. Legislation was enacted to reduce the frequency of industrial strikes, which had been such a serious feature in the French situation, by the imposition of a system of arbitrators and super-arbitrators. This programme was by no means immediately effective. In November came a law to establish a forty-four-hour six-day week, and to permit overtime while limiting the amount of extra pay received for it. Protest against this legislation took the form of the general strike of 30 November 1938. Drastic action by the government quickly broke the strike, however, and thereafter strikes became very infrequent. The effect of the new labour legislation and of the improved industrial outlook is illustrated by the fact that, while in 1937 over 300,000 workers had been on strike at one time or another, and in 1938 nearly 400,000, in 1939 practically no strikes were reported. Further, there was a progressive increase in the number of hours worked:

Percentage of French Labour occupied per week

	Less than 40 hr. (%)	40 hr. (%)	More than 40 hr. (%)
1938 monthly average	18·3	77·7	4·1
January 1939	13·0	68·8	18·2
February 1939	11·1	65·4	23·5
March 1939	10·5	67·5	22·0
April 1939	8·6	64·3	27·1
May 1939	8·6	56·6	34·8
June 1939	7·5	53·3	39·2
July 1939	6·9	49·8	43·3

In spite of the lengthening of hours of workmen employed in France during 1939, and in spite of the elimination of strikes during the year, industrial improvement in France was such that unemployment decreased rapidly throughout the first eight months of the year.

On 12 November 1938, M. Reynaud, Minister for Finance, published an analysis of the economic position of France. Its clarity and clear-sightedness created a very favourable impression. He proceeded to apply a programme of more liberal credit, economical administration of public revenues, budgetary reform, encouragement to capital to seek investment in France, and a labour policy calculated to soften the rigours of recent labour legislation—all these formed part of a three-year programme. By May 1939, M. Reynaud was able to report that considerable improvement had taken place, and the plan seemed well set to continue. Features of the changed position were: (1) the return of large sums of gold which had been in flight to foreign countries, and the release of hoarded gold; (ii) an end of franc speculation; (iii) the greater ease by which the treasury was able to meet its needs; (iv) the considerable increase in savings deposits; (v) the fall in interest rates; and (vi) the rise in stock-market quotations—fixed interest securities by 9.83%, others by 11.22%. Industrial activity increased and unemployment declined; the amount of coal mined rose and imports diminished. Industrial exports increased, thus reducing the adverse balance of trade. The extent of the recovery of business can be seen by the following indices of activity:

	October 1938	March 1939
Production index	81	92
Textile index	82	95
Metallurgical index	66	81
Steel production	541,000 tons	668,000 tons

Automobile sales rose from 50,000 vehicles in the first quarter of 1938 to 61,400 in the first quarter of 1939. Owing to this revival of business, receipts from indirect taxation were able to increase. Wages, enlarged by overtime working, were able to rise faster than prices rose.

Later on, steps were taken to enable French industry to adjust itself to war preparation. The government arranged to control the direction of workers into industry. In order to prevent any undue increase in consumption, overtime rates were not to apply up to forty-five hours weekly, although steps were taken to prevent too sudden a reduction in the prosperity of the consumption goods industries. To avoid the danger of inflation which might follow from a heavy increase in government expenditure, money was to be diverted into the exchequer by a special armaments tax of 1%, by control of profits in industries working on war orders, and by the abolition of the wheat and meat subsidies.

In short, the period begun in April 1938 with the establishment of the Daladier Government, to be followed in November by the appointment of M. Reynaud as Minister of Finance, marked the initial phase of a new French economic policy. The errors and uncertainties of the Popular Front regime were progressively eliminated, and experimental methods of relieving economic ills were abandoned for more orthodox methods. These methods, however, involved a more rigorous fiscal policy, a more enlightened financial programme, and a more clear-sighted approach than those of the governments which had preceded the Blum regime. The outbreak of war cut short the new stage in French economic policy.

In the spring of 1938 Hitler invaded Austria, thus for the first time crossing a frontier. The weakness of the reaction of France and Britain, and the acceptance of the *Anschluss* by Italy, convinced the rulers of Germany that the next step could be safely taken. A campaign for the redress of the grievances of the German citizens of Czechoslovakia was launched. The world noted that France allowed the conduct of the negotiations to pass into British hands, although France was the ally of Czechoslovakia and Britain was not. France was, at each stage of the negotiations, less resolute, not more resolute than Britain, and if Munich was a fault, the French share in it was greater than the British. Particularly ominous was the bitterness with which the main parties of the right, and the pacifist elements so powerful in such left organizations as those of elementary school-masters and lesser civil servants, attacked the 'war-mongers'. The policy of Germany and Italy found the most extravagant support in the Paris press. Some of that support was bought, but some of it was a genuine reflexion of bitterness and horror at the thought of another war for any reason, for any cause.

But Munich at least awoke France to her danger, and she reacted vigorously to Italian claims for Nice, Corsica and Tunis. Desperate and belated efforts were made to rearm. The German occupation of Prague in 1939 was a sign too obvious not to be read. The conduct of negotiations with the Soviet Government was again left mainly to Britain, as was the policy of guaranteeing Poland. The announcement of the Russo-German Pact (23 August 1939) was taken as a sign of certain war. Yet M. Bonnet, the Foreign Minister, and some of his colleagues sought a way out. Only reluctantly, belatedly, did France follow the British lead and declare war on Germany.

CHAPTER VI

DEFEAT AND RECOVERY

1. OCCUPATION AND LIBERATION

IN the face of her old enemy, France was for a time united. The Maginot line seemed to prevent attack from the east, and seemed to give time to equip an army and an air force while the full strength of the British Empire was being mobilized. But France was totally unprepared for the kind of war which was loosed on her when the Germans invaded Holland and Belgium (10 May 1940). It was a war of tanks and planes, and France was greatly inferior in tanks and hopelessly inferior in planes; her army, too, was outnumbered by an enemy incomparably better equipped. When the main British force was evacuated from Dunkirk, and the best equipped French troops had been destroyed or taken prisoner, the game was up in France. Paris fell and the government took refuge in Tours and then in Bordeaux. The roads were covered with millions of fugitives, fleeing for the second time in a generation. The President of the Republic and the Prime Minister were ready to sail to Africa and to carry on the war from overseas. But Marshal Pétain and General Weygand, confident that Britain was doomed to speedy defeat, insisted on asking for an armistice. It was granted on onerous terms, and France officially withdrew from the war. Germany retained over 1,500,000 French prisoners-of-war, and occupied a considerable stretch of French territory. The costs of the occupation were to be borne by France, as well as a heavy indemnity. An armistice was also concluded with Italy, who had entered the war on 10 June.

The government adjourned to Vichy, the new capital of that poor third of France which was left free from direct German occupation (Fig. 35). There, on 10 July, the Senate and Chamber met as a National Assembly, conferred dictatorial powers on Marshal Pétain, and suspended the Republic. The Third Republic, born in the defeat of 1870, fell in that of 1940.

The Vichy Government came into existence on the assumption that Germany would win the war. Its object was to keep France out of further fighting and to save her, as far as might be possible, from German interference; at the same time it hoped to rebuild the French State on foundations more authoritarian and clerical than those of the Third Republic, which defeat seemed to have discredited.

The main problem of the Vichy Government was how to meet the constantly increasing pressure of German demands. Immediately after their victory in June 1940, the Germans pursued a policy of industrial pillage and spoliation: large quantities of machines, tools and scrap were immediately removed to Germany. French industrial activity was for a time completely disorganized. But German economic policy was, from the outset, not wholly predatory. It was also concerned with the task of determining which factories in the conquered areas could be operated to help the German war effort. In September 1940 all industrial firms within occupied France were ordered by the German authorities to carry on; if they were unable to do so, the Germans in many cases put in a manager. Factories in the northeast, abandoned during the hostilities, were started as soon as possible either by the French owning companies under German supervision or by German firms. In Alsace-Lorraine, industrial enterprises were incorporated into the economic regime of the Reich. Unoccupied France was in urgent need of work and of raw materials, and these could often be obtained only if factories executed German orders. Soon economic collaboration with the German war effort was extended to the whole of France.

But there were French men and women who refused to assume that the war would be won by Germany. They were given a lead by a young general, Charles de Gaulle, who had escaped to England, where he organized refugees in the Forces of Free France and whence he broadcast appeals for resistance against the Germans. Gradually an underground resistance movement organized itself in France. After the German attack on the U.S.S.R. in June 1941 it was given a new impetus by the accession of the French Communist Party. In May 1943 a

National Resistance Council was formed, first under Jean Moulin, then under Georges Bidault, to co-ordinate the resistance groups and to bring them to some extent under the authority of General de Gaulle.

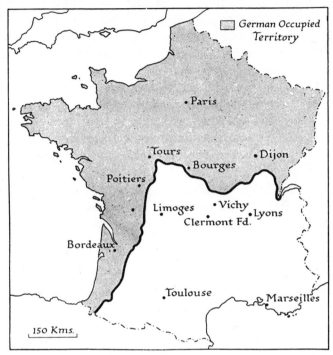

Fig. 35. The Armistice of 1940

It is interesting to compare this with Figs. 20 and 21.

When the expeditionary forces of Britain and the United States landed in French North Africa in November 1942, the representatives of the Vichy Government offered no resistance, and before long what amounted to a Provisional Government of France was set up in Algiers, with General de Gaulle at its head and a Consultative Assembly behind it. Half the members of this Assembly were representatives of the resistance movement inside France, the whole of which had since November 1942 come under German occupation.

On 6 June 1944, after intense aerial bombardment to destroy the German communications, the British and American offensive was launched in Normandy. Once again a battle crucial in the world's history was fought on the soil of France. The allies quickly succeeded in clearing the departments of Calvados and the Manche, though nearly a month passed before they could gain a foothold in the port of Caen. The climax came in mid-August when the remains of the German army in Normandy were destroyed and the allies made a successful landing on the Mediterranean coast round St Raphael. The Germans now realized that they must withdraw from the whole of France. On 19 August the French resistance leaders called a general insurrection in Paris, and after four days' fighting the Germans were evicted. On 23 August the joint victory of the resistance movement and the invading armies was symbolized by the entry into Paris of a French armoured force under General Leclerc.

Nearly twelve months were to pass before the last of the German units left France. It was a year of misery and grandeur. On the one hand, hunger, dislocation, fighting round isolated ports (Bordeaux was not liberated until April 1945) and ill-feeling between Frenchman and Frenchman—between the 'resisters' and those who had collaborated with the Germans; on the other, a sense of liberation and a feeling that France was born again. The three great powers in October 1944 officially recognized de Gaulle's Government, now removed from Algiers, as the Provisional Government of the French Republic, and in November the National Consultative Assembly held its first meeting in Paris. Preparations were soon on foot for the election of a Constituent Assembly, an election in which the right to vote would be extended for the first time to French women.

2. THE FOURTH REPUBLIC

Liberated France was in no mind to reconstitute the Third Republic. That regime was discredited by the collapse in face of the German invasion in 1940, and the political parties which had been most closely associated with it—particularly the

Radical Socialists—had disgraced themselves most completely by collaboration with the Germans. The general elections, held in October 1945, returned the parties which had associated themselves with the resistance. First came the Communists and their fellow-travellers with 160 seats, then—surprisingly, because they had hardly been known before the war—the Progressive Catholics led by Georges Bidault, whose party was called the 'Mouvement Republicain Populaire' (M.R.P.), with 152 seats, then the Socialists and their adherents with 146. Together they were supported by almost three-quarters of the members of the Assembly, and it was inevitable that the government should consist of a coalition, presided over by General de Gaulle. The General soon found the holding together of such an unruly coalition too much for him. He resigned in January 1946, but tripartite government continued and was responsible for a number of memorable changes, including the nationalization of many industrial and financial institutions and the drafting of a new Constitution. This Constitution was accepted by referendum in October 1946, and the Fourth Republic was inaugurated.[1]

The Fourth Republic turned out to be much more like the Third than the authors of the Constitution of 1946 had intended. The old dominance of Parliament over the cabinet was supposed to be checked by allowing the President to dissolve Parliament and call new elections in certain well-defined circumstances, but the Assembly found ways of forcing the cabinet to resign without precipitating its own dissolution. In the lifetime of the Fourth Republic, governments were no stronger and no longer-lived than they had been under the Third. Tripartite rule of Communists, Socialists and M.R.P. survived in one form or another until May 1947, but then government fell into the hands of a succession of coalitions known as the Third Force. These were united in little but their determination to resist the other two forces, the Communists on one hand and the Gaullists

---

[1] On the establishment and first years of the Fourth Republic, see Dorothy Pickles, *French Politics* (London, 1953) and Philip Williams, *Politics in Post-War France* (London, 1954).

on the other. General de Gaulle founded in April 1947 a *Rassemblement du Peuple Francais* (R.P.F.) which he intended to be a rally, cutting across party lines, of all Frenchmen who stood for strong patriotic government, but which soon turned into a right-wing political party not unlike the others. The Communist Party was coming more and more obviously under Russian dictation, but it continued to poll something in the region of five million votes and to be the strongest party in France.

The Third Force had a comfortable parliamentary majority over either Gaullists or Communists, but it was unable to hold together on any positive policy. The Socialists were too much afraid of losing working-class votes to support measures which had, a 'bourgeois' ring about them; they frequently withdrew their support and precipitated cabinet crises. The M.R.P. was too Catholic to feel comfortable with its Socialist colleagues and too socialist to agree with the Radicals and right-wing elements who were increasing in votes and influence as time dimmed the memories of collaboration with Nazi Germany.

The greatest dispute between the Socialists and the M.R.P. was on the question of Church schools which had caused so much trouble under the Third Republic. The republican principle was that there should be no religious teaching in the state schools and that the state should give no grants to private schools, the vast majority of which were Catholic. But times had changed. The Vichy Government had given liberal support in public money to the Catholic schools, which now could hardly exist without it. The rise in the birth-rate during and immediately after the war meant that there were more children than the state schools could possibly accommodate. The state needed the Catholic schools, and the Catholic schools needed public money. After bitter and protracted debates, two measures allowing a certain amount of public money to reach private schools were finally passed in 1951.

If one thing was certain from the political experience of the first years of the Fourth Republic, it was that the Constitution of 1946 must be amended so as to give more stability to the government; but of the nature of this amendment there was no sign until 1958.

Compared with the political development of France after liberation, the economic development was heartening. The fighting in 1944 had destroyed or damaged 55,000 factories and business houses, 135,000 agricultural buildings and 2,000,000 dwelling houses, and the loss to communications included the destruction of some 4000 kilometres of railways and more than 7500 bridges. What was more serious, the four years of German occupation had deprived French factories of raw materials and power resources, and had put a stop to productive investment and technical progress. To revive productive capacity, a plan for modernization and re-equipment (known as the Monnet Plan) was put into operation. Thanks in part to American money, it was largely successful. By 1953 the French miner was raising more coal than in 1938. France's output of electrical energy was doubled. Industrial production, which was only one-half that of 1938 at the time of the liberation, had surpassed the 1938 level by 50% in 1953.

It was a remarkable recovery, but it was confined, by and large, to the sphere of heavy industry and to large-scale undertakings. In agriculture, commerce and the production of consumer goods, achievement was not so striking. France was still a country of 'small men', of men determined to be their own masters. In 1953 there were two and a half million farms in France, more than half of them worked by one or two persons and only 8% of them employing more than five labourers. Instead of providing revenue, French agriculture was receiving much more in state subsidies than it was paying in taxes. One-third of the farms were condemned as too small and too inefficient to be economic, but a fantastic network of price-fixing, tax exemption, protective tariffs and subsidies prevented the weakest from going to the wall. It was the same with the processing industries and commerce, a huge section of which was still in the hands of the one-man business. Half the total of one million industrial establishments employed not one single wage-earner. Of the total of rather more than one million commercial undertakings, 700,000 employed no wage-earner. And France, to a greater extent than Britain, was now a nation of shopkeepers: there was one retail business for every thirty-two members of the population in 1953, when in Britain there was one for every 100.

3. FOREIGN POLICY

The foreign policy of France after the liberation showed a singular consistency. Through all the changes of government until 1954 it remained in the hands of one or other of two leaders of the M.R.P., Georges Bidault and Robert Schuman. It rested on two assumptions. The first was that the closest alliance with Britain was essential to French security. France took the initiative which led to the Dunkirk Treaty with Britain (March 1947) and to the Brussels Treaty with Britain, Belgium, Luxemburg and the Netherlands (March 1948), and France was a prime mover in the negotiations which culminated in the North Atlantic Treaty (April 1949) linking the Brussels Powers with the United States, Canada and others in the strongest military organization that had ever been put on foot in time of peace.

The second assumption was that even the strongest alliance could not prevent France from becoming a battlefield again in the event of future German aggression and that there could be no preventing such aggression by disarming and penalizing Germany as had been done under the Treaty of Versailles. It was realized that the solution to the German danger, as to the more immediate Russian danger, lay in binding the European states together in some sort of partnership which might lead to the merging of national sovereignties in a United or Federal Europe. With this aim in view, French statesmen put forward a number of constructive ideas which led to the formation of two new international institutions and to the outlining of a third.

The Council of Europe was founded in May 1949, its aim being, as declared in the first article of its Statute, 'to achieve a greater unity between the Members for the purpose of safeguarding and realizing the ideals and purposes which are their common heritage and facilitating their economic and social progress'. By 1950 the Council was established in Strasbourg with thirteen member-states, including the Federal Republic of Germany. Linked with this institution, which the French intended to become a sort of Parliament of Europe, was the Coal and Steel Community. This grew out of a declaration by Robert Schuman in May 1950, and through the vision and pertinacity of Jean Monnet. It turned into a supra-national organization consisting of representatives of France, Federal Germany, Italy, the Netherlands, Belgium and Luxemburg and was intended to eliminate the danger of the Ruhr arsenal under German sovereignty and to raise the European standard of living by increasing productivity, removing trade-barriers and reducing prices.

If the Coal and Steel Community, which began as the Schuman Plan, was an attempt to Europeanize the German armaments industry, the European Defence Community, which began as the Pleven Plan, was an attempt to Europeanize the German army. It was first proposed by M. Pleven in August 1950 when the American Secretary of State surprised the world by announcing that it was the United States Government's desire that Federal Germany should be rearmed and prepared to take part in the defence of the West against Russian aggression. M. Pleven's original proposal was that every member of the European Defence Community except Germany would retain an army under its own national sovereignty as distinct from the forces it contributed to the European Army. Germany, having no national army, would put all its forces under supranational control, and these would at first be a comparatively small proportion of the European Army.

The French soon had second thoughts about the European Defence Community. It became clear that the Germans intended to play a much more dominant part in it than M. Pleven had envisaged in 1950. It was also realized that France would be unable to arm and to man forces sufficient to form both an independent French army for service in Indo-China and elsewhere overseas and also an army which would be a preponderant element in the European Defence Community. When, after two years' negotiation, the E.D.C. Treaty was at last signed, an immediate attack by Russia in the west was no longer feared. The French Parliament was now reluctant to ratify the Treaty which its government had initiated and signed; after two more years of hesitation it turned the Treaty down.

French foreign policy may not have been glorious in the post-war years, but two solid achievements had been made. Alliance with Britain had been cemented as never before, and the age-long quarrel with Germany and the Germans had been resolved by the new approach to partnership.

4. THE FRENCH UNION

The French colonial empire emerged from the war severely shaken. The overseas territories had been cut off from the mother country at a time when they were used to sending between a half and two-thirds of their exports to France, and to drawing on France for more than a half of their total imports. In many quarters, movements for national independence had been ripening and in the Levant they had borne fruit: Syria and Lebanon became sovereign republics. Immediately after the liberation France found trouble everywhere in her empire, ranging from discontent in West Africa, revolt in Madagascar and agitation in Tunisia, Algeria and Morocco, to open war in Indo-China.

The Constitution of the Fourth Republic envisaged a new relationship between France and the colonial empire, which was expressed in the term *Union Française*. Two new advisory bodies were set up in Paris. The first of these, the High Council of the Union, consisted of representatives of France and of the Associated States—ideally the Protectorates of Indo-China, Morocco and Tunisia, but the two last refused to associate themselves. The second, the Assembly of the Union, consisted of representatives elected by the French Houses of Parliament and an equal number of representatives elected by the overseas territories including the Associated States, the colonial possessions and the departments of Algeria and the four 'old colonies' which ranked as part of metropolitan France. How important these advisory bodies and the new elected assemblies to be set up overseas would become, no one could tell. All eyes were on the troubles which overwhelmed the Union after 1948 in North Africa and Indo-China.

In North Africa the trouble arose from the fact that the French would go no further than to promise the Muslim majority equal rights with the small European community; to do more seemed absurd while North Africa was still dependent for its economic prosperity on French settlers and administrators, and the Muslim natives still lacked ability as well as capital. But this would not satisfy the Muslims, whose nationalist parties— the Néo-Destour in Tunisia, the Messalists in Algeria and the Istiqlal in Morocco—all insisted on a greater Muslim share in government.

The first North African crisis arose in Morocco. France's position in this Protectorate rested on a treaty of 1912 under the terms of which the Sultan of Morocco was recognized as a sovereign whose signature was necessary to every law and whose authority was to have the support of French arms. But although sovereign in law, the Sultan was not sovereign in fact. Power lay with the French garrisons on the coast and with the Berber tribesmen in the mountains. The Sultan could be useful to the French in giving the blessing of Islam and the countenance of legality to their conduct in Morocco. The French had great gifts to bring, gifts of engineering, building and agriculture and a genuine civilizing mission. But as often as not the government in Paris was not behind the settlers, entrepreneurs, missionaries and administrators, and these men on the spot were apt to take the conduct of affairs into their own hands. Paris was inclined to starve its representatives of funds and to handicap them with orders which, though often enlightened and 'progressive', were felt to be restrictive. A tradition grew up among the French in Morocco of ignoring orders from Paris. Before and during the First World War Lyautey defied his government again and again, and after the Second World War Marshal Juin acted as if he saw himself as a second Lyautey. This insubordination spread down the ranks of the administration to such an extent that the French Government could not be sure that its most determined policy—if ever it could make up its mind on such a policy—would be carried out. The Frenchmen in Morocco were determined to get the Sultan's signature to decrees suppressing the Istiqlal and all nationalist movements. When in 1953 it was clear that they could not succeed, they deposed him through the convenient agency of a feudal chieftain from Marrakesh. This breach of the Protectorate Treaty augured ill for the future of the French Union.

A similar Protectorate Treaty signed with the Bey of Tunisia in 1881 had been broken by France and the Muslims were in revolt even before the Second World War. The French had dissolved Néo-Destour and arrested its leader, Habib Bourguiba, as early as 1938, but terrorism and counter-terrorism increased after the war. It was obvious that Muslim nationalism presented a problem for France throughout North Africa.

The trouble in Indo-China was even more acute. When the French returned after the Japanese surrender in 1945 they found a nationalist movement organized by the League for Vietnamese Independence (Viet-Minh). The French failed to take it seriously, thinking that a military expedition would be enough to repress it. But this military expedition had the opposite effect: it convinced a great number of natives that Viet-Minh was their only champion and it turned Viet-Minh's leader, Ho Chi-Minh, into a national hero. The French bungled their diplomatic dealings with Ho Chi-Minh, whom they regarded, very rightly, as a Communist, but failed to see that in the eyes of the Vietnamese people he was a nationalist first and last. All that the French did in the political field was to make promises which nobody could believe and to set up a government under a native prince, Bao Dai, whom few people could regard as anything but a French puppet.

When the Chinese Communists reached the Indo-Chinese frontier in December 1949, the tide of war began to turn against the French. They tried to seal the frontier against Chinese infiltration and they failed. Viet-Minh could now rely on China for arms and supplies, and by 1951 the French, who had already suffered 100,000 casualties, including 25,000 dead and missing, were obliged to call on Britain and the United States to help them to hold the fort in Indo-China. The British, who had come to terms with Asian nationalism in India, Ceylon and Burma, and the Americans, who had recognized the sovereignty of the Philippines, could point out that the French had made grave political mistakes in 1945 and 1946; the French could reply that after 1949 the only bulwark against Communism in the whole of South-East Asia was the front in Indo-China and that France was no longer strong enough to hold it alone. The French had to fight the war with no other allies than those they could muster among 'loyal' elements of the native population. In the summer of 1954, when it became clear that the French could not hold the Red River, a conference was held in Geneva attended by the Foreign Ministers of the United States and Britain, of the Soviet Union and Communist China. At this conference a cease-fire agreement was reached. The outcome was the division of Vietnam into two states. North of the 17th parallel there was a Communist state under the Viet-Minh. South of that line there arose an equally nationalist state; it was under American subvention, while its northern neighbour lived on aid from Communist China and the Soviet Union. France had lost Indo-China. More than that, the drain of military manpower had left her unable to play her full part in European politics, the drain of money had weakened her efforts towards economic recovery at home, and the loss of prestige gave the lie to her pretensions to be an imperial power elsewhere in the overseas world.

Pierre Mendès-France, the Radical prime minister who had brought France out of the Indo-China war, was determined to reach a settlement in North Africa. He flew to Tunis and asked the Bey to appoint representatives with whom France could negotiate. This was a preliminary to granting self-government, although it was 20 March 1956 before France recognized Tunisia as an independent sovereign state. A few days later Tunisia's first general election brought Bourguiba into power.

What was sauce for the Tunisian goose must be sauce for the Moroccan gander. The French Government negotiated with Morocco's nationalist leaders in August 1955 and agreed to the recall of the Sultan Sidi Mohamed. In the following March, Morocco too became an independent sovereign state.

It was obvious that the Muslims of Algeria would demand what the Muslims of Tunisia and Morocco had gained, but the French did not regard Algeria in the same light as their former Protectorates. Algeria had never been a Protectorate. It was not even a colony; constitutionally it was part of France. There were 1,200,000 French settlers in Algeria—including settlers from other European countries who regarded themselves as French—and they felt themselves to be superior to the Muslims, whose population was increasing at the rate of nearly a quarter of a million a year and numbered about 9,000,000 by 1958. When the Algerian nationalists broke out in revolt in 1954, the French attempted to suppress them by force. It was an ugly guerilla war with atrocities on both sides, and although France stationed some 600,000 soldiers in Algeria, there seemed no possibility of a victory by arms. In their frustration, French officers in Algeria blamed their government—or rather the lack of government, for since 1954 every French Government seemed weaker and less decisive than the last.

On 13 May 1958 a group of officers under General Massu, the parachutist-commander, carried out a *coup d'état* in Algeria in conjunction with the settlers' leaders. They set up Committees of Public Safety, extended their rule to Corsica and seemed to be threatening France herself. They were clamouring for the rule of Charles de Gaulle. On 27 May the French Parliament, rather than face the risk of civil war, voted de Gaulle into office as Prime Minister, with powers amounting to those of a temporary dictator. This was the end of the Fourth Republic.

CHAPTER VII

GAULLIST FRANCE

1. ALGERIA

GENERAL de Gaulle had been returned to power to solve the Algerian problem. The paradox was that no-one knew precisely what his Algerian policy was, and since this uncertainty gave de Gaulle a freedom of manoeuvre he needed he was in no hurry to dispel it. But it seems likely that even in 1958 he had decided that the war could not be won, and that the best possible solution would not be the 'French Algeria' the army and settlers wanted, but an Algeria connected in some looser way with France. As always with Gaullism flexible tactics went along with a fixed strategy, but in any case de Gaulle would have had to act carefully. He was manoeuvring between two diametrically opposed forces, the French army determined on total military victory, and the Algerian rebels willing to settle for nothing less than full independence. Even in metropolitan France public opinion was polarized, with the right-wing majority (including the powerful Gaullist party) in the new Parliament taking a harder line on Algeria than the country at large.

De Gaulle had two immediate objectives: to reassert the Government's control over an army that had increasingly tended to act independently, even insubordinately, and to bring the rebels to the conference table. The latter failed in October 1958, as it was to in June 1960, because the French understandably insisted on a preliminary cease-fire before negotiations took place. The former seemed more successful. Within a year the great majority of senior officers concerned with the May 1958 rising had either retired or been posted out of Algeria, and civilian control of the administration appeared to have been re-established. De Gaulle felt himself strong enough to take his first major step forward. In a Press Conference in September

1959 he outlined three possible choices for Algeria. It could remain French (in the sense of a French Algeria strictly subordinate to the mother-country), it could become totally independent or it could achieve a certain degree of autonomy while remaining linked with France. De Gaulle as evidently preferred the third alternative as army and settlers did the first, and spent the following year in an attempt to find some political 'third force' in Algeria, unconnected with the rebels, with whom the French Government could negotiate and build the future state. He had painted the darkest possible picture of the results of total independence, but the mere mention of the word was too much for the settlers. In January 1960 they took over the centre of Algiers, aiming to rally the army to their side and replay May 1958—but this time against de Gaulle. The rising was premature. De Gaulle, with public opinion in France massively behind him, stood firm as the various Governments of the Fourth Republic had not. But as the rising fizzled out in an atmosphere akin to farce, one ominous feature became clear. Certain army officers had been involved, specific units at least benevolently neutral. Briefly de Gaulle found it necessary to back-track, and in March toured army bases in Algeria, somewhat equivocally emphasizing the permanence of a French presence in that country. At almost the same time he started— abortive—negotiations with the rebels, and in November took a second step forward, mentioning for the first time an Algerian republic 'that might someday exist'. For his opponents the writing was on the wall. Confirmation seemed to come when de Gaulle made what turned out to be his last visit to Algeria in December. Muslims in Algeria publicly demonstrated their support for the President—but also for the rebels. The 'third force' was dead, if it had ever existed. At the same time the settlers and many army officers were convinced that de Gaulle was preparing to sell them out, and saw the referendum of 8 January, in which 75% of metropolitan French opinion voted in favour of de Gaulle's Algerian policy, as proof that they were on their own. So, on 22 April, four former Generals flew into Algiers and units of the army took over the city. The putsch was tactically efficient and that was about all. Its leaders had counted on the active support of certain crack units and the obedience of the remainder. They had forgotten the very human tendency, even among the military, to sit on the fence; omitted to take French national-servicemen into account (and they were unanimously and often actively hostile to an adventure that seemed to threaten civil war); overlooked what de Gaulle, accurately if immodestly, called the major factor—himself. The revolt collapsed after four days. Some of its leaders returned to face trial and imprisonment in France, the remainder deserted to join the O.A.S., the so-called Secret Army.

De Gaulle, now accepting that total French withdrawal from Algeria was inevitable, re-opened negotiations with the rebels. At first they made little progress, but then a new factor emerged, the O.A.S. De Gaulle had wanted to finish the war as quickly as possible but with the best obtainable terms. The rebels, on the contrary, had believed that time was on their side. Increasing and indiscriminate O.A.S. terrorism in the cities of Algeria and even, to a lesser extent, in France itself acted as a catalyst. It convinced the rebels that the French government was a far preferable interlocuter than the O.A.S. was ever likely to be, and that the sooner they came to an agreement with de Gaulle the better. In March 1962 a cease-fire was signed and a provisional Algerian Government formed. The war was over. De Gaulle, seen so widely as the saviour of French Algeria in 1958, had proved to be its liquidator.

The final peace terms were no triumph. France agreed to an almost total withdrawal from Algeria, in return for certain guarantees, most of which were nebulous at the time and forgotten shortly after: but then as de Gaulle said in another context, 'treaties are like young women—they last just about as long as they last'. They have added to the whole controversy about de Gaulle's handling of the war. Was it a masterly exercise in *realpolitik*, a policy of sustained deception or simply a case of blowing in the wind? But the questions are immaterial —it was peace. After more than fifteen years of almost un-interrupted warfare, France had at last cut her colonial losses.

2. THE GAULLIST STATE

For all its immediate importance, Algeria was a side-show in de Gaulle's eyes: what was central was the reaffirmation of the State's authority through the remodelling of its institutions. The new Constitution, approved by an overwhelming vote in September 1958, radically shifted the balance of power from Parliament to the executive as a whole and President in particular. Parliament no longer initiated policy, it could no longer choose the Government or elect the President; increasingly its role was that of an echo-chamber.

The new presidential powers were imposing. They were also less relevant than the character of the man who wielded them until April 1969. General de Gaulle became President in December 1958. Superbly conscious both of himself—*moi, général de Gaulle*—and his mission, he gave his office and in consequence French political life as a whole a highly personalized flavour. But Gaullism was not merely a man, it was also a movement whose final manifestation was the new Gaullist party the General inspired (but did not create) in 1958; and a mystique, a style of government based on de Gaulle's vision of himself as a rallying-point for Frenchmen of all political shades. De Gaulle disliked the traditional political intermediaries and preferred direct contact with the nation at large. This accounts for his exploitation of the government-controlled media, in particular television. It also explains the frequent use of the referendum, theoretically a device which would allow the entire electorate to express its opinion on one specific issue, but increasingly used to provoke a direct vote of confidence in de Gaulle himself. Finally, it explains the logical if unconstitutional decision in 1962 that the President should be chosen by the nation at large and not by a restricted college of notabilities. The Algerian war emphasized this personal style, because de Gaulle alone took the important decisions, as was very evident in the crises of January 1960 and April 1961. But Algeria was also an issue that cut across party lines. The right had seen de Gaulle as the guarantor of French Algeria, the left as the only man they thought strong enough to ward off the threat of a military take-over and give Algeria its freedom. Until 1962 therefore de Gaulle had something like an all-party appeal, attracting voters right across the board (the Communists not excluded). When the Algerian war ended the traditional parties expected a return to normalcy, but by then the situation had changed. The President who had been thought of as above party was in the process of becoming a party leader—and he had what was virtually a majority party to lead.

The Gaullist party had won nearly two hundred seats in the 1958 election by ruthless exploitation of de Gaulle's name. The enthusiasm was not mutual. De Gaulle had no wish to be the prisoner of one party, much less one so vociferously in favour of French Algeria that it might curtail his freedom of action. He wished instead to form a Government resting on as broad a base as possible. As a result, and to their chagrin, the Gaullists received few cabinet offices in a Government that included both Socialists (until early 1959) and members of the centre M.R.P. (until May 1962). But when in October 1962 the opposition defeated the Government in a vote of censure, de Gaulle dissolved the Assembly and moved towards a closer identification with the Gaullist U.N.R. In the subsequent elections the Gaullists and their allies increased their seats to 270: more important, the President had ceased to be an arbiter. The American-style presidential election of 1965 confirmed this, and by 1967 when the next legislative elections took place de Gaulle had become a party boss. As a leading opposition spokesman put it, 'once upon a time there was de Gaulle—now there are only Gaullists'. In terms of a Gaullist mystique that saw the General as the embodiment not of a party but of France as a whole this was a paradox. The events of 1968 were to underline it.

Although Gaullism attracted a good deal of left-wing support it really acted as the unifier of the right, giving France something she had never had before, a modern and powerful conservative party. It was logical therefore that the opposition tried to achieve a similar degree of unity. Since no single opposition party had the slightest chance of achieving power on its own some kind of coalition was inevitable. There were two alternatives, and both were tried. First, there was the possibility of an alliance pivoting on the centre M.R.P. and including the non-Communist left. This was broached unsuccessfully in 1963. Then there was the possibility of an alliance of all the left, including (however loosely) the Communists. This was the way in which the left fought the elections of 1965, 1967 and 1968. Until 1968 the results were satisfactory, but there was one major drawback. It was the Communists who provided the electoral muscle—but the more they succeeded the more frightened the non-Communist electorate (their partners included) became. The opposition could not succeed without the Communists; they appeared almost equally unlikely to succeed with them. Even so it looked by 1967 as if French politics were becoming increasingly polarized, with a unified party of the right being opposed by a coalition on the left. The Anglo-Saxon analogy however is misleading. Neither the Gaullists nor their opponents could be identified with a precise political platform. The Gaullists spent ten years discussing not their programme but the iniquities of the preceding regime. The opposition, with rather more justification since they were unable to agree on any detailed programme in common, were reduced to demanding a blank cheque from the electorate.

Then came the summer of 1968. Student riots in Paris and elsewhere in early May escalated into a general strike of unprecedented size, affecting almost everyone from automobile and aircraft workers to footballers and dancers in the Folies Bergère. The government seemed powerless. Gaullist distrust of the traditional intermediaries, whether political parties or trades-unions, had come home to roost; it was symptomatic that the students parading triumphantly through Paris should never have considered going by way of the Chamber of Deputies, as it was that the majority of the strikers should turn down the settlement their union leaders had made in their name, demanding—and obtaining—one even more advantageous. The whole French establishment was caught on the hop, the Government left without anyone with whom to negotiate. The left prepared to fill this void and take over power. De Gaulle, dramatically, disappeared. Ten years almost to the day after the Algiers *coup* had put de Gaulle into power, it seemed as if the combined action of students and workers was to replace him.

It did not work out that way. De Gaulle returned to Paris (he had been consulting French army leaders in Germany) to propose elections, and a public increasingly afraid and disapproving of industrial disruption and student violence gave the Gaullists a landslide victory. For the left it was an electoral disaster and a deserved one. It had neither anticipated nor understood the 'May Revolution'; for all its revolutionary rhetoric it had envisaged taking over power too late and too timidly: the rhetoric remained to damn it for an attempt it had never seriously made.

May 1968 was a watershed for the Fifth Republic, and not just because of its effect on the left. It demonstrated the bankruptcy of two basic Gaullist claims. For ten years the Gaullists had made political capital out of their assertion that the traditional public parties were outmoded, irrelevant. Perhaps they were: but the Gaullists had forgotten that their own party during the decade since 1958 had also become traditional. More serious was the humiliating revelation that the stable and even authoritarian state the Gaullists claimed to have created could apparently be at the mercy of mere university students. Both indicated the fundamental weakness of de Gaulle's regime, its lack of communication with the nation at large, an ignorance that bred complaisance and, worse, credulity. In 1940 de Gaulle's had been a voice crying to the *maquis*, by 1968 it was crying in a wilderness of the Gaullist party's own choosing — and in a regime in which communication is one-way only, the barricades may seem the only answer. Finally, for all the party's electoral triumph, a massive 357 seats, de Gaulle's own myth was shattered. The 'man who was France' had become the leader of the right wing. He had also become expendable, because M. Pompidou's handling of the crisis had shown that the seventy-eight-years-old General was no longer necessary. The signs had been there before. The vote for de Gaulle personally had declined from over 90% in the referendum of April 1962 to 54.5% in the final round of the presidential elections three years later, falling to just under 47% in the final referendum of April 1969. At the same time the Gaullist party progressed from 20% of the votes cast in the legislative elections of 1958, to 32% in 1962, 38% in 1967 and 44% in 1968.

De Gaulle stayed on as President until April 1969, but it was a twilit period. He had, by his own confession, lost control even over his own cabinet during the May 1968 crisis. Perhaps he revenged himself when he replaced Pompidou as prime minister in June, but Pompidou already had a reputation and an independent power-base. From June 1968 de Gaulle struggled against a combination of political and economic events he could neither control nor perhaps comprehend. He had announced a referendum for the spring of 1969, on regionalization and the reform of the Senate, the upper (and ineffectual) house of Parliament. It was an ill-chosen mixture followed by a lackadaisical campaign. De Gaulle had threatened to resign should the referendum fail. It did. De Gaulle left the Élysée: henceforward Hamlet was to be played without the prince.

3. FOREIGN POLICY

France, de Gaulle had written in his memoirs, could not be France without grandeur; one reason for reforming the State was that only a strong Government could carry out the forward foreign policy which grandeur demanded. In the contemporary context this meant a role in foreign affairs independent of the super-powers, the leadership of a united Europe which would act both as a counter-attraction to the super-powers and as a means of bridging the gap between them. It was a strategy that rested on a well-defined Gaullist doctrine. In a world in which de Gaulle believed the nation-state to be the only reality, and international affairs in consequence a jungle of competing egoisms, ideologies were unimportant. A movement like Communism, for example, was merely the transitory cover for the—

quite natural and traditional—national aspirations of a Russia or a China. The corollary was that alliances might be tactically imperative, but they were not eternal; foreign policy might mean flirtation, it could never mean marriage. So de Gaulle, whose energetic support of the Americans during the Cuban missile crisis of 1962 surprised even the beneficiaries, could refer a mere four years later to the Cold War as being 'derisory'.

Even before the end of the Algerian war the consequences of this doctrine had become clear. Since an independent foreign policy meant that France should have the military strength to defend herself, de Gaulle underwrote the initiative taken just before the Fourth Republic fell, and went ahead with constructing a French nuclear deterrent. The first French atomic bomb was exploded at Reggane in the Sahara in February 1960. And because national self-interest in Gaullist eyes made the Western Alliance seem both unsatisfactory and inefficient, de Gaulle removed part of the French fleet from N.A.T.O. control in July 1959, the first step in a process that was to lead to almost total French withdrawal from the alliance less than ten years later. These were mere warning shots. In May 1962, with the Algerian affair finished, de Gaulle spelt out France's mission. She was to be the leader of a Europe independent of the power blocs. Just what kind of Europe this would be and how de Gaulle would go about constructing it remained to be seen.

There was one embryonic European organization in existence, the Common Market. Given de Gaulle's dislike of supranational organizations it may seem odd that he accepted it, but he did so very much in his own way. He accepted the E.E.C. as an economic community but also as a potential framework for his Europe, in the sense that he saw it as a convenient mechanism for conventional diplomacy. What he could not accept was the idea that its secretariat was a supra-national body which had the right to impose its decisions on the member-states—the reason for French withdrawal from the controlling council of the E.E.C. for six months in 1965. But there were other angles to the Common Market. The first was the problem of British entry. De Gaulle twice vetoed this, in 1963 and 1967. There were specific reasons, British economic performance— or lack of it—and British diplomacy, which had havered over the problem of Europe since the war, and having been dilatory about entry in the early 1960s tried to force the pace the second time round. There were also underlying ones. De Gaulle considered Britain a satellite of the United States whose entry into the E.E.C. would make nonsense of an 'independent' Europe; and British entry would have spoilt the Franco-German tête-à-tête which through superior and more spectacular diplomacy France dominated until 1968. For the key to Europe was West Germany, a powerful and increasingly rich state (in 1959 the German gross national product per head exceeded the French for the first time) and France's only rival in Western Europe. There were two options open to de Gaulle. He could build his Europe in connexion with the Federal Republic, or he could contain it by going over Germany's head and dealing directly with the Soviet bloc. To put it another way: given the conditions of the early 1960s France could placate the Federal Republic by adopting its hard line over Eastern Europe; suppose those conditions changed—and ideologies in de Gaulle's eyes were mere sometime things—France could work for a European detente and the eventual reunification of Germany by negotiating with the Soviet bloc. As it happened de Gaulle played both these options and played them successively.

Franco-German relations reached their peak in 1962, with Chancellor Adenauer's visit to France and de Gaulle's triumphant return visit to Germany. They were consummated in the Treaty of January 1963. From then on they stalled. In 1964–5 therefore de Gaulle played his second card. For the next three years there was constant and cordial contact between France and the Soviet bloc, culminating in de Gaulle's state visit to Moscow in summer 1966 and Kosygin's return trip to Paris that December. The cordiality remained on the surface. However much the Soviet satellites might welcome de Gaulle's own independent line within N.A.T.O. it was never very likely that they could—or indeed would—follow his example within the Warsaw Pact. The idea of building an independent Europe on a Franco-German tandem had failed because it was based on a misconception, because of all Western European states the Federal Republic for reasons both of security and survival was the most dependent on the United States. The dream of a detente which would allow the formation of a Europe 'from the Atlantic to the Urals' broke on a similar miscalculation, that Soviet policy had sufficiently changed to allow the satellites to cut free, and broke dramatically with the Russian invasion of Czechoslovakia in August 1968.

In any event Gaullist foreign policy had become increasingly incoherent, a matter of isolated initiatives rarely followed through. There had been the futureless recognition of Red China; the sudden interest in Latin America, as suddenly forgotten; the unpopular stand against Israel during and after the Six-Day War; the gratuitous 'Vive le Québec Libre' of 1967 which infuriated the Canadian government but brought no benefit to the French-Canadians. What coherence there was lay in France's increasingly critical attitude towards the United States. One indication was the elaboration of a strategy that rationalized the cost and ultimate inefficacy of the French nuclear deterrent by a policy that proclaimed France to be prepared against all comers whether from East or West. Another was the sustained campaign against gold which de Gaulle announced in early 1965, an offensive designed to force a devaluation of a dollar seen as yet another sign of an American hegemony. The last was the mounting official criticism of American policy in Vietnam. But there was another side to French foreign policy, its constantly enlightened attitude towards the 'Third World' and former French possessions, in Africa in particular. The Algerian war neither prevented the other French African states from achieving their independence almost painlessly within two years, nor stopped France from enjoying good relations with Algeria and the other Arab states after 1962. The link was partly cultural, and if French hostility to the United States could be seen here too, much of France's influence could be traced to a belief in a cultural mission that was sincerely held and skilfully implemented.

The year the answers came was 1968. The Russian invasion of Czechoslovakia bankrupted Gaullist foreign policy; the events of May made nonsense of the Gaullist claim to have established an unprecedentedly stable regime, and the financial crisis that followed removed the third plank of Gaullist doctrine, the strong franc. With 1968 the credibility of what had been in any event a hazardous claim also disappeared: that France could be the leader of Europe.

4. SOCIETY AND THE ECONOMY

Whatever the failings of the Fourth Republic, the economy had not been among them. France's industrial infrastructure had been rebuilt almost from base, and from the early 1950s the annual rate of economic growth reached and remained around 5%. This achievement had been partly masked because it had taken place beneath a blanket of inflation, a chronic financial instability largely caused by the cost of continued colonial wars. It had also taken place inside a closed economy, something the Common Market was bound to change. Even so the Gaullists inherited a fundamentally healthy situation, along with two bonuses. The first was the disguised devaluation of the franc which had been carried out in 1957. Followed a year later by de Gaulle's own devaluation (and introduction of the New Franc) it meant that the franc became undervalued and therefore attractive, and stayed that way until sterling was devalued in its turn in 1967. Even more luckily this coincided with a sharp rise in the world trade in manufactures. The result was a boom in French exports, which nearly doubled in value in the six years 1963–8. French reserves, particularly in gold, rose from almost zero to a healthy surplus, while French industry moved with unexpected ease into an open market, jettisoning the controls that had cocooned it for so long.

By 1963 signs of overheating were apparent, by 1966 the situation was turning sour. Industrial production had slowed down, gold reserves had ceased to grow, and the franc was showing signs of strain. Labour relations deteriorated as worker discontent grew with successive austerity measures, and unemployment rose. There were therefore solid enough economic reasons alone for industrial unrest by May 1968. But what the workers gained in the Grenelle agreement between Government and unions at the end of that month (the guaranteed minimum wage was increased by over one-third, and across the board salary increases averaged 15%) the franc lost. It would in any event have been in trouble now that the threat of inflation was added to political uncertainty. Speculation against the franc made the situation critical, but although the stop–go measures the Government introduced did nothing to cure this de Gaulle obstinately refused to devalue a franc he saw as yet another symbol of French prestige. Only in August 1969 with de Gaulle safely out of the way did the new Government recognize the facts of life and devalue.

In their first ten years in government the Gaullists' achievement had been almost as remarkable as the claims they made for it. Industrial production had increased by one-half, gross national product was over one-quarter as high again in 1968 as in 1963 and the French economy seemed on the whole successfully integrated in the Common Market. It was therefore unlikely that even the 'May Revolution' would do more than cut back further expansion. It did something rather different, triggering off a boom that put past achievements in the shade. Superficially the recipe looked much the same, another series of parity changes temporarily favouring the franc, another export-led boom (exports rose by 70% in the four years from 1969). But this concealed important differences. The nature of those exports had shifted away from food and processed goods to industrial products, and their destination was different too. In the early 1960s almost one-third of French exports had gone to the franc zone, the French equivalent of the sterling area. Today the figure is under 10%, and almost half France's exports go to her original E.E.C. partners. This was a development that antedated 1968, but the 'May Revolution' had more direct results. Wage increases led to a consumer spending spree which in turn forced French industry to expand its capacity and step up investment; between 1969 and 1971 industrial investment rose by 20% or more each year. They also took much of the tension out of the industrial scene, although there were other factors here. The first was the genuine if not altogether altruistic effort by the new French Government to substitute dialogue for confrontation in industrial relations. The other was the traumatic effect of the May events on the trades-unions. They were in any case weak (only 20% of the labour force in France is unionized, half the British figure); for most of May 1968 they had led their troops from behind, and they lived with the nightmare of a possible replay. As a result, from May 1968 to spring 1973 almost all was quiet on the industrial front.

The economy was not, of course, entirely a success story: there were both imbalances and inequalities. Should the Common Market be taken to imply industrial concentration on a large scale France still had a long way to go. Even in the 1960s it was still the land of the small and often the family firm, with one-third of all wage-earners employed in concerns with less than fifty workers, one-fifth in those with less than ten. In spite of mergers, notably in the steel and automobile industries, there were few giant combines. Increased competition had meant that some of the smaller and less efficient French firms went to the wall, but although French managerial expertise could sometimes do wonders even with those that survived, it was noticeable that those most competitive under the new conditions were often those that had been most competitive before—France's economic development in the first fifteen years of the Common Market has borne a slight but disquieting resemblance to the parable of the talents. Similarly, a high degree of technical virtuosity and success in new prestige fields like electronics and aeronautics could not disguise the decline of the old 'Monnet industries', coal, iron and steel. The Government had over-invested in these after the war; they were now caught in a spiral as productivity rose, demand decreased and large numbers of workers were laid off: in the coal mines of the Nord alone the labour force was cut back from 240,000 just after the war to 90,000 in 1968.

This emphasis on industry itself implies the extent to which France had changed. As late as 1954 over one-quarter of the population was involved in agriculture; France was a peasant nation in the sense Britain had hardly been since the eighteenth century. This was a problem the Gaullist Government, helped by a new and better-educated generation of farmers, went a long way towards solving. It both encouraged the exodus from the land (which at one stage ran at nearly 150,000 persons a year, so that a farm closed down about every ten minutes) and its amalgamation. The percentage of the working population involved in agriculture dropped from twenty in 1962 to twelve ten years later—and the value of French agricultural exports doubled. Even so, France still has too many farms. One-third of those existing are probably too small to be economically viable, their owners, as the proverb has it, being reduced to starvation on earth in order to celebrate in heaven—and since one in every five farmers is over sixty-five years of age, such promotion may not be long in coming.

The sheer size of the exodus from the land both benefited the economy and changed the face of the country. And because the movement from the land got under way so late it provided a massive pool of labour just when the economy most needed it. Rural emigrants in the 50s and 60s (like immigrant workers in the 70s) could be directed to developing industries rather than channelled into traditional and over-extended ones. Because the unions were weak, they could also be shifted around to meet demand without too much fear of demarcation disputes. The exodus also meant that what had been until quite recently a rural or small-town country has become increasingly urbanized. In the forty years after 1914 the urban population grew by seven million: in the next twelve years it grew by as much again. This was the result not merely of a more mobile population, but of the most important single development in post-war French history, a rapidly increasing one. Between 1944 and 1969 the population of France rose by ten million, to a figure of fifty-one millions—almost as much as it had grown in the previous one hundred and fifty years. There were marginal factors (the massive repatriation of French Algerians in 1962, for example) but the main cause was that the 'baby boom', which in common with other European countries France experienced at the end of the war, has been sustained far longer, so that one in three of the population is under twenty years of age today.

Inevitably this has affected the whole structure of French society and in certain cases almost broken it at the seams. The 300,000 secondary-school pupils of 1939 had grown to two million by the 1960s, the 122,000 pre-war university students doubled in number by 1960 and doubled again in the next seven years. Indeed, 1972 was the first year in living memory in which student numbers did not increase. The need for new schools and universities, for more teachers and facilities of every kind was acute, but the Government did little and—as May 1968 was to prove—did it too late. The housing problem was similar but worse. Although France had suffered far more war damage than Britain, although nearly two-thirds of existing housing ante-dates the First World War, since 1945 the French have built fewer new homes than the British: one-third of these have gone to replace buildings that had become totally uninhabitable, and too few have been inexpensive enough to meet demand where it really matters. The Gaullist regime did make some effort to provide low-cost subsidized housing, but the congeries of high-rise apartment blocks built in the outskirts of Paris and other major cities produced social stresses so acute that the programme was discontinued in 1973.

Unglamorous sectors of the economy like housing and education might not get their fair share of a growing national cake. The same was true of whole regions. The new prosperity emphasized a development that dates from the last century, the division of France into two zones by a line running roughly from le Havre in the north to Grenoble and then to Marseilles. Eighty per cent of France's industrial production, almost all the major cities and the most intensively farmed land lies east of this line. Two-thirds of the country's agricultural population, the least profitable farms and two major problem areas lie to the west. Both Brittany and the Massif Central have an agricultural population far higher than the national average. They also have additional drawbacks. In the Massif Central an ageing population farms uplands so inhospitable that one observer thought that only rape could make them fertile. In Brittany the fragmentation of holdings and lack of home-based industry led to a steady haemorrhage of the working population. But whereas the only future for the Massif Central would seem to be that of a tourist attraction, Government-inspired industrial development, and particularly the build-up of Rennes as an electronics centre, has given Brittany new life.

There is an older and even more intractable division, that between Paris and the provinces. Paris is by far the largest city in France, already five times as populous as any rival in the nineteenth century, nearly ten times today. It is not only the administrative and cultural capital of France but its most important industrial centre. In the last century there was some logic behind this. Today there is none. As a result Paris has the worst population, housing and traffic problem in the country. The average pace of automobile traffic today (nine kilometres an hour) just about equals that of a horse-drawn traffic in 1900; central Paris is more densely packed than either central London or Manhattan; and in the extended Paris region half the dwellings were built before 1914, the same proportion have no inside sanitation and two-thirds have neither bath nor shower. During the last twenty years there have been serious attempts at cutting back Paris's growth, and as a corollary encouraging that of the provinces. There have been measures designed to discourage further economic concentration in the capital, to move existing industries out and to foster investment in the provinces. This has meant modifying France's traditional unit of local government, the department. Since these had been created during the Revolution it was hardly surprising that they no longer reflected social or economic realities. In 1964 the Government superimposed twenty-one new economic regions on the existing ninety-five departments, and gave them their own 'counterweight capitals'. It also defined areas for special development and offered a complex series of financial incentives to encourage firms to move into the provinces. Progress has been real but hardly rapid. This is partly because some of the new regions seemed artificial constructions (why divide Normandy into two, for example?), partly because Paris-based firms were unwilling to move any further than the periphery of the capital, but also because decentralization stalled on the traditional unwillingness of French government to delegate authority. Since 1800 Paris has been the apex of a highly centralized administrative system (it is perhaps symptomatic that even the administration of decentralization is centralized—in Paris). General de Gaulle and his successor both talked of regional reform as vital to France's future. Neither de Gaulle in 1969 nor M. Pompidou four years later was willing to give the regions the substance of power, in particular budgetary independence. But without this, decentralization could be no more than a convenient political charade.

In the 1950s the average British family was one-quarter as prosperous again as its French counterpart. Now the opposite is true. But real though it is, French prosperity has not been evenly shared out. Management—on every level—has gained far more than workers, skilled workers more than unskilled, workers in the private sector more than those in Government-controlled concerns, industrial workers more than agricultural, Frenchmen more than Frenchwomen and the French more than the foreign worker. Since 1968 the Government has taken steps to redress these imbalances: the minimum guaranteed wage, for example, has risen faster than the average salary, and in the year from July 1972 rose by as much as 20%. It has been handicapped by the French tax system, in which direct taxation on income plays a far smaller part than in most of industrialized Western Europe. This tends to favour the rich—the credibility of M. Chaban-Delmas's vision of a 'New Society' broke on the disclosure that he had, *and quite legally*, paid no income-tax on his salary as prime minister for three years. But more central has been the Government's declared economic strategy. For all the talk of social justice that followed the elections of 1969 and 1973, a policy that demands a high growth-rate while cutting back inflation has to sacrifice something: and too often this has meant sacrificing the sick, the old and the poor.

You cannot, as the student slogan of 1968 had it, fall in love with a growth-rate. That year the students were not on the barricades only because they wanted to change their syllabus (although they did); the workers were not asking only for more take-home pay (although they were). Both groups wanted a *qualitative* change. They went beyond immediate demands to question the system as a whole. The final paradox of Gaullism has been that the leader who preferred *le franc* to *les Français*, who preached the need to build not super-markets but 'cathedrals for the future' should have presided over a country that was discovering the delights of a consumer society; and that a significant section of the country should hold the Gaullist regime responsible at once and contradictorily both for the existence of this society and for its inadequacies.

POSTSCRIPT

AFTER DE GAULLE

The main problem of Gaullism after de Gaulle has been not so much survival as definition. May 1968 undercut the General's claim that France's choice was between himself and chaos, if only because the French had experienced both simultaneously. In addition, M. Pompidou's handling of both crisis and elections had shown that there was a natural successor. After the General's departure M. Pompidou won the presidential election almost by default. The centre candidate, the President of the Senate and interim head of state, made a promising start but then disappeared behind his campaign's low profile; the left were still so divided by the previous year's events that they fielded no fewer than four candidates; with 60% of the votes cast M. Pompidou got home confortably. *Après-gaullisme* was installed with the Gaullists' man in the Élysée, and the party a majority in the Assembly.

The new President neither dismissed the old Gaullist faithfuls, whose loyalty had been to the General in person, nor changed the fundamental Gaullist options. He merely isolated the first and attenuated the second. A good deal of Gaullist policy and practice had been already proven a failure by 1969. M. Pompidou set out to liquidate the rest. Certainly a great deal of the difference was one of style, but then style had been a Gaullist characteristic. Relations with the United States were normalized, those with France's Common Market partners improved, most notably when in January 1972 France accepted Great Britain's standing application to join the E.E.C. There was enough here to discontent those Gaullists who clung to the vision of a united Europe under French leadership, a 'third force' in international affairs. Worse was to come. A Gaullist minister might refer to the Soviet invasion of Czechoslovakia

237

as a mere 'traffic accident'; it nevertheless put a temporary stop to plans for an East–West detente. When they were renewed, it was by means of a German and not a French initiative —Herr Brandt had stolen the Gaullists' clothes. Then came the successful Nixon–Brezhnev talks in spring 1973. Officially the French Government could do no less than welcome them. On a less official level there were Gaullists to see them as the justification of the General's worst fears, the super-powers coming together over a disunited Europe.

But two characteristics of Gaullism had not changed: there was no tampering with the sacrosanct French nuclear deterrent, as the Mururoa tests in the summer of 1973 showed; and there was no transfer of power from the President to Parliament. Indeed, M. Pompidou was relatively more powerful even than his predecessor. This was dramatically illustrated in 1972. The prime minister, M. Chaban-Delmas, had run into difficulties. There had been a crop of scandals involving individual Gaullist M.P.s, more than a hint of inflation, and the referendum on widening the E.E.C. had been received with massive apathy, nearly two out of five voters abstaining. Something had to give, and in spite of a massive vote of confidence in the Assembly, it was M. Chaban-Delmas. In July 1972 M. Pompidou replaced him.

This reminder of their impotence distressed a Gaullist party already confused by a presidential policy that seemed to have abandoned the General's policies in practice while still appealing to them as propaganda. And the party was further dismayed by the revival of the left. The left took three years to recover from the shambles of 1968–9, but when recovery came it was swift. In summer 1972 M. Mitterand's re-vamped Socialist party reached agreement with the Communists. This was more than an electoral alliance, it was an unprecedented agreement on a blueprint for a future left-wing government. Ironically, while it made the united left a credible alternative Government for the first time, it probably ensured that this credibility would never be tested in office. It enabled the Gaullists, once again, to raise the spectre of a Communist France, and led to a massive switch of uncommitted centre votes to the regime. As a result, although the left got almost exactly the same number of votes in the 1973 elections as their opponents, they received something like one hundred less seats.

The 1973 elections were hardly a victory for either side. The Gaullist alliance kept its majority in Parliament, but the Gaullist party itself was now no more than the majority within this alliance. The left, and in particular the Socialist party, had done far better than in 1968, or even 1967. But it still seemed unable to get the clear majority of votes which, with France's two-tiered electoral system, would be necessary for it to win. Nor did the elections solve France's main constitutional problem. Almost all power was in the President's hands. He could ignore or railroad the Assembly as he chose. And this meant that even if the left won a clear majority of the popular vote, there was no obligation on the President to accept a left-wing Government. It was the second strand in '*la société bloquée*', the stalemate society. France was prosperous, but this prosperity unduly favoured the haves at the expense of the have-nots. France was politically stable, but this apparently involved a Gaullist monopoly of government. In an advanced industrial society these may no longer be recipes for revolution: they remain an infallible source of frustration.

INDEX